D1568257

The Last Romantic

The Last Romantic
A Poet among Publishers

The Oral Autobiography of
JOHN HALL WHEELOCK

Edited by MATTHEW J. BRUCCOLI
with JUDITH S. BAUGHMAN
Foreword by George Garrett

University of South Carolina Press

© 2002 University of South Carolina

Published in Columbia, South Carolina, by the
University of South Carolina Press

Manufactured in the United States of America

06   05   04   03   02   5   4   3   2   1

Library of Congress Cataloging-in-Publication Data

Wheelock, John Hall, 1886–1978.
    The last romantic : a poet among publishers : the oral autobiography of John Hall
Wheelock / edited by Matthew J. Bruccoli with Judith S.Baughman ; foreword by
George Garrett.
        p. cm.
    Edited from Wheelock's own edited transcription of interviews conducted for the Oral
History Research Office at Columbia University in 1967.
    Includes bibliographical references and index.
    ISBN 1-57003-463-X (alk. paper)
    1. Wheelock, John Hall, 1886–1978. 2. Poets, American—20th century—Biography.
3. Publishers and publishing—United States—History. 4. Editors—United States—
Biography. 5. Charles Scribner's Sons—History. I. Bruccoli, Matthew Joseph, 1931–
II. Baughman, Judith. III. Title.

PS3545.H33 Z47 2002
811'.52—dc21   2002008026

Editorial work on this volume was sponsored by the Center for Literary Biography,
Thomas Cooper Library, University of South Carolina.

Frontispiece: John Hall Wheelock (courtesy of Charles Scribner's Sons)

For Joel Myerson
and for
Rodger Tarr

Time has a valve.
　　　　　　　　—John Hall Wheelock

Contents

Illustrations

Foreword

There are certain points, and this is one of them, where anecdotal evidence becomes something much more than itself, more than the dropped names and recovered faces of prominent or notorious public figures, more than a dazzle of amusing anecdotes, more than personal observations and lively hearsay. It all depends on the qualities and character of the speaker, the point of view and reliability of the narrator, the earned credibility of the chief witness. When these things come together it is a rare enough event, though familiar and even traditional from the classical era up to the edge of our own times. In our time—an age of spurious celebrity, of advertising and clever public relations, of "spin" and symbolic and insubstantial gestures, false confessions and short memory, of the making and breaking of icons and reputations, it has become much more complicated and requires more skeptical reservations. Yet, even so, it remains possible for a gifted and honest witness to transform personal memory into public history.

This oral history, the lively and extended testimony of John Hall Wheelock, precisely demonstrates that point. He tells us much that he remembers and he shares with us directly the world as he knew it and his life in it. And because it was for him primarily a literary world, what we have here is a significant contribution to our American literary history.

John Hall Wheelock (1886–1978) is, as you will quickly see, an excellent witness. In his nineties he was still writing poems, judged now to be among his finest in a long career that began in childhood, surfaced first in *Verses by Two Undergraduates* (1905), a joint effort with his best friend, Van Wyck Brooks, continued and ended in the same year as his death with the publication of his fourteenth and fifteenth books of poems: *This Blessed Earth: New and Selected Poems, 1927–1977* and *Afternoon: Amagansett Beach*. As our population grows older, there may well be other poets who will live and create over a longer lifetime—one thinks of Stanley Kunitz, who began writing poetry much later in his life than Wheelock—but Wheelock's career as poet remains truly remarkable. Wheelock, looking back over his shoulder at a full generation of nineteenth-century poets (as a child he sees

George Garrett

Walt Whitman standing at the rail of a ferry boat, sees Swinburne wearing a turban, walking on the sidewalk), among his own contemporaries seems to have known almost everybody (T. S. Eliot, Vachel Lindsay, Wallace Stevens, Sara Teasdale, Marianne Moore, Elinor Wylie, Edwin Arlington Robinson, Edgar Lee Masters, Edna St. Vincent Millay, and many, many others); and, as a working editor, one who published new poets as well as more prominent and mature masters (Conrad Aiken, Louise Bogan, Phelps Putnam, Sara Teasdale, Howard Moss, Peter Viereck, John Peale Bishop, Rolfe Humphries, Oscar Williams), he was acutely aware of all the trends and fashions in the new American poetry and of the poets who were creating it. He served as the editor for the eight volumes of the Scribners *Poets of Today* series (1954–1961), a series devoted to the discovery and publication of new poets. Probably more than he, or anyone else, could imagine at the time, he helped to shape the future of twentieth-century American poetry by judiciously selecting and publishing twenty-four first collections of poems. Three individually copyrighted book-length collections were bound together in each volume of the *Poets of Today* series. These came from a large number of submissions. During those years, no question, Wheelock had a look at almost all the potential first books of poems. The poets that he elected to publish in that series are widely various in their ways and means, distinctly different from each other and from the aesthetics of his work as well. These poets and their poems are linked together by talent and promise and demonstrate conclusively Wheelock's ability to recognize excellence where he found it. He lived long enough after his retirement and the end of the *Poets of Today* series to see for himself what became of his poets, a good number of whom went on to earn prizes and honors: May Swenson, Robert Pack, Louis Simpson, Joseph Langland, Donald Finkel, David Slavitt, James Dickey. He was able to say, as he says here—"All my poets turned out well."

If someone should ever trouble to study Wheelock's record as a poetry editor, comparing and contrasting his choices with those of other editors at the same time, bearing in mind that then, as now, all these editors would have had roughly the same manuscripts to consider and evaluate, that almost all first books by new poets passed under their noses, Wheelock's editorial choices and his *Poets of Today* series will be seen as being at once wonderfully eclectic and powerfully influential. Moreover it can be persuasively argued that since the series ended, ending the publication of three new poets annually, the poetry scene has never been quite the same.

In short, John Hall Wheelock played an active role, a major part, in the literary world that he here bears witness to.

But there are other things that make his life and contribution, celebrated in this oral history, pertinent to us here and now in the new century. One of these things is his long association with the publishing firm of Charles Scribner's Sons, where he began as an employee of their bookstore (1911–1926) and went on to hold important editorial positions in the firm for many years, retiring as editor in chief in 1957. Those years, from the bubbling and booming 1920s up to the edge of the 1960s, were a vital time for Scribners and, indeed, for the whole American publishing and literary scene. With trade lists that included F. Scott Fitzgerald, Ernest Hemingway, Thomas Wolfe, Marjorie Kinnan Rawlings, James Jones, Nancy Hale, and Alan Paton, Scribners had much to do with the shape and substance of American letters in that era. As a firm with a considerable backlist, they also played a part in conserving the literature of the recent past. Thus Wheelock's double vision, his view fore and aft of the world of poetry, was complemented by his editorial point of view.

Wheelock's inherent modesty, and a natural shyness that adds credibility to his observations and comments, taken together with an old-fashioned code of good manners practiced by his generation of American gentlemen, inhibited, indeed forbade him from aggressively asserting his own importance or taking credit even when much credit was due. He was a good company man who worked well, as a teammate, with the famous Scribners editor and presence of the period—Maxwell Perkins. There is no telling, then, how many books he worked on, helped to shape and bring to life. We do know the books of his own (not counting his poetry) that he was given credit for: *A Bibliography of Theodore Roosevelt* (1920), *The Face of a Nation: Poetical Passages from the Writings of Thomas Wolfe* (1939), and *Editor to Author: The Letters of Maxwell E. Perkins* (1950). He is also listed as a translator for *Happily Ever After: Fairy Tales Selected by Alice Dalgliesh* (1939). He is the author of *What is Poetry?* (1963), a slender and intense gathering of essays and lectures defining his own *ars poetica* and examining the place of poetry in our time. The reader will note that Wheelock was surprised at the successful sales (more than twenty thousand copies) of this little book and a little disappointed, too, that it sold so much better than his books of poetry.

Wheelock's career as a poet was a long and somewhat complicated one. Early on his work was widely praised and admired. With his emphasis on the music of poetry and on traditional rhythms and forms, he was, at first, seen as a bright exemplar of the great conservative tradition, building on the foundations of the late-nineteenth-century poets, especially those in Britain and in Germany. The modernist revolution, the emphatic arrival on the scene of T. S. Eliot, Ezra Pound, Wallace Stevens, William Carlos Williams and the others, placed Wheelock and many of his friends and peers on what seemed to be the losing side, soldiers for a lost cause. By 1936 he had published eight books of poetry, presenting a very large number of competent poems out of which critics have reckoned maybe a dozen or so to be first rate and lasting contributions. But time has its way with winners and losers, heroes and lost causes. Wheelock lived a long time, and even as he aged he continued to grow as an artist, not changing his antimodernist mindset, but gradually refining his craft and his voice until he could explore and exploit the full potential of the powerful formal verse that he had been master of. In the important essay on Wheelock's poetry listed below, poet and critic Henry Taylor celebrates "in a spirit of gratitude" the rare achievement of a poet who had "come to write, in his seventies and eighties, work that constitutes one of the most notable achievements in our literature."

The reader will note soon enough in Wheelock's story that everything else, including things he did well and seems to have much enjoyed, was subordinate to his love of poetry. He was, first and foremost and always, a poet. The undeniable accomplishment of his late poems was earned by a lifetime's dedication.

Wheelock, having joined Scribners early in the century and worked there through the high holidays of literary quality and the steady, if modest, profits, retired just before the deluge, the sea change in global publishing that witnessed the rise of conglomerates triumphing over family and independent ownership and next suffered through a relentless dumbing down of literature. The goal, the prize these corporate giants had their eyes on, was double-digit profit percentages at whatever cost. When Wheelock worked at Scribners, they still maintained the custom of afternoon tea. The new and savage breed, already whooping and circling the old-fashioned wagon train, scorned the habits and practices of their elders, publishers like Scribners, as being not much more than "a literary tea party."

The stories and details of his publishing career at Scribners are fascinating, brewed with honorable nostalgia, though next to no sentimentality. Wheelock kept his common sense and irony and makes some fun of himself and his firm for blithely turning down any number of good and/or successful works, among them Erskine Caldwell's *Tobacco Road*, Malcolm Lowry's *Under the Volcano*, Robert Musil's *The Man Without Qualities*, and Céline's *Journey to the End of the Night*.

Stressing the importance of his literary vocation, I have said too little about Wheelock the man. Of course he speaks clearly for himself with eloquence and elegance. Remember, for it is easy to forget, that in the context of an interview/oral history this is a man spontaneously responding to questions and *talking* to us. His early life and the family history are an American story set firmly in the nineteenth century and focused, as his youth was, on the turn of that century into the next one. How much we have changed, for better and for worse, since then! As much so as any novelist of the times—and, yes, I include James and Howells and Wharton—his story, this oral history, dramatizes the expectations and demonstrates the assumptions and ideals, the manners, the basic ideas of acceptable and unacceptable behavior, and the wit and humor of those times, much of which was fading, if not already lost and gone even as Wheelock arrived at his maturity. All that bulk and solidity—heavy furniture and heavy people, domestic objects of all kinds, the elaborate houses, the clothing, the brutal medicine, the horses and buggies, the chuffing locomotives pulling behind them, bathed in clouds of cindery black smoke, the clanging passenger trains that took them from here to there, the great ocean liners hooting in harbors—all these might as well have been made of thin air, no more than a light morning fog at the mercy of the rising sun. There are some places here where Wheelock seems to be describing a foreign country and its alien people. The old world is, in some of this context, somewhat restored. And our new world is viewed from a slightly different standpoint than our own. All of which is the gift of good history.

One great strength of this oral history is the fact that John Hall Wheelock was blessed with an extraordinary memory, a power he sustained into his old age. His powers of memory were enhanced by the kinds of memorization routinely required in the schools in his childhood days and were refined by his unusual ability to remember accurately large patches of poetry of all kinds. He seems to have created much of his own poetry, over the years, by heart and stored it in memory before actually writing it down on paper. It is a method that well serves the special music and clarity of his poems. Late in this oral history he refers to this process, noting that he created poetry while walking on the beaches of Long Island, then "wrote" it in New York City: "Sometimes I would bring back with me to the city, carried in my head, as much as four weeks' work, knowing that if I were run over by a truck (I actually used to worry about this), all this work which seemed so important to me would be lost. I always was very reluctant to put new work down on paper, because, you see, as long as you have a poem fluid in your head, there are so many choices that can be made with regard to all the possible alternatives." Memory is not a burden, but rather liberating, then, setting the poet and the man free to explore the continually changing present and to expect the future, sooner or later, only when it arrives. So the past comes alive, becomes, then, part of the everlasting present in this story, and with it comes a wonderful cast, a whole gallery of interesting people, rogues and heroes, famous or obscure, early and late, all of them interesting, all of them justly spared from oblivion. And at the center of it all, like a classic circus ringmaster, stands the author, someone worth remembering and altogether worthy of our best attention.

A Postscript

Although Wheelock's poetry has not lately received the kind of critical attention it certainly deserves (though perhaps this book, at least indirectly, will encourage some of that), it was well and widely reviewed in his lifetime, especially in the early years; and he earned major prizes and honors throughout his career. For an early appraisal see Louis Untermeyer's "John Hall Wheelock" in *The New Era in American Poetry* (1919), pp. 215–230. In my judgment, the best contemporary piece about the poems of John Hall Wheelock, and it is first-rate, is Henry Taylor's "John Hall Wheelock: Letting the Darkness In," in his *Compulsory Figures: Essays on Recent American Poets* (1992), pp. 207–233. An excellent general piece on the man and his work, by Robert H. O'Connor, appears in *Dictionary of Literary Biography, Volume 45: American Poets, 1880–1945, First Series*, pp. 429–34.

Wheelock appears as a major figure in a superb poem by David R. Slavitt, "Elegy for Walter Stone," which first appeared in Slavitt's *The Carnivore* (1965).

I need to add the fact that John Hall Wheelock was my first editor and selected my first book, *The Reverend Ghost*, for the *Poets of Today* series. Young and ignorant, I knew little or nothing about his life and work, but Wheelock was a sympathetic and helpful editor, and I remain deeply grateful for his kindness and attention, and I honor his memory.

George Garrett

JOHN HALL WHEELOCK

The prepublication history of this book began in 1957 when I was a graduate student at The University of Virginia. Fredson Bowers, my dissertation director, who was married to Scribners author Nancy Hale, ordered me to invite John Hall Wheelock to give a reading for the Graduate English Club. While Mr. Wheelock was in Charlottesville, he told me about working with F. Scott Fitzgerald on *Tender Is the Night*—testimony included in this book.

A dozen years later I became a colleague and friend of James Dickey at the University of South Carolina. Mr. Wheelock had published Dickey's first book, *Into the Stone* (1960), in the Scribners *Poets of Today* series. Jim and I shared an admiration for Thomas Wolfe, and Jim reported to me Mr. Wheelock's statement that he had done more work on Wolfe's books than had Maxwell Perkins. When my wife and I edited *O Lost,* the uncut text of *Look Homeward, Angel,* I researched the mythologized history of the novel's publication. In the course of my investigations I checked for material on Charles Scribner's Sons in the Columbia University Oral History Research Office, where I found this extraordinary dictated autobiography of John Hall Wheelock.

As I read the transcription for the first time, I formed the intention of publishing excerpts that provide an inside view of Charles Scribner's Sons during its glory years under the editorial direction of Maxwell Perkins. But it became evident that the entire document is valuable for its record of John Hall Wheelock as an American Man of Letters—in addition to its importance as literary history.

That Wheelock was speaking for the record and expected his recollections to be made public is established by his words "By the time this interview is released . . ." in his 27 March, 1967 dictation; however, he stipulated to Columbia University that "no use of any kind whatsoever is to be made of this memoir until January 1, 1990." It is overdue in 2002.

Wheelock was the only first-rate American writer to have a distinguished lifetime career in publishing. At Scribners from 1911 to 1957 he progressed from the mail-order department of the bookstore to editor, succeeding Perkins as editor in chief in 1947; he served as a director of the firm and as its treasurer and secretary.

Wheelock published his first collection of poetry in collaboration with Van Wyck Brooks in 1905 while they were Harvard undergraduates; his fifteenth volume of poetry appeared in 1978, the year of his death at ninety-one. He witnessed the metamorphosis of verse from late romanticism to high modernism and knew many of its practitioners well. Wheelock was an inside witness to the movements of American literature during his lifetime.

Literary historian Jay B. Hubbell, who greatly admired Wheelock's poetry, joked that before World War I the history of American literature was the history of Harvard College. John Hall Wheelock's recollections of his years in Cambridge and his undergraduate friendships document the confirmation of his poetic vocation at Harvard. It is permissible to wonder how he would have turned out if his Harvard friend Perkins had not told him about a job at the Scribner bookstore.

M. J. B.

Editorial Note

These interviews were conducted by Mary R. Hawkins for the Oral History Research Office at Columbia University in 1967, when John Hall Wheelock was eighty years old. The tapes were transcribed by an unknown person, and the transcription was sent to Wheelock in October. On 15 December he reported to Mrs. Hawkins:

> I have finished work on the transcript, and I have to confess I took such a dislike to myself on reading it that I wish it could be destroyed. Of all the vain, conceited, self-important, muddled, inaccurate, self-contradictory and wordy persons, I there reveal myself as the worst. As I said before, you are the only one in the interview who makes sense.
>
> You and Miss Mason will be horrified to see how drastically I have rewritten the whole thing, correcting misstatements, inaccuracies, contradictions, verbosity, repetitions and, above all, my dreadful monotony in the transitions: my "Well"s, my "Of course"s, my "You know"s, "I mean"s, etc. etc.—the general second-rate slackness and egotistical smugness of my speaking style. I dare say making all the changes I have indicated in the transcript will be too laborious and costly a re-typing job and the only thing to do will be to ditch the whole thing. So much the better. I shouldn't be willing to have the thing read, in its original form, as I recorded it, even in the year 3,000.
>
> Let's leave the matter alone until after Christmas, when I'll turn the transcript over to you or to Miss Mason, as you may elect.[*]

Allowing for the diffidence of an elderly gentleman, Wheelock's communication clearly does not request or instruct the Oral History Office to destroy the interview: he wanted his edited transcription retyped to replace the original document. This was not done. Wheelock's preserved marked typescript is an unfinished task. He did not rewrite "the whole thing"; and it was not ready for publication.

The editors have constructed a reading text from Wheelock's edited transcription and have checked it against the recordings. The interviewer's

[*]Columbia University Oral History Research Office archives.

questions and interpolations have been removed; duplications have been cut; interrupted anecdotes have been combined; factual errors have been corrected in page notes; unnecessary words (*and, of course, you know, I mean*) have been eliminated; false starts and digressions have been removed. No additional material has been interpolated, although necessary missing words have been supplied. Some repeated points have been retained to preserve the conversational flavor of Wheelock's recollections.

■ ■ ■ ■

I acknowledge the help of Ronald Grele, David Skey, and Mary Marshall Clark at the Columbia University Oral History Research Office. Judith S. Baughman, my rod and my staff, never comforts me. Barry Blose at the University of South Carolina Press saw this volume through production and publication.

M. J. B.

Charles Scribner's Sons

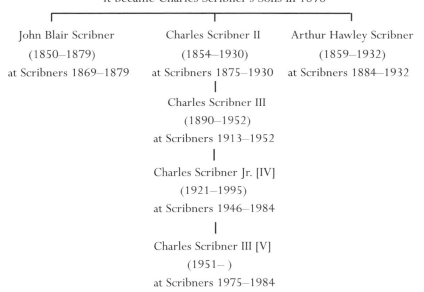

The Proprietors

Charles Scribner (1821–1871)
founder of firm in 1846;
it became Charles Scribner's Sons in 1878

John Blair Scribner	Charles Scribner II	Arthur Hawley Scribner
(1850–1879)	(1854–1930)	(1859–1932)
at Scribners 1869–1879	at Scribners 1875–1930	at Scribners 1884–1932

Charles Scribner III
(1890–1952)
at Scribners 1913–1952

Charles Scribner Jr. [IV]
(1921–1995)
at Scribners 1946–1984

Charles Scribner III [V]
(1951–)
at Scribners 1975–1984

In 1979 the company merged with Atheneum; in 1984 it became a subsidiary of Macmillan. Since 1984 the Scribner imprint has been subsumed successively by Macmillan, Maxwell Communications, and Simon & Schuster.

The Editors Featured in Wheelock's Memoir

W. C. Brownell (1851–1928), literary advisor and book editor
(1888–1928)

Edward L. Burlingame (1848–1922), first editor (1886–1914) of
Scribner's Magazine

Robert Bridges (1858–1941), assistant editor (1887–1914) and editor
(1914–1930) of *Scribner's Magazine*

Maxwell E. Perkins (1884–1947), advertising manager (1910–1914)
and book editor (1914–1947)

Roger Burlingame (1889–1967), book editor (1914–1926)

Charles F. Dunn (1875–1962), joined Scribners in 1900 and was the
first reader for more than fifty years

Burroughs Mitchell (1914?–1979), book editor (1946–1977)

The Last Romantic

I WAS BORN ON THE NINTH of September 1886 at Far Rockaway, New York. The Wheelock family goes back to Ralph Wheelock, who came to this country, not with the fashionable *Mayflower* crowd, but about the same time. I always like to recall that he was a classmate of John Milton's at Cambridge, before he came over to this country. Also I'm very proud of the fact that among my ancestors was Eleazer Wheelock, who founded Dartmouth College and who was a great friend of the North American Indians. He translated the Bible into the "Seven Tongues" for the Seven Tribes, and many treaties were negotiated by him with the Indians because they found they could trust him.

Wheelock College was founded by Eleazer Wheelock, strangely enough, in East Hampton, Long Island, where we have a country cottage, and where I have spent most of my summers for the past seventy-eight years. My father was actually born in England, while his father and mother were abroad—my grandfather was over on business. William A. Wheelock was his name. My father was William Efner Wheelock.

My mother was born in Dublin, Ireland, one of eight children. Her father was a Presbyterian clergyman from Armagh, where he had a church. Later he was called to a church in Dublin, and then was called to the Fifth Avenue Presbyterian Church in New York, on Fifth Avenue and Fifty-fifth Street. My mother's father was John Hall, after whom I am named. He was a very popular preacher, a great big man, six foot six, and very much sought after in other pulpits, as well as in Presbyterian. He was a very obstinate man, but courteous. When he was shown the vestments that they wanted him to wear in the Episcopal Church, he always asked one question: "Is it obligatory?" Then he would add, "Because if it's obligatory, I'll not do it." But if they said, "Dr. Hall, it's entirely as you please," he would do it, out of courtesy.

He was a chancellor of New York University. My father's father, William A. Wheelock, was a chancellor of the New York City College. And I'm very proud of both men, because both of them started from scratch as poor boys with nothing. William A. Wheelock worked his way through New York City College by waiting on table and doing various menial jobs; and my grandfather John Hall, my mother's father, worked his way through Trinity College at Dublin in the same manner. They both started from nothing. My grandfather William A. Wheelock ended up as director of the Equitable Life Assurance Company and of the Central National Bank.

Now, just to say a word or two about my immediate ancestors: my father was a strange man. He studied to become a physician and set up practice in New York. He had graduated from the College of Physicians and Surgeons after leaving Yale. He soon gave up the practice of medicine, however. He was not well suited to it; the sight of blood made him uncomfortable. Then he studied law. He passed his degree for the bar and set up his practice as a lawyer. He got the money from his father. By the time my father had become a physician, his father was already director of the Equitable Life Assurance Company and a rich man, according to the standards of those days. In fact, he gave my father a job as examining physician at the Equitable Life. My father disliked it because he had to deal with some rather objectionable types, candidates for insurance, many of whom tried to bribe him to put them through. He was a very fastidious man. I suppose if he hadn't had a rich father, he couldn't have afforded to be so fastidious.

He gave up the law because he loved being outdoors and couldn't stand the confinement of a law office. Then he studied botany, took a doctor's degree in botany, and was appointed as assistant, up at the Bronx Botanical Gardens, to Dr. Britton, who was head there. There again, the confinement of the life and the fact that he knew his father was able and more than willing to take care of him weakened his interest. He retired and devoted himself to his passion, which was the French horn. He had begun early in life, and he really became a master of that very difficult instrument, so much so that sometimes when one of the four French horns of the Philharmonic gave out, he would be asked to substitute.

The family on my mother's side was Protestant Irish, from the North. Her mother's name was Bolton, Emily Bolton, and she married a rich landowner named Irwin who was shot by his tenants during the potato famine. It was some years after that she met my grandfather John Hall, who was then a young clergyman preaching in Dublin, a little bit younger than she was. They were married. She'd had three sons by Irwin, and she had four sons and a daughter by her second husband, John Hall. My mother was the youngest. The distinguishing things about my mother, I would say, were her gentleness and patience and extreme intelligence. She was a tremendous reader and had a passion for poetry, so that early, as children, my brother and I had to recite and learn by heart a poem a week. At first we hated it, but we got to like it, and I think that's how my interest in poetry began. I probably inherited some of it from her. John Hall, my grandfather, also was a poet. He wrote poems for the religious-theological magazines of the day, which were very widely read, and for those old magazines like *The Independent, The Outlook,* and other ones.

John Hall, my maternal grandfather after whom I am named, was a mysterious figure to me, as a boy, and to my brother. He was born in Armagh, Ireland, a poor boy, so poor they often didn't have even enough to buy shoes. He worked his way through Trinity College, Dublin, and graduated with honors; then he was called to the First Presbyterian Church in Armagh. He was greatly beloved by his congregation there. I don't remember how long he was pastor there, but we have a most beautiful sideboard, reaching way up to the ceiling, in our country house at East Hampton, which was presented to him by a loving congregation, when he was called to Dublin, as pastor of the most important Protestant church in Dublin, the First Presbyterian.

When I knew him, he had, of course, been called from the Dublin church to the fashionable pulpit of the Fifth Avenue Presbyterian Church at Fifth Avenue and Fifty-fifth Street. We went to service in that church in the morning, every Sunday, and then moved over to the manse at 712 Fifth Avenue for lunch. My grandfather appeared to advantage in the pulpit. He was an enormous man, six foot six, I believe, and very gentle, but gave the impression of great strength too. He was a man of mystery to my brother and myself, because of his awesome presence in the pulpit and his kindly and, at times, mischievous charm, when out of it. We were very young when we first went to church. We were allowed to play on the floor of the pew, if we kept quiet. Every now and then we'd sit up and see our grandfather reach out his great arms in some gesture of appeal. His fame rested on his preaching more than on anything else. He had a remarkable voice, and was known as "The Golden-Voiced Preacher."

After having seen him in his majestic role in the pulpit, we regarded him as an entirely different person after he passed from the church to the manse through a little door in the wall. We used to wait there, near that door, till he came through in his black cassock, very, very warm from the exertion of preaching, and disappeared, while we sat down in the library waiting for him to come back. There we were surrounded, when we were old enough to read at all, by books that piqued our curiosity. There was one book called *Dogmatic Theology,* which aroused our interest because of its first syllable, and another one called *Nosology,* which we thought must be about noses. He would greet us in the library and talk to us a little bit about the sermon. Did we remember the text? He was quite direct and simple. He would tell us to be good boys. This didn't worry us too much. We found him fascinating.

Then at lunch, which was downstairs, Grandpapa did all the carving. My grandmother drew him out and let him do most of the talking. We didn't understand much of what he said, but we did feel a strong attraction to him. He had a mischievous sense of humor. He was overweight, and he had a heart condition. His wife, my grandmother, usually went ahead of him, very majestically and slowly, up the stairs, so that he would have to follow very slowly. She blocked his way. He would wait at the foot of the stairs until she got to the top, then he would run up, two steps at a time.

He did have in his congregation people who were well known at the time. One who eventually made his home in Chicago was a man named Cyrus McCormick, who founded the International Harvester Corporation and was the inventor of the McCormick Reaper. I remember he sometimes came to dinner at the manse when we were there, and he had the curious habit of requiring a bowl of hot mustard water to put his feet in when he was at dinner, which intrigued my brother and myself. He became a famous and wealthy man because of his invention.

My grandfather wrote books, too, and gave my brother and myself several books. One was called *Talks to Boys,* which we found a little oppressive because the emphasis was so much on being good. I think it was not strange that we were so much influenced by him, in spite of all this. He had enormous personal magnetism.

My grandfather was with the Fifth Avenue church for thirty-eight years. He published books, as well as poems in various religious magazines. He was appointed Chancellor of New York University, and he preached a great deal at Yale and issued a book for the Yale students, too. He was, all in all, a very influential man in his time. But by the end of the thirty-eight years, his congregation had become more modern-minded; young people had come in, and they found him old-fashioned. They wanted a different kind of preacher, and they wanted choirs and vestments and all the trappings. My grandfather was very stubborn about it all, and eventually he was asked to resign by one faction in the congregation. They suggested his retirement. Anyway, they succeeded in ousting my grand-father, and then another section of the congregation, extremely loyal and devoted to my grandfather, got hold of him and told him to reconsider his resignation and remain. It was a mistake, because the people who wanted him out were determined to get him out. They did, and he went home to Ireland that summer. He always went home every summer, took all his family with him to Europe. They would go to France or other countries but always end up in Ireland. He went back to his old home in Ireland and died there, I really think, of a broken heart. Of course, he had this heart condition anyway, and the whole grief of the thing was probably too much for him.

One of my few memories of being absolutely overwhelmed by the impressiveness of a service was at my grandfather's funeral in that Fifth Avenue Presbyterian Church. They brought his body back, and the funeral was there, and the church was jammed with people. They sang all his favorite hymns—"In the Cross of Christ I Glory, Towering O'er the Wrecks of Time" and "The Church's One Foundation" and some of the Isaac Watts hymns.

Well, that's all I wanted to say about my maternal grandfather, Dr. John Hall. He did make a great impression on my brother and myself, although many of the things he talked about bored us as boys, and many of the things that he believed we were unable to believe. But I could see, later in life, how fortunate he was in that he could believe them and that my grandmother could believe them, because when Grandpapa Hall died, in Ireland, people said it was the happiest death they'd ever seen. He sang part of the time, knowing that he was about to rejoin people he loved and that my grandmother would follow him soon and they would be reunited in another, better world. His faith sustained him throughout his entire life. My mother inherited, and showed me once, a little notebook which he'd kept, in which he'd jotted down his feelings when he was going about on his pastoral duties. Although he weighed, I think, nearly two hundred fifty pounds, he climbed to the top of the stairs of little rickety buildings and visited every one of his parishioners, rich and poor, twice a year. This notebook was crammed with soul-searchings: of how unworthy he was, of how he must try to do better about this and about that, and so on; there were poignant prayers—evidently of a suffering man, ridden with guilt, and yet sustained by this absolute faith.

My father was a great admirer of him, yes. My grandfather was very fond of my father. They got along beautifully. My grandmother Hall was a very attractive woman, but she was what might be called a strong-minded, as well as a high-minded, woman. She was older than her husband and ruled him a good deal; also, she had an imagination that enabled her to believe anything she wanted to believe.

My father and mother had only three children. I was the eldest. My brother Almy, named after William Almy Wheelock, his paternal grandfather, died at the age of nine. I was a year older than he was, and we had been very companionable. His death was a terrible blow and shock to me at the age of ten.

Then there was a sister, Emily. She was twelve years younger than myself, so she must have been born in 1898. Emily, without our knowing it, had been a mental case from childhood. We all marveled at her extraordinary whimsicality and strangeness. But as she grew older, she began to show definite signs of mental upset which, as usual, the family is never willing to think of as mental upset. We just thought, "That's Emily's charming whimsicality."

She married a very fine man, whom, I think, she was not in love with. Anyway, she left him on their honeymoon, came back to New York and took a room in a hotel across the street from the house where my mother was living, and where I was living, for I was not yet married, and she got a great deal of pleasure from looking out of the window and watching us going in and out of the house, under the misconception, in our minds, that she was in Bermuda on her honeymoon. Well, there were things like this that she did. Her husband came back to New York and said that in spite of the way she had treated him, he was willing to take her back, wanted to take her back. But she wouldn't hear of it. Eventually they were divorced. Long before that, in fact, some two or three weeks after the marriage, she had discovered that she was pregnant, and she had a daughter, Sally.

After my mother's death in 1938, my sister Emily became more and more peculiar, until finally it was obvious that she was completely psychotic. And the family lawyer, whom she had called on several times and talked to very strangely, called me up and said, "You'll have to do something about this." That very night when I came home and went to her apartment to see her, I found her in the act of—I don't know what, but all the gas jets in the kitchen stove were open, and she and the child were there alone. I discovered this, and she was very embarrassed and said that she'd meant to light the gas right away but had got a telephone call. I realized that I would have to spend the night there. To make a long story short, in the end she had to be committed to the New York Hospital. I went up to see her every week, and it was so agonizing an experience that the doctor said, "You accomplish nothing. She just hangs on to you." When I'd try to go, she'd be clutching my knees, lying on the floor and pleading with me not to leave her in this dreadful place. "What *are* you doing to me?" she would cry. I couldn't stand it, and they said it only made her worse. So in an effort to get it all out of my mind, I went abroad, and when I was in London, I had news that she had escaped from the hospital and gone to the top of this building where she had spied on us, on Sixty-third Street—it's called, I think, the Barbizon-Plaza—and had thrown herself from the roof and was killed instantly.

■ ■ ■ ■

One of the things my mother told me, which made quite an impression on me, was that my birth was a very difficult one and that she heard during her suffering, which was very prolonged, the sound of grasshoppers and crickets. The sound seemed to become monstrously amplified in her hearing, in her pain. And it's a strange thing that long before she told me this, these insects, which I've heard in East Hampton and which I've written so much about in my poems, had a peculiar effect upon me. One of my best-known poems is called "The Divine Insect," which is what I called one of these cicadas as a boy, because of its clear, high monotone that always made me think of eternity or something endless and far away—and it seemed as though this might be tied up in some way with what my mother had gone through when I was being born. At least she thought so.

We had at home, one of the first human beings I remember, apart from my parents, a German nurse, Lydia—to me a most beautiful woman. She always has remained so in my mind, with dark hair, and very, very sweet, very, very firm, too, as a nurse. One of my earliest memories is having Lydia take me into Central Park and hearing there some sort of a siren or whistle. It may have been the deep bass whistle of a steamer in the distance—I hear them now, before they depart—or it may have been the noon whistle. But this has made those sounds have a special meaning for me that I can't quite define, because they are tied up with early memory. I was very much attached to Lydia, more than Almy, my brother, was. I was in some ways almost more attached to her than I was to my mother. She must have left perhaps when I was four or five. Then after that, we had governesses, always Germans. In those days—that was some time ago—it was the thing to have not French but German governesses, and they always had to come from a certain part of Germany, from Hanover, where the purest German is spoken. I learned German, very early, and I could speak it just like English. I can read it like English even now. Well, then, I remember Lydia with especial affection, almost as if I'd been in love with her.

My mother told me various amusing stories about myself. One was that I was so solemn as a child that she didn't dare to be left alone in the room with me. She felt more comfortable if somebody else was in the room. Another, that she asked her father, the clergyman, Dr. John Hall, "How shall I tell the child about God?"—or, the children, my brother included. My grandfather said, "The next time you're in the country, in the summer, on a beautiful star-clear night, just take the boy under the stars."

I have to add at this point of the story that I couldn't pronounce my own name, Jack, so I called it "Datch," and my mother took me out first, as the eldest, and held me up under this glittering inverted cup of stars, and said, "Who made all this?"—which was what my grandfather had told her to say. And he'd added, "The child will be made very thoughtful by this question." My mother said it again, and I didn't say anything. She turned my head up and said, "Who made all this?" And I immediately answered, "Datch!"

We were in East Hampton. You see, not being in school in those early years, we'd go down in May and wouldn't come back till November, because my father loved trees and gardens and all the things that I speak of in my poem about him, called "The Gardener." He was already retired from everything, you see, but he practiced every day on his French horn for at least two or three hours.

I had been ill from the time I was born. I was born as a "blue baby," with a valvular lesion of the heart, because my mother had had rheumatic fever while she was carrying me. It was thought I wouldn't live. I didn't suffer from the valvular lesion, but I did suffer in childhood from the most terrible colics, as they were called. I remember during all those years there were periods, probably three or four times a year, when I had these attacks, and I was blamed for crying and screaming, because it was thought to be colic and they said, "Don't make such a fuss about a little colic. Lots of children have colic." But for two or three days I wasn't allowed to have anything except milk toast and boiled milk. I would spend my time making lists, as I got a little older, of delicious things to eat, in order to satisfy my ravenous hunger vicariously.

My brother and I were sent to a school on Forty-second Street called Miss Miller's School, a private school which faced what was then a reservoir, where the New York Public Library is. When my brother was nine, I must have been ten—therefore it must have been 1896—we both had attended an organization called the Knickerbocker Greys, a military organization for boys, supposed to be very good for them because they were drilled in the armory down at Lexington Avenue and Thirty-fourth Street by soldiers—drill formation and squads and all the maneuvers that teach soldiers how to move in unison. We were both of us rather gentle boys —rather timid, I might even say—because I remember some of the other boys would gang up on us and follow us all the way home, coming up very close to us and snowballing us, and we never threw any snowballs back. We just went ahead, anxious to get home as soon as possible. This was the time when we were allowed to go and come from school without a governess, and of course in those days, crossing streets—— Well, you could cross Fifth Avenue at almost any place or time without even looking very much to one side or the other, traffic was so light.

This horrible measles epidemic broke out there, spread among the boys of the Knickerbocker Greys—a singularly virulent form of measles. My brother and I both came down with it. I don't remember just when it struck, but I know it was before Christmas, and my brother was bedridden and struggling with this thing. After the measles the only casualty I suffered was one perforated eardrum, which has made me slightly deaf in my left ear. But Almy went on into the regular pattern they so dreaded. He had rheumatic fever after the measles, and then the rheumatic fever damaged his heart. He developed pericarditis and endocarditis and a terrible St. Vitus, and this was going on all winter long, from before Christmas right up to June.

My father was a morbidly sensitive man, and, as often happened when anybody in the family was sick, he himself got sick and went to bed. My poor mother had this desperately sick boy on her hands and a husband who was neurotic and just went to bed, went all to pieces. He couldn't bear it, the thought that this boy might die. He was ashamed of himself for not being able to be more—— But he couldn't help it.

So I was sent away to my grandmother's. My grandfather, William Almy Wheelock, had a lovely place—it was lovely then—at One Hundred Fifty-fifth Street and the Hudson River. There my father had grown up as a boy, had had his boats—his canoes and rowboats. He was one of the few men who ever paddled all around the island of Manhattan in a double-paddle canoe. He was an athlete. At Yale he was—well, I've seen photographs of him that horrified my mother, looking like Sandow,[1] with these enormous muscles on his chest, in his arms.

So I was sent up to my grandfather's, which really meant living with my grandmother, because my grandfather was driven by his coachman and his team downtown to Wall Street every morning, and didn't come back till evening. Every evening when he came back, he brought fresh flowers to my grandmother. He was most gallant, so terribly in love with her his whole life long. I was lonely, and I was heartbroken about my brother's illness. He had been my principal comrade. And I wrote him a letter almost every day. I think most of them he probably was not even allowed to see. My mother very faithfully wrote me, did everything she could to try to help me with my awful homesickness, but I never can forget that winter. My grandmother was very sweet, but a rather austere person. However, she got me interested in Audubon, Audubon's birds. She and my grandfather had been friends with Audubon, who lived near them, and I saw those fascinating colored plates of Audubon's—not in the big folio, but in the quartos—and I started drawing pictures of birds with crayons that my grandmother gave me. She encouraged me in this, and I've been interested in birds since a child. I knew a great many birds from East Hampton, and I made these pictures, and then, having noticed that in the Audubon book each bird's picture was covered with a bit of tissue, I covered my pictures with toilet paper—which was the only tissue paper I could get—much to my grandmother's amusement.

Well, then, this went on all winter. Almy and I had been very close. We loved East Hampton, which we always referred to as "the dear country." It's the same house and the same place that my wife and I now spend our summers in, so I have seventy-eight years of association with it, and it's been the source of—— Almost all my poetry has been written there, or a great deal of it. I remember that coming back to New York was, for my brother and myself, a form of degradation, after the sea and the dunes and the house with the beautiful trees and gardens that my father had created, and no other house visible from where we were in deep country. Coming back to New York, the sound we hated most of all was the "clop clop clop clop" of horses' hooves on the pavement. That represented to us the dreariness of New York. And then of course school and the confinement of these tall rooms with their high ceilings and the big curtains hanging—the gloom of it all.

I was allowed to come home. Preparations were under way which I hadn't been told about. My brother was over his illness, but he was going to be an invalid. He would have to be confined to a wheelchair for the rest of his life because his heart had been so badly damaged. The doctors had said, "You've got to take him to the country. He will need to live permanently in the country." My father had chosen Morristown because there were friends there, and it was not too far from New York, about thirty-five miles—Morristown, New Jersey.

A special car was rented from the railroad, and the doctors—two doctors and a nurse—went down with Almy and my mother and father and myself to Morristown. My father had rented a house there. Just why he rented that particular house, I don't know. Perhaps he couldn't get anything else. It was up on a hill, on the wrong side of town, with a level waste of land stretching away in the distance where there were dumps from the town, and you went up to it by a long winding road between yew trees. It looked very much like the kind of house that Charles Addams would draw in *The New Yorker,* gloom and horror, with little pinnacles and turrets—one of those absurd monstrosities of that period, with a verandah running all the way around. It did have an orchard of apple trees and a stable. And there we were.

My brother was put in the best room in the house, and a nurse was with him at night, and my mother took care of him in the daytime. And a week after we had arrived there, he died. He died of general uremia, from failure of the kidneys. I was in the room at the time, and this was very bad and unfortunate for me because I never forgot it, and it filled me with a horror of death. My mother was in the room, and my brother, who was not allowed to move very much, and was supposed to be resting from the journey, sat up and said, "Glass of water." My mother rushed out to get the glass of water, leaving me alone in the room, and suddenly Almy looked up and cried out, "Look! Look, Mama, how beautiful!" And with that he had a convulsion, a perfectly colossal writhing and wrenching of his whole body as if he was struggling to get out of it. And he fell back dead on the bed. I saw all this. I was ashamed because I hadn't done anything to help him. I turned away and covered my face with my hands in horror.

Then, after the funeral services, we came to New York with the body, and I remember the horror of seeing my brother's casket put into the baggage car, which of course is where they always put them. This was my brother being put into a baggage car. We went out to Woodlawn Cemetery, to the family plot there, and I saw the casket lowered into the ground.

Then we came home to Morristown. And through some lack of imagination on my parents' part, they put me into *his* bed in *his* room, where I'd seen his dead body lying for three days! And I couldn't sleep. I just could not sleep. I got up night after night and knocked timidly on the door of my father's and mother's room, but never with enough force to really wake them up, feeling so ashamed to be doing this—and above all feeling the deepest sense of shame that I should be afraid of my own dear dead brother. I couldn't admit this to anyone, except to myself.

Well, finally, I got ill. I lost weight, and I got nervous, and my father forced a confession out of me. I was amazed how kind he was. "Why, of course," he said, "how stupid of us not to have thought of this." He didn't take me out of the room—he had some idea I had to fight it out—but he came and moved into the room and slept with me. Of course that made everything all right. As I say, it was the best room in the house that they were giving me. He stayed with me for several weeks, and I had got over it long before that. It was so comforting having my father there that I never told him that he could go now.

Well, one of the things that was curious about both my brother and myself—— I might say, my brother was the popular one in the family, and with other boys. He was more adventurous than I was and much more popular than I was. I was rather shy. I was rather the introverted type. Almy was an extrovert: very good at roller skating, for instance, which I wasn't good at, and always bringing friends home, which I never did. I never had the slightest feeling of jealousy about this—I admired him so much—but it certainly was true. And then also, of course, it was held against me that I behaved in such a cowardly way when I had these attacks of so-called colic.

We came from a very religious background. My mother was the daughter of the manse; my father had been brought up very strictly. I remember his telling me that he was never allowed to look at his toys on a Sunday, and that if he ever, by mistake or through naughtiness, took toys out of the closet—which was usually locked, but if it was left unlocked and he took the toys out—he was forced to walk backward holding the toys behind his back and drop them in the closet. And we, as boys, at East Hampton, for instance, even in the summertime, were never allowed to go the beach or to go swimming or to read any book except a sacred book or to hear any music except sacred music on Sundays. We had to go to church in the morning, and we had to go to the chapel for prayer meeting in the afternoon, and we had to go to Sunday School; and we both had to learn the *Shorter Catechism* and the *Larger Catechism,* and I still know them by heart.

And yet, from the very beginning of childhood, neither of us believed any of these things, any more than I do now.

I don't know what it was, but I know, for instance, that we never believed in Santa Claus, even when we were very small. And darling Mother, who really it seems to me was the dearest mother anyone could have had—she was so strong and yet so gentle, so full of love—she would hang up our stockings most carefully, while we lay in bed. We never slept a wink the night before Christmas. We'd close our eyes tight and lie quiet so as not to hurt Mother's feelings, and she would hang the stockings up over the fire-place, and the next day we would make all sorts of sounds of delight because Santa Claus had brought us this or that, knowing perfectly well, of course all the time, that there was no such thing as Santa Claus. And I knew perfectly well that Christ never walked on water and that the body is not resurrected after death—and, in other words, both our feelings from the very beginning were that there is just one universe and that is the natural universe, and there is nothing supernatural. That, I think, is rather strange for children to have sensed. I did, and do, admire Christ very much as a man, as a personality, and as a teacher; but I never for one moment thought that He performed the impossible, the miracles, or did any other sleight-of-hand tricks.

We stayed in Morristown. My father'd got the bit in his teeth—— He was back in the country. You know, he hated the city. When he was in the city he never did anything but practice on his French horn or sit with his head in his hands in gloom. There in Morristown he began making this place just as beautiful as he had made the East Hampton place. He had a gardener to help him. And I was sent to Mr. Talmadge's School in Morris-town, a school down in the town which—fortunately for me—was attended mostly by boys from the town. It was a private school. The butcher's son went to it, other boys, sons of the local tradesmen went, and it was good for me to meet these boys and to mix with them.

Now, coming to the gist of the matter, these colics of mine got worse and kept me out of school three or four times a year; and about a year and a half after my brother's death, I had a particularly violent attack, and the pain became so intense that I remember lying on my bed and—my poor father, who was so neurotic about illness, almost out of his head himself—and begging my father to kill me: "Kill me, Father!" I screamed. I couldn't stand it, it was so awful—writhing on the bed. Why he didn't give me morphine (as a doctor, he could have), I don't know, but, anyhow, he sent for the family doctor, the same man who had delivered my sister, Emily.

She was born while we were in Morristown. You see, we'd moved there when I was ten, and she wasn't born until I was twelve.

The doctor came, and he said, "Why, this boy's got peritonitis! His appendix has burst. He's already suffering from general sepsis, from blood poisoning." I wasn't told this, of course, but he added, "He's within a day or so of death. Something's got to be done and done quickly."

He gave me morphine, and all my pain ceased. A surgeon was sent for, Dr. Abbey, a very eminent surgeon who had specialized in the then rather rare operation, appendectomy. There were no Sunday trains to Morristown; they shared in this general puritanical feeling about Sunday. The surgeon had to drive all the way out in a buggy with his anesthesiologist, and I was operated on on the kitchen table. They gave me ether. It is a brutal thing; they never would dream of doing it today. They had nothing better in those days. My father held me down on one side, my mother on the other. The nurse held one leg, and the anesthesiologist tried to hold down the other, and I just strangled to death—at least that's how it seemed to me. They put this cone over my head, and I couldn't get any air. Then suddenly I was in a big revolving steel tube with steel dragons whirling around in it screaming, and I was the only soft living thing in this tube, and then I blacked out.

About twenty-four hours later I came to and saw two figures, immobile, seated at my bedside, and I thought: "I'm dead. And these are statues in the mausoleum." I was so wretched from the headache and the vomiting that came on soon. If you've ever been dead drunk, it's just like a very bad hangover from that. And these figures came to life almost immediately and tried to help me. And I got over it. But they had to leave the wound open for—I think it was for two months—to drain the pus away, from the peritonitis. The worst of it was that the flesh kept growing over, what they call "proud flesh," and it had to be burned off with nitre every once in a while, and the dressings were almost as bad as the operation itself. They offered me a whiff of ether each time before the dressing, but I now had such a horror of ether that I refused it. I just had to stand the probing around in this big wound.

Well, I got over it. I remember my father—such a strange man—even the day after, two days after the operation, he couldn't sleep, and he got up early in the morning and came to my room and wheeled my bed around to the other side of the room so that I could see what he said was a particularly beautiful dawn: "I want you to see this." And I was way beyond caring about dawns! But that was the way he was.

I could hear his French horn when I was getting well. First I hated the sound of it, and then I loved it—playing Beethoven melodies and Schumann and Brahms, some of those wonderful horn passages and, above all, the melodies of Mendelssohn, which, if I run them over now in my head, bring all my childhood back to me.

I read a great deal, and my brother and I had had to learn all these poems by heart, and I could say them over to myself. Some of them were poems that didn't mean much to us. I remember one that I particularly disliked, "All are architects of Fate / Working in these walls of Time."[2] What could that mean to a child? We read, of course, *Alice in Wonderland* and *Through the Looking-Glass.* We read all the books that one reads in childhood, or did in those days—*Davy and the Goblin.* . . .[3] My mother read to me when I wasn't up to it, and sometimes she'd read, and I would fall asleep while she was reading. She would go right on, and I would wake up, and there she would be, still reading.

I got over it. Then there began a new period in my life. I'd always been timid, and in a way cut off from other boys. Now, I was going with a gang. Our place was chosen as the haunt where the gang met. And our place had slopes down which we could coast, and it had an orchard where we could climb trees. Sometimes there would be fourteen or fifteen boys there. I still remember the names of some of them. They wouldn't mean anything, of course—Biggie Watts, who had only one leg and the other was a wooden leg, which caused much amusement when a snowball struck it with a resounding thud. And Kid Waller and Baby Waller and the two Poore boys, and, oh, there were fourteen or fifteen of them.

I went back to school, but the great thing was the restoration to me of the normal pride of a boy. I became almost a leader for the time being and a favorite of the other boys, partly because they met on our place, my father's place. I was known as "Burly." That was my nickname. All the boys called me Burly. I was fairly heavy, after I got well, a little overweight. I took pride in my nickname, never having had one before. I took pride in the experience of normal companionship with a lot of boys.

I went back a grade, but only temporarily because then I was moved up to my normal grade. I'd learned a great deal from the governesses that we had. We had one governess, Fraulein Maison—she was Huguenot; Maison, you know, the French word for "house"—who was a regular martinet, so much so that my mother dismissed her when she found out how she treated my brother and myself. For instance, if you put elbows on the table after being forbidden to do this, when you weren't looking she'd grab your arm and jam it down on the funny bone. And she would box your ears. We were so afraid of her that we never dared tell our parents what was happening. My mother found it out one day (oh, Fraulein Maison had cruel and unusual punishments) and dismissed her immediately. I remember the day after she'd gone—this was at East Hampton—my brother and I climbed the old oak tree and all the high branches that she had forbidden us ever to go on, and as we did so we wept. It was so poignant, violating all the rules laid down by this pathetic, stern, rejected person whom, in spite of everything, we'd grown fond of.

I soon went to the boarding school that is situated on the outskirts of Morristown, between Morristown and Boonton, in beautiful country, with the Boonton hills blue in the distance. That was the Morristown School, run by three Harvard men, all of them athletes—Francis Coll Woodman, who had been stroke on the Harvard varsity crew and captain of the football team; Thomas Quincy Browne, who had been coxswain of the crew; and Arthur Pierce Butler, who had been on the crew also and had been a very fine baseball player. I was not a boarder. They had day scholars, and a bus came and collected the day boys and took them up to the school, which was about two miles from our house.

I had a very, very thin time at that school because it was athletically minded, and I liked to moon around. I liked to go out in the woods or go down to the farmhouse at the foot of the hill and eat chocolate cake that the farmer's daughter sold down there. And I was writing poems. I think my first one that I recall was written when I was nine. I'd been reading a great deal of Sir Walter Scott, *The Lady of the Lake,* also the novels, but the poetry was what appealed to me most of all. I wrote a poem about a stag that my mother thought was wonderful, and when I say it to myself now, I realize how kind she was. It was a terrible jingle. But I remember it: "The stag is on his weary way, / He will neither stop nor stay; / When he heard the hunter's horn, / He jumped as if pricked by a thorn, / Threw out his heels and dashed away, / Down through the forest and out to the bay." Oh, awful!

I think that's the first poem that I remember consciously having written. I had been trying to imitate the great poets, and I kept right on with it, and I was in full flood when I was at the Morristown School. There it was disapproved of. The rules there were that when the boys were out on the football field practicing, those who were not on the football team must stand on the sidelines and cheer the boys on because we were told the most terrible rubbish, such as: "These boys are giving all that they've got for you and for the honor of the school. Now, the least you can do is to stand by and shout, 'Rah, rah, rah!'" And I was against all that, and I didn't hesitate to show it. I was very unpopular at school. And then the worst blow of all fell. My Latin teacher, who was the one teacher whom I respected and who had aroused my interest in the subject of Latin, Latin poetry and Greek poetry, liked the translation I had made of the first book of Ovid's *Metamorphoses* and told me that he was printing it in the school paper, *The Morristonian*. And I was horror-struck. I said, "Oh, please don't do that! Why, they'll murder me here, the other boys! That'll be the last of me!"

"Well," he said, "I'll tell you what I'll do. I'll leave your name off. But I will have to say, because it's really not a strict translation, 'A paraphrase from Ovid's *Metamorphoses* by a third-former.'" So it appeared as that, and of course the other boys found out, and I remember a man named Tommy Birch, who was on the football team of the school, coming up to me and saying, "Did you write that stuff in *The Morristonian?*" And I hotly denied it. "You did so!" he sneered. "No, I did not. I know nothing about it. I don't know a thing about it."

"You're a liar! You wrote that, you sissy!" I thought he was going to strike me in the face, because they had no discipline in that school at all. The hazing was perfectly awful. However, he refrained. And emboldened by that, I went on, and I had quite a few poems in *The Morristonian* with my name. And I have had an offer from a very eminent book dealer here in New York who said if I would get that copy of *The Morristonian* with that first published poem of mine, he would give me seven hundred fifty dollars for it. The book dealer was the Seven Gables Bookshop, just off Fifth Avenue.[4] Well, I have a copy of that issue. My mother did bookbinding and weaving and other things. She faithfully bound together all the copies of *The Morristonian* that had anything in them by her darling.[5]

There were just a few things about the earlier days in New York that I thought might be amusing. The great excitement of the year was going to East Hampton, and I remember the landau coming up to the house, and driving to the Long Island ferry, all being magically transported over to the Long Island Railroad—and then not to East Hampton, because they didn't yet have a railroad station there, but to Bridgehampton—and then driving, coach and four, with a man blowing on a coaching horn, to East Hampton.

I had been reading about Columbus and his men when they first discovered America falling to the ground and kissing the earth. It was in May, and everything was deep in mud. I was in a white sailor suit that my mother particularly liked us to wear, and I jumped down—thinking I was doing a heroic and beautiful thing—and threw myself face down and kissed the earth. I got a severe spanking instead of all the admiration I had hoped to arouse.

Also, at East Hampton I was terribly admiring of Christ, and I thought, "I'm going to try to be like Him." I tried to be Christlike all that week, until my father came to me and said, "Jack, what *is* the trouble? You're acting very strangely, and I'm getting awfully tired of it." He said, "Be yourself," although I'm sure he never used that phrase. But you see, there were so few ways in which I could show that I was behaving like Christ. I mean, I could only do it by always insisting that I wanted very little dessert or none, and that everyone else must have this or that first, and could I run errands, could I do this, and getting in everybody's way, you know, like the clown in the circus.

I was given music lessons as a boy, on the piano, and I used to love to improvise by the hour, and of course my mother thought this was marvelous. My father took a rather dim view of it, being much more musical than my mother, and he said, "Why don't you learn how to play the piano properly? Never mind about the improvisations." Then the teacher I was given took away all my interest in the piano. She said, "You must hold your hands like this. I'm going to put a penny on each hand, and you must be able to play without the penny falling off." And I lost all interest in piano-playing and gave it up.

My father never had any use for poetry except that of Shakespeare and Goethe. He read German; he'd spent some time in Germany. All medical students had to learn German so that they could read German medical books. But he made fun of me. He used to hear me in my room, as a boy, reciting my poems to myself in the way that poets do recite, and it sounded a good deal like praying, and he used to poke fun at me, saying, "What were you praying about in your room this afternoon?" And I was very embarrassed and wouldn't admit that I was saying my poems to myself. Then he wrote a poem, making fun of my poetry, and the first line of it, I remember, was: "When through the dusk the blundering twilight stumbled—" That was his idea, you know, of the sound of poetry. Also he wrote a very lovely poem of his own about a lark's nest that was spared by the mowers who came to mow our meadow in front of the house. These huge machines had carefully gone around one place where there was a little lark's nest, leaving it in the center of the field untouched. You know, that poem was exactly the subject that Robert Frost much later made into one of his most beautiful poems called "The Tuft of Flowers." I think my father's sonnet (I still have it) is lovely in its feeling, but of course unskilled. It's the poem of an amateur—the same sort of job that I would do if I tried to make a hat.

He never praised a poem of mine, except one. He did like certain of the modern poets. For instance, he was very much fascinated by Edgar Lee Masters's *Spoon River Anthology,* with those very grim, realistic, disillusioned portrayals of the terrible things that go on in a small western town. He was impressed by Robert Frost. I wrote a poem that came out in the *Yale Review,* when I was, oh, I don't know, twenty-five or so. Anyway, my father read this poem and spoke to me about it, and said—he never praised too much, but he said, "I like your poem in the *Yale Review.*" It was the first time he'd ever liked anything of mine, and I was immeasurably proud. It meant more to me than all the praise that my mother always showered on everything I did.

I went to college in the fall of 1904, graduating from the Morristown School, but without diploma. My marks had been good, although not particularly distinguished, but I was not given my diploma because of "lack of school spirit, and untidiness." So I went up to college without the diploma. I passed my College Board examinations and entered Harvard with one boy from the Morristown School, Maunsel Crosby, whose father, Ernest Crosby, was at that time quite a well-known reformer, a poet, and the son of the Howard Crosby who had been a great friend of my grandfather John Hall, both North of Ireland men.

My father was feeling poor that year, 1904. I forget when it was that my grandfather Wheelock died, but I think it must have been just after my grandfather Wheelock's death, and the estate wasn't settled yet, and business —They'd been going through a panic. I remember that my grandfather, I was told, had walked the floor all one night during this panic, not knowing whether the Central National Bank, of which he was director, was going to pull through or not.

So my father said, "We'll have to economize a little," and I got one of the poorest rooms in Cambridge, in Holyoke House, which is not in the Yard. It's outside—nothing the matter with it except it's a rather dingy brownstone house. My father, as you probably have gathered from what I've told you about him, was a rather special kind of man. He was a very solitary man. He was devoted to his family. He had only one friend that I know of, another doctor. My father was not a man who was skillful in arranging things, like getting a room—he didn't pull wires, he didn't have anything of the politician in him—so he had just got whatever he could get without too much trouble. And there I set everything up, and I started smoking a pipe, because I thought that was the thing to do. My father had never smoked, and I remember my mother telling me how she had said, when they were first married, that she liked a man to smoke a pipe, and he'd said, "I will take it up for your sake." Then nothing happened, and one day she asked him, "When is this pipe smoking going to begin?" "Oh," he said, "I've been doing it every morning. I get up every morning before you get up and smoke it for half an hour." My mother was very much amused.

Well, when I entered Harvard, my only friend there was Maunsel Crosby. He was in fashionable Beck Hall. His family was very well off indeed, for Ernest Crosby had married a Schieffelin, a very idiosyncratic woman, but a woman of great wealth, so that he could indulge his passions for being a reformer. He was a disciple of Tolstoy and often visited him in Russia. Ernest Crosby wrote Walt Whitmanesque verse that wasn't very good but was very noble, very idealistic, and so on.

However, I soon met my best and dearest friend at a punch night given by *The Harvard Monthly,* one of the undergraduate magazines. There are two, the *Advocate* and *The Harvard Monthly.* The latter, by the way, had been started by the philosopher George Santayana in my birth year, 1886. Each autumn this periodical gave a punch night at which candidates for contributorship to or for editorship of the magazine, and literary men in general, gathered, and I went. I was rather a shy boy. It was in the very beginning of my freshman year that I saw, standing in the room where we all were, a man who attracted my attention right away because he seemed even shyer than I was. There was something about his look that interested me. Summoning up my courage, I went up to him and spoke to him. This was Van Wyck Brooks. And we became friends. He turned out to be infinitely more mature and sophisticated than I was. I remained very immature. In fact, I still am. That's one reason perhaps why I feel younger than I am. I've never completely grown up.

Van Wyck was living in diggings somewhere on Charles Street, I think, an inexpensive room that he had heard about through somebody. Van Wyck and I started seeing a good deal of each other, and there at college I made other friends who as time went on became lifelong friends. One was Francis Biddle, who later became U.S. attorney general, and his brother, George Biddle, the painter, who's remained a closer friend than Francis because Francis lives in Washington while George lives in Crotonon-Hudson. Two other classmates became lifelong friends—the composer George Foote and another composer, Charles Seeger, who later became a musicologist and at one time was professor of music at the University of California. His son is Pete Seeger, the banjo picker.

Harvard had the elective system. You could choose anything you wanted in your studies. The college had a remarkable faculty at the time. Santayana was teaching there and Josiah Royce, William James, Hugo Münsterberg, Nathaniel Shaler, George Lyman Kittredge, and Charles Townsend Copeland, who was sort of the pet of the students. I don't think he was a great scholar, but he was an odd interesting man, Charles Townsend Copeland. There also was the famous Irving Babbitt who had such an influence at one time upon the ideas of Van Wyck Brooks. I found college simply marvelous—after having been through the dreariness of the Morristown School—then suddenly to find that I was living in my own separate place and was treated like a grown-up human being and was allowed to choose from these wonderful courses. Now I began actually to work at my studies, though I never could have been a scholar, really, because I was always writing verse, and that took up so much time.

I majored in English. I found when I went in that the Morristown School had prepared me so badly that although I was publishing poems in the magazine all the time, the school never gave me a certain course in advanced English that I would have had to have in order to escape the Harvard course English A, a freshman course that all freshmen had to take who hadn't taken advanced English in high school. So I had to go through English A, and I think probably it was very good for me. You had to write a theme every day, except Saturday and Sunday, and then every six months you had to write a thesis. That was a course that Kittredge ran, and he was very strict. I loved it at college. After the Morristown School, it was like a release from prison, having these friends. I didn't see much of my friends except at college, because in the summer we were at East Hampton.

The first poem I published while at college was published in *The Harvard Monthly.* At first I wouldn't submit any poems to any of the college magazines. Van Wyck Brooks, who was so much more mature than I, said, "Now, you've got to send out poems to these magazines. That's the way you begin." I agreed with him, but I didn't ever tell him that I wasn't going to do it, because I thought: "What would happen if they declined a poem of mine? I wouldn't be able to stand it." I was afraid. The rejection would be so awful. But then Van Wyck began having poems published. Do you know, I know all his poems by heart. I just can't forget them. They're not particularly good poems, but my memory for that sort of thing—I just can't shake them off. I try to forget them, but I can't.

Finally I felt I must too. So with great fear and trembling, I sent a poem called "Silence" to *The Harvard Monthly,* a short two-stanza poem— the first poem I had sent them. I waited a long time and I thought, they're going to reject it, what'll I do? Fortunately, I hadn't told Van Wyck I'd sent one in; I'd just lie up and down and say I was sticking to my guns. But they took it.[6]

> Sweet Music revels in her own delight,
> And sighs, "O slavish Silence—short-lived death
> Of airy splendors—how my whispered breath
> Hath slain thee wholly, as the dawn the night!"
>
> Even with the words the sound of them has passed:
> Quietness dims hushed voices till they cease,
> Soothing their aching beauty into peace.
> Silence remains, inexorable, vast.

So from then on, I sent them poems, and some of them were rejected, and it didn't make any difference because I'd already been accepted.

The man who was the editor in chief at that time was Swinburne Hale. He later married Inez Mulholland, the great feminist. He was a poet, but he never went on with it. He became a lawyer and made a lot of money. The secretary of the *Monthly* was a man who became quite well known, but not as a poet, although he began as a poet, Hermann Hagedorn. He became president of the Roosevelt Association.[7] My friend Van Wyck Brooks began as a poet, not at all as a critic or an essayist. He wrote political poems. He wrote a very prophetic poem about Korea—"Not omenless, the finger that points across the sea, / Where the angry storm dogs linger / In the leash of destiny. . . ."

In our freshman year, Van Wyck and I issued together a pamphlet called *Verses by Two Undergraduates.* Out of modesty we didn't put our names on it—and also I think we felt that was a wise measure. Of course this was printed at our own expense. We had saved up the money. Van Wyck was a man who was practically—— I don't know how he ever went through college; he never had any money. His father had committed suicide after a failure in one of the panics. He was a Wall Street man. Van Wyck had a wonderful mother who did everything she could for her two sons. Anyway, Van Wyck was always borrowing from me and used to be so annoyed

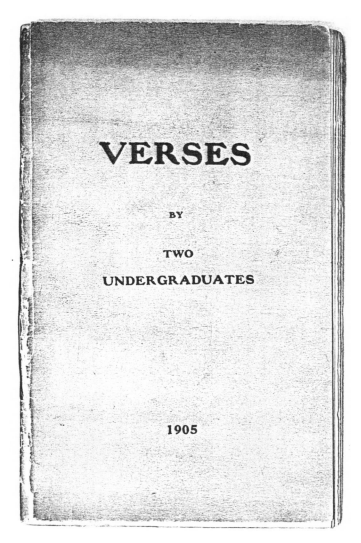

VERSES

BY

TWO

UNDERGRADUATES

1905

ABOVE AND OVERLEAF: *Verses by Two Undergraduates* is the first book for Whee-lock and Van Wyck Brooks (Matthew J. and Arlyn Bruccoli Collection of F. Scott Fitzgerald, Thomas Cooper Library, University of South Carolina)

While we were still freshmen at Harvard, Van Wyck Brooks and I, who had been writing verse for ten years or more, were certain that we were destined for great things. Rather than wait for a publisher, we decided to take the world by storm with <u>Verses by Two Undergraduates</u>, of which 100 copies were printed, at our own expense, nearly sixty years ago. The poems of Van Wyck Brooks appear on the right-hand page, throughout; mine, on the left-hand page. I still know most of the poems by heart. If memory serves me, 6 copies in all were sold.

John Hall Wheelock

October 8,
1963

when I'd take out a small purse and pick out the money, and he'd say, "Jack, don't ever hand out money like that. If a man asks you—a friend asks you—for a loan, just go to the bureau drawer where you have all your money and pull out a bunch of bills and hand them to him. Don't even look at them." He said, "You've got to learn to be a good fellow." I felt like saying, "Well, I never borrow from you." He said, "Money is a mere convenience. You must never take it so seriously." I thought, "It's a great convenience to you, but. . . ."

This pamphlet. Van Wyck, who was the more mature, intelligent man, said, "Of course, we'll have to put it on sale. The next time you go to New York, you take it in to Brentano's and to Scribner's bookstores and place some copies with them. What you do is to ask whether you can place it on consignment." So I went to Brentano's, and they didn't want it. They said, "We can't be bothered with these paper things; they get all messed up." However, they took five copies, and Scribner's took, I think, five copies. I'm not sure. But they didn't succeed in selling any, of course. I had eventually to take back these very messed-up copies. That is now an item that was listed in the Seven Gables Bookshop rare-book catalogue about two years ago, I think, at three hundred dollars.

These were poems that we'd written before we went to college. Van Wyck was very much in love with the woman whom he married, and I was very much in love with the woman to whom I am now married—just sheer luck that I am, because we weren't married until 1940, and in the meantime she'd been married to somebody else. Van Wyck's poems were mostly written to Eleanor, and my poems are mostly written to Phyllis. Also there were philosophical poems. My poems—let me get this right— my poems are on the left-hand page, and Van Wyck's on the right-hand page.

We issued them in the spring, I think in January or February of 1905, which was in our freshman year. We didn't make any stir of any kind whatsoever. But one of my poems was reprinted in what was then *The New York Evening Post,* with a brief comment saying, "Doesn't the following poem by a young undergraduate have rather unusual quality?" That was a poem called "Song on a Line from Shakespeare," and that line I afterwards found was my own. I thought I'd heard it in the theater. I went to see *Richard II*— Richard Mansfield was starring in it—and where Richard is in his tent and the ghosts come and speak to him, I distinctly heard the line, "Sleep on, I lie at heaven's high oriels," and I thought, "My God, what a beautiful line! I've got to write———" While I was in the theater, I made the poem, not quite sure what "oriels" are, and I looked the word up when I got home, and it was all right; it was a window, a bay window—just what you could look down from. It was published in *The Harvard Monthly* as "De Coelo" with the subtitle "Song on a line from Shakespeare."

> *"Sleep on, I lie at heaven's high oriels,"*
> Over the stars that murmur as they go,
> Lighting your lattice-window far below
> And every star some of the glory spells,
> Whereof I know.
>
> I have forgotten you long, long ago,
> Like the sweet, silver singing of thin bells
> Vanished, or music fading faint and low.
> *"Sleep on, I lie at heaven's high oriels,"*
> Who loved you so.

Then the letters began to come in, from various people saying, "Where is this line? We've been looking in the Shakespeare concordance, and we don't find any such line." I went to Kittredge about it. He said, "There isn't any such line in Shakespeare." I even wrote, at his advice, to the Mansfield Company, to see if what they called their working sheets showed that they had introduced some other Elizabethan line there. No, there was nothing of the sort. I must have heard something else and given it that form. But it's so puzzling, because I wasn't at the time familiar with the word "oriels."

In my second book, *The Belovèd Adventure,* where I first collected the poem, I called it "Nirvana." In a later book, *Poems 1911–1936,* I renamed it "Song from Heaven," and in *Poems Old and New,* it appears as "De Coelo." It's just a short two-stanza poem. I have never to this day quite believed that that line wasn't spoken in the theater, because the actor spoke very clearly, and I heard: "Sleep on"—this was to Richard in his tent, he was sleeping—"I lie at heaven's high oriels." This was the ghost speaking.

In my sophomore year I was made an editor of *The Harvard Monthly.* But I began having many poems in the *Advocate,* as well as in the *Monthly,* and I also wrote short stories for the *Monthly* under another name. The name was a silly one—Murdock was the last name, William Murdock. I thought: Wheelock, Murdock. Also I had a lot of poems in a third magazine that had sprung up, run by a man who later became a famous radio

Wheelock (front row, center) as editor of *The Harvard Monthly*, 1908

John Hall Wheelock

commentator. It was called *The Harvard Illustrated Magazine,* and his name was Kaltenborn—Hans von Kaltenborn.

The Harvard Monthly was the very highbrow magazine founded by George Santayana. The *Advocate* was the older, better-known magazine that had been going on I think before 1886. I had poems in all three magazines, and Van Wyck even more than I did. Then in my junior year I was made secretary of *The Harvard Monthly,* and in my senior year I was made editor in chief. It meant reading the manuscripts that the students sent in and passing on them.

Another thing that I've forgotten to say, a most grievous omission— Another man whom I met at Harvard and who became one of my most intimate friends, just as intimate a friend as Charlie Seeger or George Foote, perhaps not quite as intimate as Van Wyck Brooks, was Edward Sheldon. I roomed only during my sophomore year with Maunsel Crosby. In my junior year, Ned came to me and said, "I don't want to disturb anything, but why couldn't you and I room together? Do you think Maunsel would mind?" I thought he would, probably, because although we really didn't have much in common, still we'd both come up from school together. However, I got out of rooming with Maunsel, and Ned and I roomed together. Ned's great passion was writing. He had many very brilliant stories in the *Advocate* and in the *Monthly.* He graduated from Harvard in three years summa cum laude. He was already passionately interested in the theater, and while he was taking a fourth year to get his M.A., Mrs. Fiske came up from New York and while at Boston accepted an invitation to tea at the Stylus Club, a little undergraduate literary club, which I belonged to, and Ned also. Mrs. Fiske was bored to death with us there. The conversation had died, and she was silent, tapping her heels on the floor, and we were all very uncomfortable. We went for Ned because everyone knew Ned could do anything. When Ned appeared, he immediately hired a big limousine, took Mrs. Fiske all over Cambridge, showed her Longfellow's house and the other historic sights. He also showed her the scenario of Act I of his play *Salvation Nell.* She took the play on the strength of that one scenario, and the play was produced with enormous success in New York the year after Ned got his M.A.

Minnie Maddern Fiske was one of the great actresses of her time, like Sarah Bernhardt. She was considered the greatest American actress. I don't really think she was; she was very idiosyncratic. She was always "Mrs. Fiske," and that seems to be a fault of many American actresses—the inability to forget themselves in whatever part they are playing. She starred in this play which she'd taken on. Ned had of course submitted the scenarios of the other acts as he finished them, and then he had submitted the finished acts themselves. I think it was a four-act play—it was at least three acts— in the great school of Sardou and the French melodrama. It was a story of a Salvation Army girl, with many street scenes. Ned was the first play-wright to bring that sort of thing onto the stage, the sort of thing that Elmer Rice has done more recently. *Salvation Nell* was a smash hit; it made Ned a great deal of money.

In my junior year and during what was my senior year and was for Ned a postgraduate year, we roomed together in Prescott Hall, one of the unfashionable halls, very nice, over near the big Memorial Hall, where we used to have breakfast. My freshman year I ate all my meals there. It was the most inexpensive place. It was like a big cathedral, with these tables. It was a church, and these round tables——— It still is a church. The round tables held, if I remember rightly, eight people, and at our table two of them were Negroes—most delightful men, both of whom later made their mark. One was Alain LeRoy Locke. He eventually became a profes-sor at Howard University. The other man was a writer, Benjamin Brawley, who became a leader in the Negro movement. He became a professor at Negro colleges and wrote many sociological books that were published by Macmillan. None of the men at that table of eight had any feelings what-soever about eating with Negroes. In fact, we found the Negroes among the most interesting men at the table. But the Negro waiters who waited on us in that big place objected to it and said they weren't accustomed to "waiting on niggers." That's a situation you often found in those days.

I became a member of the Stylus Club, and I was elected president, and I was so immature that I didn't know what to do. I went home and I couldn't sleep. The next night I couldn't sleep. I was frightened at the idea of being president, and I spoke to Van Wyck about it, and Van Wyck couldn't even understand what the trouble was. He said, "What are you frightened of?" I said, "I don't know, but I can't sleep." He said, "Oh, don't be silly. There's nothing to it at all. You just get up and you preside at the meet-ings." I said, "Well, what do I say at the meetings?" "Say anything you want," he said.

It was just a small club, in a building that we rented. We had a woman who worked in the little kitchen there, just to give us tea, no meals. The custom was to go down there for drinks or tea. We had a locker. You know, Cambridge was dry. In Massachusetts they had local option. We had a locker with our liquor there. You were taken in in your freshman year.

You could go there any time, all through your college days. But if you didn't get in in your freshman year, you didn't get in at all. It was a nice group. They were the people I've spoken of, Edward Sheldon and George Foote and Charlie Seeger and Van Wyck Brooks and a man named Harold Bell, who was something of an aesthete; it was quite an interesting group— both the Biddles.

I belonged to all the literary societies; later in my junior year I was taken into the Signet, and then in my senior year into the senior literary club called the OK—whose only purpose, so far as I could see, was to get drunk. And we certainly did. We had dinners about once a month and usually ended up with some of us parading up and down on the table. I remember reciting a whole blank-verse Greek tragedy I'd written, that I thought would knock them out—and nobody paid the slightest attention to it. They were all too drunk even to listen. And I was drunk myself. We did an awful lot of drinking at Harvard in those years. I learned how unpleasant it is to pass out, unconscious, as I did twice, I think. Ned was wonderful on the first occasion. We came back from Boston in the car of Harold Bell, and they had the curfew then, and we ordered a lot of liquor so as to have it before curfew, and just when the hour came and we were going to leave, I had got up on a chair to recite something, and when I wasn't looking Harold Bell filled up my glass with straight whiskey. Then he said, "Bottoms up, we're going home now," and I in my drunken state drank this down. We got in his big car and went over the bridge, and as we drew near Cambridge, I thought I was dying. The whole world was just fading away, and I was awfully afraid. But Ned got me out of that car; he got me into the apartment; he undressed me and put me to bed. He wasn't a particularly strongly built man. He didn't give me any remedies. He didn't send for a doctor. I might have died that night, easily, from such an overdose of a narcotic. I came to in the morning—but, oh!

Santayana made a deep impression on me. He was a very remote man. You couldn't get at him. Even when he lectured, he looked out the windows, at the other side of the hall, never at the students. Some of us were passionate admirers of his sonnets. He wrote superb sonnets. He's still one of the best sonneteers that ever wrote, although he's rather forgotten at the moment. And he gave teas in his rooms, to which he invited some of his pupils, and I was lucky enough to be invited. There he got us to talk and read our poems. There he showed a different side. But for the most part, he was very remote, and as you know, he left the United States, after being there as teacher for a good many years, and he never came back. He boasted that he didn't leave a single friend behind. He went to live in England, and then later he went to Italy and lived in the convent of the Blue Nuns in Rome, where he died. And I became his editor at Scribners for many years.

Then, Josiah Royce——— I never had any personal contact with him nor with William James. James was the most fascinating person at Harvard. His lectures were wonderful, and his warmth—it was really very exciting to listen to him. Kittredge amused us all. He was supposed to be the most learned man in Cambridge, in Anglo-Saxon and all the old languages. He also was something of a showman, and he used deliberately to —I caught him at it one time, I know he did it on purpose—stumble as he went up on the platform, and then just catch himself, whereupon a titter of laughter would spread through the room among the students. Then he would turn around, furious—"Who laughed then?" You know, it was all a showpiece, but it endeared him to the men, who thought it was genuine.

They didn't have creative writing courses (that dreadful phrase) in those days. We had these English courses, and we had courses in certain periods of literature. There was a Professor De Wolfe who covered the period from Samuel Johnson's time on, and there were other very interesting courses, but nothing in the way of composition except English A, in which you had to write a theme every day. I wrote poems instead of themes, and they allowed me to do this.

I could have taken German, and it would have eased the work very much because I knew German well. But I'd read so much German poetry and prose already. Now during all these years I was writing more and more verse and particularly at East Hampton in the summers. I left college about the middle of June, or sometimes a little earlier, and then we were all there at East Hampton until the end of September, and I lived in a perfect trance—I don't think anyone ever had such a wonderful youth as I had—of poetry. I discovered many new poets. I had been reading Browning and Tennyson and of course the older poets, the Elizabethan poets, the metaphysicals, but now I suddenly discovered Rossetti and Swinburne and Morris and Yeats and Henley and the more modern French poets and German poets. I always read a great deal of German poetry. And I was just in the right mood. There was the sea as background, the sound of the sea, and I was young, and I fancied myself very much in love, and this flood of marvelous poetry that kept washing over me—it was almost unbearable. I was writing reams and reams of verse through it all.

JOHN HALL WHEELOCK

Born 1886, at Far Rockaway, L. I. Prepared at Morristown School. Home address, 5 Morris Ave., Morristown, N. J. Stylus, Signet, O. K.; Hasty Pudding Club, Phi Beta Kappa, Musical Club, Dramatic Club, Monthly, Class Poet. Degree cum laude.

From the 1908 *Harvard Class Album*

I graduated in 1908, not with any special distinction. I graduated cum laude. But I was Class Poet and editor in chief of *The Harvard Monthly* and Phi Beta Kappa, and I was a member of the Hasty Pudding Club. I was not taken by any of the Greek-letter societies. In fact, none of our literary group was. We were told—Hermann Hagedorn came to us and warned us—"Do you know what they call you, all through the college here?" I said, "No." "You are known as 'the intellectual snobs.'" We thought, that's magnificent!

I didn't know whether I would get my degree or not. I had had two conditions, algebra and geometry. I had worked the algebra off, but the geometry I never worked off, and I was never told whether I would get my degree or not. When we went to the hall where you get your diplomas on commencement day, I was uncertain about this. And yet, I couldn't help thinking that a man who was Phi Beta Kappa, Class Poet, editor in chief of *The Harvard Monthly,* and contributor to the *Advocate* and the *Illustrated Magazine,* and cum laude in his courses couldn't be refused a degree. And sure enough, there my diploma was, waiting for me.

[20 February 1967]

AMONG THE AMUSING EVENTS AT HARVARD was the initiation into some of the literary societies. There were three of these, the Stylus, the Signet, and the OK. The Signet initiation I remember distinctly because it was quite overawing to a young man. We had expected—the two other candidates and myself who came in at the same time—that we probably would be subjected (so we were warned) to very drastic physical dangers and horrors of one sort or another. But on the contrary, we came out into this beautifully lighted room, and sitting before us were George Lyman Kittredge, the great scholar; William James, Professor of Psychology at Harvard; Josiah Royce, the philosopher; Hugo Münsterberg, the philosopher, I think also was there; and Charles Townsend Copeland, Boylston Professor of Rhetoric.

Then these men began questioning the candidate, each of whom came out alone. I remember the first question I was asked was by Kittredge, who said, "Spell 'syzygy.'" I couldn't spell it. He then said, "That's spelled S-Y-Z-Y-G-Y." He looked at the other inquisitors and said, "This candidate doesn't seem very promising to me."

Then one of the other professors, I can't remember which one, said to me, "Would you please let us know to which of Longfellow's sisters he addressed that beautiful line, 'Hail to thee, blithe spirit, bird thou never wert.'" And I was confused, because I knew of course that this was from Shelley's "Ode to a Skylark," and it would seem rude to catch a professor in a mistake of that sort, so I had to claim that I wasn't familiar with that, either. Then they looked very doubtful.

Then the third question was: "Could God make rocks bigger than He could lift?" I'd never heard this question before. I have heard since that it's sometimes been used by boys to stump a Sunday school teacher. But there didn't seem to be any answer to that. So I just said I couldn't answer it.

All unanimously agreed—James, Münsterburg, Royce, Kittredge, Copeland, and whoever else was there: "This man is not fit for admission to the Signet. I'm sorry that we've subjected him to this ordeal" and so on. "Next candidate, please." And I retired in the most dreadful state of shame and annoyance. Then, when they'd all listened to and been subjected, I suppose, to the same humiliation, punch bowls were brought in, and I was welcomed with the rest of them as a new member. It was run by students, and these professors were men who had been in the Signet themselves as undergraduates, and it still goes on. It has a house of its own.

I cannot remember any particularly well-known writers that appeared in *The Harvard Monthly* under my aegis. I believe Conrad Aiken had a short story or two there. There were several men who had shown great promise, one of them Charles T. Ryder, who afterwards became a physician and stopped writing. Men like that. I can't remember. I probably am missing some names—oh yes, there was a man named Earl Derr Biggers,[8] who became a very well-known Broadway figure, writing musical comedies and farces and so on, and who had a number of short stories both in the *Advocate* and in *The Harvard Monthly*.

In my senior year I was elected Class Poet, and I read the class poem in Sanders Theatre on Class Day. It's quite an occasion, you know. You have a large number of students there and their invited guests; the president of Harvard and the governor of Massachusetts and the mayor of Boston are usually there, and various distinguished editors from New York, from the Century Company and Scribners, and newspaper reporters. The poem made quite a stir—not that it was a good poem. It was not. I've never included it in any of my books. But it was a sincere poem by a young man who was very much in revolt, or thought he was, against the capitalist system of our time, and it was full of phrases like: "Out of the church's prison. The new Christ re-arisen"—telling you that you are your brother's keeper, you are responsible, and so on. It got a tremendous press because of the character of the poem. The socialist *Call* and I think also the *Masses,* I'm not sure of that, published it in toto, and the *Call* in its editorial said, "As long as this sort of thing can come out of Harvard, there's still hope." In the meantime, my parents got letters of condolence from their friends and relatives saying, "You must excuse it. He's just a young chap, and he doesn't know any better."

Well, this had been brought about by a number of factors in my life— the very strong influence upon me of my uncle Thomas C. Hall, a professor at Union Theological Seminary, which used to be a hotbed of radicalism. He had married a German and had a house in Göttingen in Germany and was caught up in the socialist movement so active in Germany at that time. Also, I'd been reading a great many books along those lines, beginning with Thoreau and going right on into Marx and some of the German novels of the period. You know, Gustave Frenssen who wrote *Jörn Uhl,* a novel about the oppressed peasantry of Germany. It all built up together into a romantic revolt, which was shared by some of my classmates, mostly a few of the younger men. John Reed was one of them.

I knew that most of the class would be very much against my poem. I was projecting my own feelings and rejoicing in the fact that I was in revolt. I was in revolt with my father and mother in those years. I remember writing a poem called "Eighteen Years Old"— that's the title of the poem, and I was that age—in which I drew a picture of myself as a martyr with my style cramped by my parents and completely misunderstood and so on, although they were the most patient and loving parents, I would say, that the world had ever seen. But that's a natural feeling in youth. There are some people who will even assert that if you don't start out that way, by the time you reach thirty you'll be so worn down that you really will hardly exist at all.

I never belonged to any of the Greek-letter societies at college, and most of my friends didn't belong. I was very much amused years later when George Biddle, my old friend and classmate, was writing his reminiscences and said to me when I had made some remark that displeased him, "Well, Jack, how can you take any pride in what we were in college— thinking about nothing but getting into Greek-letter societies and pulling wires and playing politics?" He had swung way over to left by this time. I, at this time, had tempered my radical tendencies. And I said to him, "George, I don't know what you're talking about. I didn't even know about these Greek-letter societies while I was in college, and most of my friends didn't, and I never belonged to one. I never was asked to belong to one."

But I did belong to the Hasty Pudding Club, which was a general club, and Edward Sheldon and I were taken in the very last lot. We debated whether we should accept the invitation or not; we felt so superior to it. However, Ned wrote a play for the three of us that were taken in, and I was dressed up as a chorus girl, laced into a very tight corset, and fainted in the midst of the evening. I remember that very well.

■ ■ ■ ■

One of the things that was supremely important in my life was my stay during the summers at East Hampton. When I was quite young, we used to read Shakespeare aloud in the evenings, and I was detailed off one evening to read *Hamlet*. After I'd been reading for some time my father inquired, "What edition have you got there?" He reached out, took the book, and discovered I had been bowdlerizing Shakespeare all along, so as not to shock him and Mother. I knew just what words and passages to omit, and I'm sure I omitted some that were completely innocent.

I first started writing verse when I was nine, and I kept at it all the time, just the way a drunkard keeps on drinking, I suppose, because that was my inclination. I had written a long poem while we were in Morristown, when I was ten or eleven, called "Beatissimus," which seemed to go on interminably and was really an imitation of Tennyson's "The Two Voices." And every summer at East Hampton was an orgy of poetry, and not only of writing it but reading the work of other poets, beginning with the early poets and the metaphysical poets and going on to the Romantic poets, Keats and Shelley and Byron, and Tennyson and Browning and so on, until finally, at the time of the first summer when I came back from college, I had reached the stage where I was absolutely intoxicated with Swinburne and with Yeats, but particularly with Swinburne, so much so that I got permission from my father, much against his will, to go over to England to see Swinburne. I'd written him many letters, which he had never answered, and I had written about him and published articles about him and written poems to him, in *The Harvard Monthly* and in *The Harvard Advocate,* which I sent him. I remember, in one of my letters to him, I said, "Do not answer my letters. I would never forgive you if you ever stopped to answer one." My feeling was of such worship and adoration that I couldn't bear the thought that he might ever respond in any way. But now I was bent on seeing him, and my father said, "I think it's foolish. You can go—but you'll have to go steerage." We were not well off then, and I might add, while we're talking about college days, that in college, except for a few friends like the Biddles, we were all rather poor.

Well, anyway, my father blew me to this, and I went over to England. For three days I hung around "The Pines" in London, in Putney, where Swinburne lived, before I saw him. Then, one day, I saw this figure advancing towards me. It was very disillusioning. He was extremely short. I knew he wasn't tall, but I'd never thought of him as a dwarf practically. And he was wearing a turban—I don't know why—in London. He was wearing a turban; it was midsummer and very hot, and he was talking to himself. And as he drew nearer, I felt that I was approaching God and that I was going to faint. My heart was just going like mad. But I managed to keep upright until I got to him, and I touched his coat with my hand as he passed, and that was the greatest moment of my life. I never could feel like that again about anyone or anything. I wouldn't have dared speak to him! I went home to my cheap hotel and lay on the bed, on my back, thinking about it all that day and well into the night. And I wrote several more poems to him, which I sent to him. But I'd given him the injunction, in my letter, that I would never forgive him if he answered any of them, you see.

The only other even further-back poet that I saw was Whitman. I saw him with my physical eyes, but not with my mind, because I was an infant at the time. My father was crossing on the ferry from Long Island to New York, so he told me in later years, and Walt, old Walt, was on the ferry boat. My father held me up—I suppose I might have been two years old or perhaps less—and pointed him out. He told me that he had said to me, "You are looking at Walt Whitman, a great poet." I made no comment.

The summer after my freshman year I was sent to Germany by my father, for good reasons—because I had fallen in love, very foolishly but very charmingly, I think. I came back to Morristown my freshman year at Christmas time, and in those days people used to have domestics, you know, in the house. Going upstairs to my room on the second floor of the house where we lived, I brushed past a very pretty young girl. As it turned out, she was only seventeen, a German girl. She'd come over from Germany and was acting as housemaid for my mother. And I fell in love with her instantly. That was all right.

Then, when we went down to East Hampton and she was there—she was very pretty—I was timid about saying anything to her, but I finally engaged her in conversation. We used to go out and walk on the beach at night together all summer long. Perfectly innocent. I never made any

improper suggestion or advances to her. I was much too timid and too idealistic even to dream of it. But we did kiss and embrace each other and sit
and watch the lights of ships out to sea, and I would recite Heine and
Goethe and Schiller. She was a German, and I spoke German just like English. Well, we won't waste too much time on that, except to say that one
evening a terrific thunderstorm broke out, while we were on the beach—
a wonder it hadn't happened before. It was my habit to go down on a
bicycle, and she would walk a separate way, so that we would not meet
until we got to the beach. Also, we always came back to the house separately. But that night we both came back together absolutely bedraggled
and drenched, and as I drew nearer the house, this shadowy figure loomed
upon the path—our house was very isolated. It was my father. And he was
much upset. He imagined the worst, of course. The burden of his song
was, "That you should do such a thing to your mother, in her own house,
is unpardonable! I don't see how you could do such a thing!"

I was so innocent that it never even occurred to me to make any
explanations at all. But gradually, in the course of our conversation, my
father began to realize that this was just a bit of idealistic romance that had
no—you know—no involvement physically. Yet I was terribly in love, or
thought I was. And of course, she had to go. So then my great fear was that
Else, for that was her name, would suffer for this, and I spoke to my
mother. My father seemed enormously relieved. I didn't realize until I
thought back about it in later years why he was so relieved; he'd pictured
all sorts of complications, of course. And probably I was a very timid, shy
man not to have got into those involvements.

However, Else was dismissed, and I got a promise from my mother
that she would give her a very good reference and that my mother personally would see to it that she got a good place in New York, which she
did. Then I was allowed to say good-bye to her, in the front room, the big
hall. I said, "Can't I say good-bye to her in the pantry?"—which was more
secluded. I thought in that moment of course it was the end of my life.
After Else had left, I made life miserable for my parents by going out at
night, bursting out of the house in a flood of sobs and tears. I didn't say I
was going to commit suicide, but I acted as though I were. Well, anyway,
I wrote a great many poems on this subject. You'll find them in my book
The Belovèd Adventure, poems about lost love and departure and all that sort
of thing.

Then, to end the story, during that winter after that summer, I kept in
touch with Else, and we used to meet in New York in Central Park. I had

no extra money. We couldn't go to—we didn't have movies in those days—couldn't afford to go to a restaurant. So we would just meet in the park and sit on a bench and embrace and kiss. Then I wrote a whole series of poems about that, called "Songs Beyond Death." They were the imaginary songs of a ghost who comes back and tries to establish contact with a beloved woman but can't because now he is disembodied. So that strain runs through and explains a great many of those early poems of mine.

After all this, my parents thought that it would be a good thing for me to get away for a while because I seemed to be taking things rather hard. I had told my father and mother that I wanted to marry Else. I told Else this too, but she was much more mature than I was, although she was younger, and said, "Don't be silly." I don't think that she really cared very much for me. I must have seemed very immature to her, although she was a year younger than I was.

Anyway, I was sent abroad, and that was the time when I went over alone and traveled all through Germany. It was very romantic, traveling through moonlit valleys on a local train, when I'd be the only person in the compartment. I was longing to meet some girl or woman that I could love. I never had the courage to pick up the girls in the streets who were so openly offering themselves. I tried very often. Night after night I would try. I would walk alongside, and then I'd have to go by because I didn't have the nerve. I was too shy. I went back to America without having had any adventures at all and not even a chance to talk to anyone all summer long, except waiters and conductors. I'd been given letters of introduction by my parents to German friends, and they'd written these friends, who were naturally very much offended that I hadn't taken up these letters of introduction. I was like that in youth, very stubborn and immature.

After my graduation from college—in fact, before, because my father was a farsighted man—he had had talks with the president of Cornell University, President Schurman, a neighbor at East Hampton. President Schurman, who was a wise man and knew me and had seen my poems—by this time I had a pile of manuscripts about that high; really, it was like an illness, this unpublished accumulation—said, "The thing for you to do, Mr. Wheelock, is to have your son go to Germany and get a Ph.D. That is the union card for the better teaching positions in this country, and a German Ph.D. means more than any other"—and it did, at that time.

My father thought, well, here's an opportunity. There was an uncle of mine, this same Thomas C. Hall of Union Theological Seminary, whom I previously referred to. He had been chosen that year as Roosevelt Exchange

Professor in Germany; he was having a sabbatical from Union Theological and was teaching at the University of Göttingen. He and his wife were living in the house there that belonged to his wife. He'd married in youth the daughter of a professor of botany at the University of Göttingen.

When I went over to take up my studies at the University of Göttingen, this became my home. I was a paying guest, paid very little, and I now took up my courses for a Ph.D. I did not pay much attention to my studies. I spoke German well and had no difficulty in following the lectures of my professors. In German universities they were even freer than they were in Harvard University of my time under the elective system. All you had to do was to go to the lectures. Nobody ever checked up on you, as to whether you attended or not. I spent most of my time trying to find some lovely, romantically inclined young woman and in writing verse. I certainly didn't succeed in the first because Göttingen is a small town and people weren't just lying around waiting for chance amorous encounters, and whether I succeeded in writing any poetry, of course I never shall know, but at least I wrote a lot of verse.

Then, at the critical moment, for I had been getting desperately homesick, a friend of mine, George Foote, who was studying composition, and his friend and my friend, Charlie Seeger, arrived in Germany to take up their musical studies. They both came out to Göttingen and infused me with the idea of going to Berlin, where they were going to be. In Germany, you can move from one university to another. So, my next semester, I moved to Berlin, and I was there for some time. And there I did find a young woman who, I thought, was extremely attractive. I picked her up in a restaurant. She was the mistress of a German cavalry officer who was now well on in age, a great deal older than she was. She took a fancy to me, and we had a long love affair. She had a lovely little flat out in West Berlin, in the Rosenheiner Strasse, and that became my home, at least part of the time. We'd go marketing together, and I spent many nights there. This inspired me to a great flood of poetry—241 love poems in one book, *Love and Liberation,* and none of them any good, and all deeply felt but written too hastily. I didn't get enough sleep, and I got myself into taking drugs—which at that time you could get in any drugstore without a prescription: Veronal, Trional, Sulfonal, etc. That's how I got in the habit, and I've never got out of it in all these fifty-four years.

Well, anyway, I did a great deal of writing. It was wonderful having these two friends, Charles L. Seeger and George L. Foote, with me there in Berlin. They had two grand pianos where they lived, in one of the rooms, with nothing else in the room—the clangor was magnificent when they played the two pianos together, and I heard a great deal of good music. Music is a passion of mine. I think I inherited some of my father's feeling for it.

George Foote was a man of means, and he took Charlie Seeger and myself to many concerts, for he could afford it. This brought me back to my boyhood, because my father, when I was a boy, had taken me to the Philharmonic concerts quite regularly, to the Friday rehearsals. I remember the first time I went with him. The orchestra was tuning up. I heard this confused murmur of strings and woodwinds, and I turned to my father, who could on occasion be rather stern and said, "It's beautiful, Father." His answer was, "Don't be silly; they haven't even begun yet." This wounded my feelings deeply. My father felt I was trying too hard to be appreciative, and this irritated him.

In Berlin, I heard Richard Strauss himself conduct on the opening night of his *Electra*. And I heard various French composers conducting their music. Some of them have been forgotten, others not. Debussy of course is well known, but Vincent d'Indy, for instance, I think has been more or less forgotten. He wrote a piece of music that made a great impression on me, a tone poem on the descent of Queen Istar into Hades—the old cuneiform tablets—and there is a poem of mine called "The Descent of Queen Istar into Hades" based upon his conception in the music, which is different from the traditional conception.

I was supposed to be studying. Actually I was spending most of my time with this charming woman, who was a little older than I was. I was living in a rooming house, but I spent a great deal of my time in her apartment. I didn't have to pay anything—expenses or rent or anything else. I brought her presents whenever I could, because I was very much in love with her. This went on, till finally at the end of two years, or perhaps two and a half—anyway, by 1910—my father wrote me to say, "I'd like to know how you're coming along. It might take you three years, I understand, or perhaps you're ready now to take your doctor's degree?" I had to write and say I was not any nearer my doctor's degree than I had been when I started. My father wrote back a very kind, patient letter, and said, "Well, you'd better come home." He said, "I'm sorry, but I'm cutting off your credit." I hadn't, of course, said anything about this romance.

Now I was determined to marry my Charlotte, and I told her that I was sure that when I came back to America I could persuade my father to give me enough to live on till we got started. She was a very worldly woman and quite experienced, and she was very kind, too. She listened to all this and said, "How sweet of you. I do appreciate it." Of course, she knew perfectly well that it would never come about. I, on the other hand, thought it would. I tried to stay on in Germany, and did get a job as a clerk in a shoe store, which I thought would enable me to stay on. George Foote and Charlie Seeger were staying, but they moved soon to Cologne, where they became assistant conductors at the opera house, and I wanted to stay on in Berlin to be near my beloved.

Charlotte—— I think she knew very well this wouldn't last. Well, I couldn't make the grade in the shoe store. I don't know why. I wasn't trained for that sort of work, and I probably wasn't obsequious enough or something. I did my best. I really did. I had no feeling of stigma, of revulsion at taking people's shoes off and so on. Not at all. I felt thrilled by the thought that I was doing this for Charlotte and that we would be able to be together.

But it finally collapsed, and I had no choice but to come home. George was worried about me. He was the well-off one, and he had some excuse for coming home himself, so he came home with me on the same steamer, and I remember well coming back on that steamer. Most of the time I was crying and upset and worn out anyway. When I got home to East Hampton, that was the worst summer I ever had. There in the house there was a young German governess or companion, a girl from a good family in Germany. She was supposed to be a companion to my sister, who was twelve years younger than I was.

I suddenly had to shift gears from leading the life of a married man to become a bachelor again, and in the room right next to mine was this very attractive young German girl. Nothing amiss occurred, of course, but it was tormenting to me to hear her turning around in the bed there. The result was that the situation drove me in on myself to such a degree that I spent all my time writing letters to Charlotte over in Germany or writing poems, and all the longing that was pent up and couldn't be released went into this terrible drive, this sleeplessness, one poem pouring out after another, so that I never got a chance to sleep. And I took more and more of these drugs, these sleeping pills. I got myself all worn out and ended the summer with a still greater mass of manuscripts. I didn't know how to go about it. I would just take these terrible handwritten things and send them out, and they always came back. And I had a friend at court. Richard Watson Gilder was an uncle of the girl who is now my wife, and he was a big shot at *The Century* and a poet. I even tried to enlist his help, but unsuccessfully.

Well, not to make a long story (as old Stark Young used to say) nause-
ating, I came back to East Hampton, weathered that summer through. I
don't know how I did it, because I was in such a dreadful state of depriva-
tion and so ridden by these poems addressed to my beloved in Germany,
many of which went into this enormous book *Love and Liberation*. The title
came from a German poem by Richard Dehmel, the great German lyri-
cist of that time, who wrote a poem called "Liebe und Erlösung," which
means "love and liberation." It didn't mean liberation from love; it meant
the liberation that you achieve through fulfillment by love.

Meanwhile I was carrying on a correspondence with my beloved
Martha Charlotte Zincke—I dedicated my first book to her, very dis-
creetly, under initials. We left East Hampton, and my father said to me,
"Now, look. You have disappointed me; you have not carried out the plan
that we thought would work for you, because as a professor you would
have had your summers for your own work. Now it's up to you to choose
what you want to do. If you want to live at home with your mother and
myself and work at your writing, there's always a room for you here, and
you can have your friends from New York come out and spend the weekends. But if you want to go to New York and make your own way, you'll
have to do it yourself. You'll have to earn money. I cannot support you in
New York." I said, "I don't want to live at home. I want to make my own
way in New York."

I came to New York. I bought a copy of the *Tribune,* and I found that
there was a job open on the Funk & Wagnalls dictionary. They wanted men
to write out definitions of words. To my amazement, when I went to the
Mercantile Library, where you applied for this job and where the work
was being done, where you could consult all the dictionaries—you weren't
allowed to copy from any other dictionary; it would be an infringement of
copyright—who should I find was working there but Van Wyck Brooks.
He also was unmarried at the time. I always had thought of Van Wyck as
being absolutely impractical because he never had any money and was
always borrowing from me. He proved much more worldly-wise than
I was.

We started in working on a sort of a preliminary text. I was feverishly
writing, and Van Wyck said, "Don't go so fast. Take it easy, take it easy!" I
didn't know why. "Slow up!" I did slow up. Van Wyck's advice was shrewd,
as I learned later, for we were going to be paid by the hour. By slowing up,
of course, we'd have that many hours more of paid time ahead of us. I
worked at this job with Van Wyck for a while. Then I was fired. Van Wyck

was very unhappy about this. He was a poet, too, and he reasoned, "If I were any good, I'd be fired too. For a poet to be able to do this, there must be something wrong with him." There was also one elderly man who worked with us. Well, I say elderly; he seemed elderly to me then; he was forty, I think. One night the poor devil committed suicide. And the only comment made by the head of the firm, or the man who was in charge of the Funk & Wagnalls *Standard Dictionary*—it was Mr. Funk, I think—his only comment was: "What a pity—just when he was learning our style!"

I went out and looked for another job, and I finally got a job with a firm called A. Mugford, Incorporated, 23 Liberty Street. I'll never forget it. There were three people in the office besides myself. The head of the office was Mr. Redfield, a very nice chap. Then there was a Jewish girl and a Jewish young man. The girl was the secretary, and the young man was a sort of handyman, did everything around the office. Our job was to sell advertising. In other words, we made prospectuses for various business firms. I was the outside man sent out to one place or another to try to sell them the halftone work we did. I put so much energy into this and so much enthusiasm, I visited so many places, that the boss was charmed with me though I didn't get much in the way of results because I didn't know enough about halftones. Sometimes a prospective client would say, "What screen do you use?" I didn't know what a screen was. Nobody had told me about it.

But anyway, one day when I was having lunch at the Fifth Avenue Restaurant in Madison Square—I was just beginning to have my lunch—I heard a voice calling from across the room. It was Maxwell Perkins, who was then the advertising manager at Scribners. He was not a classmate of mine. He was in the class before me. He was 1907. But he was Van Wyck Brooks's closest friend. They'd both grown up in Plainfield, N.J. He said, "Come over and have lunch with me. What are you doing?" And I told him. He said, "What? Mugford? Who are they?" I told him. He said, "Why, that isn't suitable work for you—an outside man selling advertising. You'd never be any good as a salesman."

It was true. I'd been thrown out of several offices, practically pushed out, because of my ignorance. One day I went in after we'd turned in an estimate for a job and didn't get the job, and I went to the successful firm and said to the head, "What was your estimate?" I didn't realize there was anything wrong about this. This man—a very powerful-looking man, too—came over and said, "Now, get out!" And I wouldn't get out. I felt insulted. Until I saw that he was going to kick me out, and I had to get out——well!

Interior of the Scribner Bookstore on Fifth Avenue (courtesy of
Charles Scribner's Sons Archives, Princeton University Libraries)

I had a talk with Maxwell Perkins, and he said, "There's a vacancy in
the Scribner Bookstore. I don't know how good a job it is, but why don't
you go up and try for it?" So, holding on to my Mugford job very carefully,
during my lunch hour I went. At Mugford's I was getting twelve dollars a
week, and I'd taken a room in Stuyvesant Square, upper-floor hall bedroom, which was two dollars a week. I had some money that my father had
started me off with. He gave me a bank account of two hundred fifty dollars to get started. This hall bedroom was very uncomfortable. But I managed, somehow or other.

I went and had an interview with Mr. Henry L. Smith, the then-manager
of the Scribner Bookstore. He was a very fine old gentleman, but not a
man of any great consequence. He put me through all sorts of tests: I was
allowed to come in one day and dictate some letters. Eventually he took me
on. I was to be the head of the library department. In every bookstore there
used to be a department which sold books to public, university, college,

and school libraries at a discount, a library discount, and the reason such a department was in a bookstore is that it sold not just the books of one publisher but the books of other publishers, of all publishers.

Well, I was made, supposedly, the head of this department. It was rather ridiculous, because the "department" consisted of a secretary—I remember Miss Morris, the quite pretty, rather fat, secretary—and a billing clerk. My business was to take these long lists—sometimes there'd be as many as one hundred pages of typewritten titles of authors and books without the publishers being given. We had to look all that up in the cumulative catalogues, identify the publishers, order from the publishers, get the books together, ship them out, and bill them at the different discounts.

Actually, it was the best thing that ever happened to me, because I was pretty soft. I'd been writing a lot of verse, and I'd not been in the army—we were not at war at that time—and now, I had it pretty tough. There were several men downstairs in the basement who were very familiar with my job. I came to it absolutely ignorant. Each one of them felt he should have been chosen as the head of the department. Down in the basement there they made endless fun of me. There were copies of a book of mine—I'd published only one book then, *The Human Fantasy,* a book of poems—there on the bottom shelf in the stock room in the basement.

Their kind of humor was rather tough, you know. They had a cat there named "Punch," and they would—in fact, before a lot of people, some of the salespeople, girls, too—they would say, "Well, Jack," as they called me, "see what the cat thinks of your book." And again they used to come up to me and say, "Do you think you'll ever be president, Jack?" You know, these Irishmen, packers down there, who sensed in me a sort of a college dude, a stuffed shirt. I took it all seriously and was very unhappy about it. Then sometimes they'd come up to me and threaten me, you know—"Which way do you want to fall, Jack? You want to fall this side or the other side? Count this fellow's teeth, will you, somebody? Oh, don't hit him again, he's all blood"—and so on, that line, you know. Then somebody else would shout, "Don't hit him, kick him!" And I took it all seriously, until one day when the billing clerk, to whom I'd given orders to get out a rush order and to be sure to bill it in that afternoon and get it out, just lay back and smoked cigarettes and wouldn't do anything. It came to a showdown. I lost my temper. I don't lose it often, but I did lose it very thoroughly, and it came to a scuffle, and I went right into the scuffle with him, and I was pretty strong, and I was giving him just as good as I got. And from that moment on, everything changed. Everyone took me more seriously. Also,

I learned to take their humor. The next time they came up to me and said, "Well, Jack, do you think you'll ever be president?" I said, "Well, if I get enough jackasses like you to vote for me, maybe I will." They liked that.

I was offered twelve dollars for that job, but the very first week I was there, Mr. Charles Scribner himself, this august presence, the grandfather of the present Charlie, came down from the fifth floor to tell me, "I hear you're doing well, and I'm raising you to fifteen dollars."

The Human Fantasy had been published by a little firm in Boston. I had sent out the manuscript of this book to two publishers. I sent it out first to Henry Holt and Company. This time I did use a letter of introduction given me by Mrs. Charles de Kay, the mother of the young woman who is now my wife. A dear lady, she wrote to Roland Holt, who was a personal friend. The Holts didn't see it at all. It's a narrative poem about a young undergraduate who falls in love with a shop girl. It was a story based upon my own experiences, and very noble, because it ends with their going up to her room in the evening, and then he, in a great wave of ethical compassion and nobility, decides they won't go ahead with this.

I had heard of a firm in Boston, the successors to Stone and Kimball, a very distinguished imprint, called Sherman, French and Company, who were carrying on the Stone and Kimball business and published a great many poets. They did demand a certain payment—of course in this case by my darling, indulgent mother, who adored my poetry. It sold about fifteen hundred copies. It did quite well.

I've revised it and revised it and put parts of it, a continually shrinking proportion, into successive selections of my poems, and new editions. They are poems about New York City. I transferred the scene from Germany to New York City. They were written in Germany, as were the two hundred forty-one love poems later published in *Love and Liberation*. I took over to Germany with me the substance of my second book, which was called *The Belovèd Adventure.* That book included everything that I wanted preserved from the time I had begun writing at nine.

The Human Fantasy was published in 1911 by Sherman, French. *The Belovèd Adventure* was published in 1912 by Sherman, French. *Love and Liberation* was published in 1913 by Sherman, French. In this way, I gradually unloaded this great mass of manuscript. My mother wanted to do it, and I got wonderful reviews. On *The Human Fantasy* I had as fine letters as anybody could have from important people. William Archer, who translated Ibsen for Scribners, whom I'd never met and no member of my family had met, wrote me a magnificent letter about *The Human Fantasy.* John Masefield

THE
HUMAN FANTASY

BY

JOHN HALL WHEELOCK

BOSTON
SHERMAN, FRENCH & COMPANY
1911

THE
BELOVÉD ADVENTURE

BY

JOHN HALL WHEELOCK
Author of "The Human Fantasy."

BOSTON
SHERMAN, FRENCH & COMPANY
1912

LOVE AND LIBERATION
THE SONGS OF ADSCHED OF MERU
AND OTHER POEMS

BY

JOHN HALL WHEELOCK
Author of "The Belovéd Adventure," "The Human Fantasy," etc.

BOSTON
SHERMAN, FRENCH & COMPANY
1913

Wheelock's mother paid for the publication of these three volumes. (Matthew J. and Arlyn Bruccoli Collection of F. Scott Fitzgerald, Thomas Cooper Library, University of South Carolina) wrote me about it, saying that we wanted to get the city into poetry. Richard Le Gallienne wrote me, and the most touching letter of all came to me from S. Weir Mitchell after the publication of *The Belovèd Adventure*. This book contained a long poem to a prostitute, called "The Woman in the Café," which again was full of all these very noble feelings that seem *so* old-fashioned today: "Think not dear, sordid heart, I condescend / From this high dream with you to sympathize," and so on. Mitchell was very old-fashioned, too. He was the famous neurologist and had a sanitarium where people went when they had nervous breakdowns. He wrote me a long letter. He said that this poem and other poems in the book had moved him deeply, and he ended his letter—he was then in his eighties—"Believe me, dear sir, the better man for your poetry." I think I still have the letter.

■ ■ ■ ■

Maxwell Perkins didn't edit any magazine in college, but he contributed articles and stories to the *Advocate* and *The Harvard Monthly*. He was something of a diplomat in college. I mean, he moved with the Greek-letter clubs and the correct people, and he had grandiose dreams. He always wanted to be president of the United States. His plan was that he would achieve this by entering journalism, becoming a star reporter, getting control of a newspaper, until finally he was the owner, then getting into politics with a newspaper as his organ, and becoming president.

He did join *The New York Times,* and he became a star reporter on the *Times.* He did not succeed in getting control of anything, and early in the game Scribners heard of him and invited him to come and run their promotion department, which he did. See, I went to Scribners in April 1911, and Max was then head of promotion. He didn't become an editor until 1914.

In the meantime I spent fifteen years in the bookstore, long hours, nine to six every day, including Saturdays, except during July and August when the hours on Saturday were from nine to one. I did extremely well, I don't mind saying—not by the use of intelligence, frankly, but just by dint of terribly hard work. I wrote my poems at night and on weekends.

The business grew. Of course, it doesn't sound very impressive, but when I came, they used to do about, oh, I would say eighty or ninety thousand dollars a year. This is after the discounts were taken off. I worked it up to about one hundred eighty thousand. During the First World War, for which I volunteered—I was turned down by both the army and the navy because of a valvular heart leak—we supplied all the books that went to the military camps all over the country, and the amount of work that was put on me was so great that Mr. Charles Scribner II was worried. He knew I didn't have room enough in the basement to spread out all these books. He gave me the directors' room on the fifth floor, and the poor devils down in the basement had to carry all these books up to the fifth floor in the elevator, and I would spread them out on the huge directors' tables up there. I wasn't allowed any more billing clerks. Mr. Scribner said, "I'm going to authorize you to increase the billing clerk's wages," and he used an expression that sent a shudder through me. He said, "Just sweeten him up a bit."

Mr. Scribner was a very fine man. He was a cruel man in some ways. His was the fascinating combination of cruelty and kindness. The firm was founded in 1846 by Charles Scribner I. His three sons—John, who died young; Charles II; and Arthur—were Charles Scribner's Sons. Arthur was an amiable, lovable nonentity, awfully afraid of his brother Charles, who was five years older. Charles Scribner II was one of the cleverest publishers the country's ever had, and a cruel man in some ways, as I've already said. Not so much to his employees as cruel to his brother, cruel to people in little humorous ways. He played with you like a cat with a mouse, you know. I wasn't made an editor until 1926. The year my father died I was made an editor because William Crary Brownell, the Dean of American Critics, as he was called, who had been the senior editor, had retired, and everyone was shoved up a peg, and I came to the editorial department as a junior editor. The first editorial conference that I was at was in the office of this august man, Charles Scribner II—old-fashioned, you know, a man of great authority—with all the editors, Maxwell Perkins, the advertising men, Brownell, and Roger Burlingame, all these big shots. I was trying to sell the conference a book about a man who had spent an entire summer on an island studying a bird's habits. I thought it was a fascinating book, and Mr. Scribner got me talking about it, and I did. Then he began, "What part of the island was the bird on?" "He was, I think, at the southerly end." "You mean to tell me this man followed the bird around from one part of the island to the other? How many steps did he take pursuing the bird?" and so on. He asked all these ridiculous questions. Finally, I was getting unhappier and unhappier, and terribly embarrassed, not knowing which way to turn or what to do or say, when I looked up and caught the eye of Charlie, Mr. Scribner's son, winking at me. Then I knew that this was Mr. Scribner's game. Afterwards, he invited me out to lunch. He said, "What a wonderful presentation you made. I was only joking with you."

Charles Scribner II, president of Charles Scribner's Sons, 1879–1928
(courtesy of Charles Scribner's Sons Archives, Princeton
University Libraries)

My books kept coming out, and they all sold somewhat, and they got some fine reviews. The collection of two hundred forty-one love poems got the poorest reviews. Some of the reviewers said, "A honeymoon is very wonderful, but to have to live with a honeymoon for two hundred forty-one pages gets a little bit cloying." You know, they poked a lot of fun at me. Some of the reviewers took it humorously and said, "This man must have been terribly in love and certainly terribly anxious that everyone knew about it."

Anyway, the books prospered and got good reviews. Then it was known that I read German and French and, being a poet, presumably knew something about books. All that was lacking was the trade sense of what would sell. They would send books down to me to read. The first one that I was sent was, I remember, by Emil Ludwig, a German writer. It was a book on Napoléon. It was in German, and I read it. I didn't think it was a really first-rate book, but I did think it ought to be published, and I told Mr. Scribner, "This book you should do." My report was all in writing. I estimated that the sale was likely to be quite a big one. Mr. Scribner was a little suspicious of my callowness, and sent it to the Seth Low Professor of History at Columbia University, William M. Sloane, and he read it and said, "Oh, no. This is very unsound. This is not sound history. This is a mere popularization." It was turned down—and sold afterwards almost a million copies under the title *Napoleon*.[9]

Then one or two other cases of that sort happened. There was a young man who sent in a book of poems, or one long poem, called *This Is My Beloved*. He was a Russian. His name was Walter Benton—he'd just taken on that name. I was absolutely for the book. Mr. Scribner himself looked at it, and he came across things that seemed to him to be too—— Well, of course today it would seem innocent enough, but in those days it seemed risqué, highly improper, and Mr. Scribner said he wouldn't for a moment allow the Scribner imprint on such a book. So I didn't know what to do. I'd met Walter then, and I'd also met the girl that he wrote the poem to, who was a high-class tart but very attractive, and he'd been living with her and was very much in love with her. She had no use for him, except as a sexual partner. Didn't want to get married anyway. This was wearing him down terribly, because he really was awfully infatuated with her. And his poem, which was quite beautiful, told the whole story.

So Van Wyck Brooks and I got together. (Van Wyck at this time had been released from the asylum. He was out of his head for some years.) It was while I was an editor, so it must have been after 1926. Van Wyck by this time had had a great success with his books. He'd made hundreds of thousands of dollars with *The Flowering of New England* and *New England Indian Summer* and all of that five-volume history of American literature.[10] Van Wyck and I and William Rose Benét—Bill Benét, who's been forgotten now, really quite a good poet—and Stephen Vincent Benét and others got together, and we wrote endorsements for this book, for the jacket. The poem was full of very wonderful flashes, such as comparing a falling star to somebody striking a match on the vault of heaven. Then I took it up again with Mr. Scribner, and I said, "Mr. Benton is willing to cut some of the parts that strike you as vulgar."

No, Mr. Scribner wouldn't hear of it. He said, "Any man who could write in that way, I don't—— I'm very proud of the Scribner imprint; I wouldn't sully it by having it on such a book." So that was the end of that. I took it to Alfred Knopf, and he took the book and made an absolute killing with it.[11] It's gone into, I don't know, twenty-seven, twenty-eight editions. They get it out in gift form at Christmas time.

I'll tell the rest of the Walter Benton story, while I'm at it—though it doesn't fall in this time. I was living in New York. I was alone here in the summer except for weekends when I joined my wife at East Hampton. I never got more than two weeks vacation in those days. I think the book *This Is My Beloved* and the turning down of it perhaps took place in 1935 or '36. But my having recommended it to Alfred Knopf proved to be valuable in the mid-1940s. Coming home to the apartment late one night, I found awaiting me there a case of vintage wine with a little card: "Thanking you for *This Is My Beloved,* Alfred Knopf." He's been very disagreeable to me at various times since, and I have no use for him now.

There were other books that came down to me from the editorial department at that time, while I was working in the basement, many of which I turned down, and some of which I took on, or they took on on my advice, and they fared well. So this called Mr. Scribner's attention to me as a potential editor—this and my own books. These, also, made some impression, so much so that in 1918, Mr. Scribner himself, the great man, took me out to lunch and said, "We want to become your publishers." This of course was to me like being offered the key to Paradise. So I gave them my book called *Dust and Light,* which was published in 1919—a big book, too, all the dammed-up poems. I hadn't published anything since 1913. And it sold. It went into a second printing.

I think the second printing was five hundred copies, much to the dismay of Mr. Arthur Scribner, who was great on economy. He said, "We've just come to the end of the fifteen hundred copies printed. It doesn't seem likely to sell much more, and it doesn't pay to print a small amount. Couldn't we let it rest there?" I said, "Mr. Scribner, I know it's going to sell a great deal more." He was cautious, however, so we only ordered a printing of five hundred. It sold a little over two thousand in all.

Anyway, Scribners had sent me things, and some of the things sent me I was against and some for, and they didn't always follow my advice. But, on the whole, having seen that two books, or one book at least, that I'd strongly recommended had had great success, and having seen that some that I had recommended and they had taken had been moderate successes, they thought my judgment might be useful.

I became a junior editor in 1926. By this time, Scribners had published two of my books, *Dust and Light* in 1919 and *The Black Panther* in 1922. Then in 1927 they published *The Bright Doom,* my best book to date, which did quite well. I think it sold, all in all, about twenty-five hundred. That was the year that I was invited to read the Phi Beta Kappa poem at Harvard in the Sanders Theatre before a big audience. It's *the* Phi Beta Kappa poem occasion of the year. I wrote a long poem called "Affirmation," which was a poem against the despair of our time, and ended it with three sonnets. I had a great success with it. It was published in *The Boston Transcript* and parts of it in *The New York Times,* and found a good deal of favor.

I remember when I was reading it, one thing held my attention. I looked out over the audience, a big place, and I saw a pair of very intelligent eyes fixed on me. They fascinated me, and I thought, "I wonder who that is?" It was Ralph Barton Perry, professor of philosophy at Harvard, and he seemed very much impressed, I could see, with my poem as it went on and on, and his hopes were kindled more and more: "Here's a young man who's going to give us some solution." Actually, it was a profoundly gloomy poem up to a point. It went on, and these words were just revolving around each other, in this rhythm, for no purpose that anyone could fathom, and then I came to the climax: "Yet the deep heart still knows that all is well." I had begged the question. Although it sounded so grand in the poem, all that I'd really said was that somehow, somewhere, there must be a purpose, because the thing that makes every heart beat is faith, and every living creature goes on living out of some blind faith. And in the sonnets, the same thing. I spoke of the heart in the body "jetting fierce streams of faith . . . through the unbelieving brain." I begged the question. I didn't make my philosophical point. I saw all the light die out of those eyes, and

DUST AND LIGHT

BY

JOHN HALL WHEELOCK
AUTHOR OF
"THE HUMAN FANTASY," "THE BELOVED ADVENTURE,"
"LOVE AND LIBERATION"

> *—they are still immortal*
> *Who, through birth's orient portal*
> *And death's dark chasm hurrying to and fro,*
> *Clothe their unceasing flight*
> *In the brief dust and light*
> *Gathered around their chariots as they go—*
> *—SHELLEY.*

NEW YORK
CHARLES SCRIBNER'S SONS
1919

Wheelock's first book with the Scribners imprint (Thomas Cooper Library, University of South Carolina)

I knew I'd failed. However, I had the glory of saying it, when I was young enough to be very much excited by it all.

My immediate boss was Max Perkins. I inherited William Crary Brownell's office after he retired, and his office had a couch. Just imagine it! I was just treading water all the days I was there, and at night I took work home with me, but he was able to lie down on the sofa and sleep during the daytime. You see, they didn't have so many telephones or telephone calls then.

I was reading manuscripts, and I took on manuscripts, without becoming the editor of the author. But the first contact I had—and it had nothing to do with any real editorial job—was with Edith Wharton. It must have been shortly before she died. I was introduced to her, I think by Brownell, because he said, "Here, you two poets ought to get together."

She had published several books of poems. She was most kind. Bristling in very stiff attire, she reminded me of a wasp—and a highly irritable one—but, as I said, she was very kind.

The first person I actually was an editor for was A. W. Greely. He was the Arctic explorer. They had failed to reach the North Pole but come very close to it, and they had run into trouble. They'd had to become cannibals up there. Some of their members had died, and they'd eaten them. He was writing his book on that North Pole expedition, and that was the first book I saw through the press.[12] I was editor for this very old man—he must have been nearly as old as I am now.

In those days, the big man at Scribners was Max Perkins. He had genius as an editor. He was the central figure. I've been in on historic occasions when Max showed himself completely in control of the situation. There was, for instance, the day when Scott Fitzgerald's *This Side of Paradise* came up for discussion. This was before I had become an editor, but the occasion is an historic one. What happened on that occasion followed the usual routine: the editors would find something they thought ought to be published; then they would all go—it would be arranged ahead—into Mr. Charles Scribner's office, and the various arguments, the pros and cons, would be heard, and the decision would be made finally by Mr. Scribner himself.

I understand several had read *This Side of Paradise.* I had read it, and Max had read it. It had very serious flaws in it, but it was quite obviously an outstanding work, something belonging to a new order. Mr. Scribner had read it—and he was very much against it. He said, "It's frivolous. I will not have a frivolous book like that on my list." You must remember that the books that Scribners were then publishing were books by such writers as Henry Van Dyke, Richard Harding Davis, George Washington Cable, Frank R. Stockton, John Galsworthy—all pretty much belonging to the past.

Well, then they got through with their discussion, Mr. Scribner looked up at Max, who was standing behind him, and said, "You haven't said anything, Max. How do you feel about it?" Max, who was a very silent New England type, didn't say anything for a while. Then finally he said very quietly: "My feeling, Mr. Scribner, is that if we let a book like this go, we ought to close up and go out of the publishing business." Mr. Scribner was very much upset: "What do you mean by that?"

"Well," Max said, "we can't go on publishing Theodore Roosevelt and Richard Harding Davis and Henry Van Dyke and Thomas Nelson Page forever, you know. We've got to move on with the times."

Mr. Scribner was impressed by this, and he said, "I'd like to think it over." So he did, and, at a later editorial conference, he said, "Have you any recommendations to make, Max, about changes in the Scott Fitzgerald book?" Max said, "Yes, I have. I've made———," and he had a list of the things that ought to be done. Mr. Scribner said, "All right. If you make those changes to your satisfaction, I'll publish the book." Scott was delirious with joy, and he got to work on it and made most of the changes, though he didn't make them all. And the book was published.

Then some years after that, when I had become an editor, we went through the same thing with Hemingway, when *The Sun Also Rises* came up, and we had the same discussion, but in this case Mr. Scribner said: "It's a vulgar book. There are four-letter words in it that I never would permit on the page of any book that enters a gentleman's house." Max said, "Well, Hemingway is willing to cut out some of these words." Mr. Scribner said, "Which words?" Max, who was a New Englander, rushed back to his office, got a piece of paper, wrote the words down, and handed the paper to Mr. Scribner. Mr. Scribner looked at it with that cruel smile. "Max, if Hemingway knew that you didn't dare say those words in my presence, he'd disown you!" *

Almost the most fascinating man I've ever seen was Scott Fitzgerald when I first knew him. I never knew him well, you know. I had lunch with him but never knew him really as a friend. He was most attractive looking and had something unique to himself—a good deal of reserve which hid a tremendous vehemence of feeling and also of mischief and humor. His great difficulty was that he was making a god of money. Scott felt that he couldn't be happy or at peace or write a good book until he had sold enough to the *Ladies' Home Journal* or *The Saturday Evening Post* to assure him of twenty thousand dollars for the year. Then he could settle down to write

---

*There are several versions of this famous anecdote. The most widely reported account has it that Perkins wrote the unspeakable words on his appointment calendar and that when Mr. Scribner saw the calendar he solemnly inquired, "Don't you want to take the rest of the day off, Max? You must be exhausted."

Perkins to Charles Scribner III (27 May 1926), reporting on the decision to publish *The Sun Also Rises*: "Wheelock was called in, with a curious result: I thought he had been so much out of the world on that balcony of his, + in his generally hermit like life, as to be out of touch with modern tendencies in writing + therefore over sensitive; but to my amazement he thought there was no question whatever but that we should publish" (*The Only Thing that Counts: The Ernest Hemingway – Maxwell Perkins Correspondence*, ed. Matthew J. Bruccoli [New York: Scribner, 1996], pp. 38–39.

a really good book. But he got caught up in this and in alcohol. He married a girl whom he was very much in love with, a little Southern girl, Zelda, and he got her into this alcoholic thing. She couldn't take it and had a complete mental breakdown and had to be hospitalized.

But in the years when they were at their most attractive, I remember Van Wyck Brooks telling me that at one dinner party he'd sat next to Scott Fitzgerald—Van Wyck was already known as the chronicler of New England literature—and Scott leaned down and pulled up Van Wyck's trousers: "I just want to see if you have on red flannel underwear."

Whenever Scott and Zelda went to a dinner party, mostly at the houses of people who were well-off because those were the people they liked to be with, a bedroom was reserved upstairs, and as the meal went on, usually before the end of the dinner, both of them would pass out, and then they would be carried upstairs and put to bed. This went on for years, and Zelda cracked up under it. Scott was so stricken, for they were deeply in love with each other, that he tried to give up drinking. And he did. But what was left of him was just nothing.

After he had given up drinking, he would come into the office a shrinking, timorous, shy, embarrassed man. He lost all of that Byronic boldness and flair and dash that he once had. I saw *Tender Is the Night* through the press, worked with him on it during his drinking days. He would come in in the morning, at nine o'clock. He sometimes was there before I got there, so drunk that he couldn't walk, and he'd say, "Could you help me into the library?" And he'd lean on me heavily, really on the verge of passing out; he just couldn't walk properly, he was so drunk. Then he would sit down before that proof, and if there was the slightest mistake— if a comma should be a semicolon—he'd catch every single one. His mind was just blazing with clarity. And he claimed that it only did that when he had plenty of alcohol. He was a tragic man. I think *The Great Gatsby* is his best book, a magnificent book.

Hemingway I knew even less well than Scott. Max, you know, rather monopolized Hemingway. I had thought that Hemingway was devoted to Max because Max had done so much for him. Good lord, how he worked with Hemingway—went down, you know, to Key West to stay with him when he didn't want to, when he had tons of work to do here at Scribners, left it all to be with Ernest. Yet after Max's death, Hemingway came in to see me, and walking into Max's office, which I then occupied, he looked around and sort of sniffed the air and said, "Where's Max's ghost?

I expected to find at least a ghost here"—which seemed to me a rather unfeeling thing to say.

Max knew what Hemingway, fortunately, did not know. Max had this extraordinary intuitive, uncanny thing that made him such a great editor. We always kept hearing about the books that Hemingway was working on; always next year there was to be a big one, a new big one ready. I asked Max about it. He said, "Ernest will never do anything again. He's done for." I said, "How do you know that?" Max said, "I just know. He's absolutely done for." And he was. That's why he killed himself, in the end.

An author that I did see a great deal of was Thomas Wolfe; we became friends.* His books, the principal books, were the ones that Scribners published—*Look Homeward, Angel* and *Of Time and the River* and *From Death to Morning*. It wasn't till after his death that Harper's brought out *The Web and the Rock, You Can't Go Home Again,* and *The Hills Beyond.* He used to come to the house and have dinner. I'm not a heavy drinker. I enjoy drinking, but I hate to drink too much, and I always had to drink too much with Tom. I'd have a bottle of bourbon there for him, and Tom wouldn't go home until we'd polished it off. He did a great deal more than I did, but even so it was much too much for me. I never could sleep a wink afterwards. We used to talk about poetry. Tom loved poetry. He knew English poetry right back to Chaucer, inside out, although he came from a family of rather plain people—a big family, in Asheville, North Carolina. His father was a stonecutter who made monuments for cemeteries, and his mother was a woman who had some of Tom's gift of the gab. I've never known a woman who could talk as much as she could—marvelous gossip about people in North Carolina, in Asheville.

I told him one day, "I don't know, Tom, critics say that you're something of a caricaturist, and I'm sure that you have caricatured your mother

---

*In a 12 January 1929 letter to Mrs. J. M. Roberts, one of his former teachers, Wolfe reported: ". . . before I left [Scribners] he [Perkins] went out and brought in another member of the firm, John Hall Wheelock, who spoke gently and quietly—he is a poet—and said my book was one of the most interesting he had read for years. I then went out and tried to pull myself together. A few days later, the second meeting. . . . As I went prancing out I met Mr. Wheelock, who took me by the hand and said, 'I hope you have a good place to work in—you have a big job ahead.' I knew then that it was all magnificently true. I rushed out drunk with glory" (*The Letters of Thomas Wolfe,* ed. Elizabeth Nowell [New York: Scribners, 1957], p. 170).

Thomas Wolfe (photo by Carl Van Vechten; courtesy of
Yale University Libraries)

in the character of Eliza." "I'll bring her in some time, and you can see her," he said. So one day he appeared with his mother. We went into the little library. Tom got her to sit down and pulled up a chair for me right in front of her, and he stood behind her chair, and she started in. And after the first fifteen minutes—of course, I didn't have a chance to say anything—I saw Tom winking at me. He'd absolutely got her down in his books to the *nth* degree. She never stopped talking, and when there was a pause, she would say, "A-aand . . . ," so that you wouldn't interrupt.

Why Wolfe left Perkins is a thing that most people don't know much about. It's like everything else in life: it's a complex of things. In the first place, the fatal thing was for Max to allow Tom to dedicate *Of Time and the River* to him in that extravagant fashion. Tom showed me the dedication he was going to use, and it ran four pages. Imagine, for a dedication—which is usually about a line—four pages! In this dedication Tom all but groveled. He said in substance: "If it hadn't been for this marvelous man I never should have been able to write a word. I never should have been able to finish this book. I was like a woman in labor who couldn't give birth to a child; it was killing me. And Max delivered me. He was my savior, my god—this brave man who stuck by me to the end." And it's true, Max did. They used to work many a night until eleven or later.

They would sit in Max's office there at Scribners on the fifth floor, and the night watchman, Mike, an Irishman, used to bring the elevator car up and hang it there just outside Mr. Perkins's office so that he could hear the outcries of Wolfe when Max told him what had to be cut out. His shouts of, "You butcher! No! No, that's a most important passage! That cannot come out!" Max went over every single sentence in his book to reduce these three million words to a publishable book. And in the end he did save Wolfe's life because Wolfe was drinking; he wasn't eating. He wasn't going to bed. He'd work for two or three days without sleeping and then go into a regular orgy of drink, destroying himself. But once the book was out, he became a reasonable man.

Tom wrote this absurd dedication. I said to Tom, "Now, look—you can't. You'll make yourself ridiculous. Don't do this, Tom. Think it over. Cut it down. You've got four pages here; cut it down to four lines, if you can." Oh, he was furious with me. He had this overwhelming emotion, and he wanted to articulate it. I did get it down, I think, to about eighteen lines; but even so, I knew it was fatal. Max knew it would be, too. Or, at least, I suggested to him: "Why can't you tell Tom that you won't accept anything in the dedication except just 'To my friend Maxwell Perkins'?"

But Max was a little bit hipped on Tom. He had no son of his own. He had five daughters. He had a great contempt for women, you know. He sat down to breakfast every morning with six of them. And he made Tom into his son.

Then, this is what happened. In the dedication, Tom announced to the world that he couldn't write his books without the help of Max Perkins. The reviewers kept picking this up. When the book came out, there was discussion: "I presume this also was turned out at the Scribner factory. Wolfe is incapable——" and so on. That is why Tom had to prove, to himself and to the world, that he could get along without Max Perkins.

Tom read every review, though one time he did leave America and go to England because he was afraid of reading the reviews. And he wrote back to Max—you'll find all these letters in Wolfe's *Letters*—saying that he was through, he was never going to write a word again* because he knew how horrible the reviews would be. In fact, he might kill himself. Max wrote him wonderful, reasonable, gentle letters, calming him down. And of course the book then got the most marvelous reviews. This was *Of Time and the River*.

But Tom wounded Max almost mortally. I think Max really died of a broken heart, in a sense, because this is the man he'd helped the most, and Tom was the man who turned on him. We found in Max's desk, after Max's death—he died while he was still editor—we found the terrible letters that Tom had written him and that Max was too ashamed to put into the Scribners file because of what they said. They are letters, some of them, that say: "I used to think that you were a coward because you wouldn't. . . . Now I know you're not even a coward. You're not even a man," and so on. This to the person who'd done more for Tom than any person in the world!

Wolfe discussed it with me ad infinitum before he left, and I did my best to—— You know, he was an irrational man. I used to go out drinking with Tom, and he would stand at the bar, and he'd say to me, "You see that man down there?" I'd say, "Yes. What about him?" "He looks like kind of a grey man to me. Doesn't he to you?" I'd say, "No, he looks just like any other man." "I don't like the looks of him at all. I've got a good mind to go down there and punch him in the nose." Then, if I had said to him, "Don't do that, Tom," he would have gone down and done it. So I'd just talk about it lightly and try to be humorous about it and get his mind on some other subject.

*See Appendix 2: Thomas Wolfe to JHW, 18 August 1930, and JHW to Thomas Wolfe, 28 August 1930.

He and Max worked so late one night that Max said to Tom, "Why don't you get on the train and go out with me to New Canaan, and we can go on working there? I have to get home, or Louise will be worried." So they got on the train, and while the train was going lickety-split, Tom decided he didn't want to go out to New Canaan after all and jumped off the train. Broke both ankles, of course.* Max had to get off. The train was stopped. They had to get an ambulance. You know. That's the sort of person Tom was.

Max made it his life work. He worked with Tom almost every night. Tom was the sort of person that Mr. Charles Scribner III was beginning to get rather restless about because he took up the time of all the editors and used all the offices. He was always there. He slept in the library very often. He was just exhausting everybody. Mr. Scribner began to think that Tom was wrecking the House of Scribner. But of course Tom died fairly soon after that.

Tom went to Ed Aswell when he was at Harper's, and Aswell was absolutely sporting and fair about the whole thing. When Tom insisted that he wanted to leave Scribners, Ed Aswell came to me and asked, "Is it all right for Tom to come to me? Because if you people can hold him, I'm certainly not going to———" You know, it was considered a very serious thing in publishing to steal an author from another publisher. I of course referred him to Mr. Scribner, and Mr. Scribner said, "If you want him, take him. We can't hold him."

Max knew about it, and if you ever should read my book—I have edited a book of Max's letters, *Editor to Author*—you'll see the whole struggle there going on, in Max's letters. This event wounded Max beyond words, so much so that he never would speak of it. Fortunately, as you'll read in this book of mine the very last letter that Tom wrote, on his deathbed, when he was dying from tuberculosis of the brain out West there—a marvelous letter, written when he was forbidden to write letters or even to sit up in bed—told of his gratitude to Max, asking his forgiveness, saying (I am paraphrasing this from memory): "I have met the Dark Man, and I don't think I was too afraid, and I know I have to go, but before I do, I just want to say one word to you—that you were the one that I cared the most for. I know that you were the one who did the most for me, and I want to end our correspondence with the thought of the day when we both walked

*Wolfe sustained a leg injury in Grand Central Station, but he did not break his ankles.

over Brooklyn Bridge together, and I'd finished my book, thanks to your efforts, and the whole power and the glory of the world lay there before us, and we were happy." This letter was like a blessing.*

Max began his work as an editor by standing before a lectern. In the later years, however, he sat at a desk. Max was a combination of extreme gentleness and feminine sensitivity and craglike obstinacy and puritanical severity—a mixture of the Puritan and the Cavalier. He had a terrible superego that rode him pretty hard. He had to punish himself, to stand up at a lectern because he wanted to sit down; he always wanted to do the more difficult thing. Then, he usually wore his hat in the office. I remember his wife coming in one day and saying, "For heaven's sake, Max, why do you wear your hat in the office here? It's very hot." Max liked you to think he was contemptuous of women. Anyway, this irritated him, and he said, "Oh, just for fun." Louise answered, "Well, if that's the only fun you get, you have my sympathy."

He had a sense of humor, Max did. Authors used to come in and sit there in his office. You'd see a certain type of woman, one who wrote very

---

*Providence Hospital letterhead, Seattle, Washington

Dear Max: I'm sneaking this against orders—but "I've got a hunch"—and I wanted to write these words to you.

—I've made a long voyage and been to a strange country, and I've seen the dark man very close; and I don't think I was too much afraid of him, but so much of mortality still clings to me—I wanted most desperately to live and still do, and I thought about you all a 1000 times, and wanted to see you all again, and there was the impossible anguish and regret of all the work I had not done, of all the work I had to do—and I know now I'm just a grain of dust, and I feel as if a great window has been opened on life I did not know about before—and if I come through this, I hope to God I am a better man, and in some strange way I can't explain I know I am a deeper and a wiser one—If I get on my feet and out of here, it will be months before I head back, but if I get on my feet, I'll come back

—Whatever happens—I had this "hunch" and wanted to write you and tell you, no matter what happens or has happened, I shall always think of you and feel about you the way it was that 4th of July day 3 yrs. ago when you met me at the boat, and we went out on the cafe on the river and had a drink and later went on top of the tall building and all the strangeness and the glory and the power of life and of the city were below—Yours Always

Tom

(*To Loot My Life Clean,* pp. 270–71.)

Maxwell Perkins at Charles Scribner's Sons. It was believed that he customarily wore a hat in his office to aid his deafness; but Perkins did not explain. (courtesy of Charles Scribner's Sons, Princeton University Libraries)

saleable books, sitting there with this stream of words coming out, explaining just how she came to start the book, what had suggested it to her, why she wrote it, et cetera, et cetera, Max meanwhile sitting there in absolute silence. So I asked once, "For God's sake, what are you thinking about, Max, when you're sitting there? Because I can't do it. I always interrupt at a certain point. I say, 'Well, what about it?' to bring them up short." Max said, "I have only one thought in mind. Sometimes I think about my income tax, and I can work things out in my head. Usually the only thing I'm thinking about is to be sure to ask before she goes, 'Did you put your name and address on the manuscript?' That's the only information I absolutely have to have: her name and address."

He was a good tutor to me, very good. But good in the sense that he left me alone. I turned down some very important books. I made some bad mistakes. I turned down a book that went on to have a tremendous sale when it was published. It was *The Art of Thinking,* by the Abbé Dimnet. I turned down Malcolm Lowry's *Under the Volcano,* which has become a fashionable success. He's become a "culture hero." I turned down Robert Musil; I read his book in the German, *Der Mann Ohne Eigenschaften.* I forget what the English translation title is, but it has become a classic of its kind. I turned down Céline's *Journey to the End of the Night.* I read that in French, *Voyage au bout de la nuit.* Those are the four, the biggest ones that I can think of, where I made a mistake.[13]

I had quite a lot of successes. I can't even remember all of them. Well, Marjorie Rawlings was one. I knew her quite well. She was not a top writer, but she was, at her best, extremely good. I don't know whether you know *The Yearling.* That's a good book. She was a writer capable of writing a really good book and then sitting down and doing some terrible melodramatic bit of tosh.

Then also, of course, I was particularly interested the field of poetry. I published Louise Bogan and Conrad Aiken and John Peale Bishop. Louise is a friend of mine, and Conrad is also, to a lesser degree. Louise Bogan is one of the most accomplished poets this or any other country has had. She's a purely lyric poet. She's done very little work. I don't think she's published a new poem, or a book of poems, for ten or more years, although she's now a woman of only—oh, I suppose she must be sixty-seven, sixty-eight. She was shattered by her divorce, I think. Also, she told me once that she thought men were much luckier than women. Her theory was: "Women write with their ovaries, and after menopause women are done for." I know that's not true, but that was her theory, and she has lived up to it. She was very much shattered by her divorce because she loved the man deeply. Her great flaw, if she has a flaw, has been extreme jealousy. This is strange, for she is a very beautiful woman. Tragically enough, it was this jealousy that, as far as I know, brought about the divorce.

Raymond Holden, her husband, told me that life became impossible. He was a friend of mine, too. He was a very good poet, rather overlooked at the moment. They'd go to a concert together, and he would be behaving, as far as he knew, perfectly normally; and then when he and Louise came home, he couldn't get to sleep because she'd be berating him late into the night about his having looked at a certain woman who was sitting nearby in the theater—that he was staring at her: "I know you were falling in love with her," or something like that, and "I don't know why you don't pay a little attention to *me* when we go to a concert." She'd go on and on and on, and he told me he'd found only one way to cure her of this, and that was when she was finished at about two in the morning, then he would start arguing his rebuttal and keep it up for another two hours, till she'd say, "Please stop, I want to get some sleep." He'd say, "No, I won't stop, I'm going to go right on."

You can't edit poetry. If a person needs to have his poems edited, then he's not a poet, because poets are perfectionists, and by the time they get through with all their agonizing work on a poem, either they've ruined it by revising too much or it's the way it should be. My job really was like that of a man up in the crow's nest in a ship, to scan the horizon and find the good poets and try to get them for Scribners. I was very fortunate in getting Peter Viereck and Louise Bogan and Conrad Aiken and Rolfe Humphries. I'm probably leaving out some of the most important ones.

Conrad Aiken didn't live in New York much of the time, but I know him quite well, and I've had some fine letters from him about my own work. Louise Bogan I know very well. Peter Viereck I know well. I know Louise Bogan's poetry will last because she writes absolutely perfect lyric poetry. There is no other woman, or man, who's written more flawless lyrics, except possibly Léonie Adams. She, also, has stopped writing.

Personally, I think that the finest woman poet of her time was Sara Teasdale. I knew Sara very well, better than any other writer or poet, largely because she admired my work so much. There was a group of poets that came out of St. Louis, poets and writers, from the region around St. Louis: Edgar Lee Masters was one; Zoë Akins, who later became a playwright, was one; Sara Teasdale was one; and Orrick Johns. There were a number of them. I can't remember the names of all of them.

I became friendly with Sara when she wrote me a "rave" letter about my first book, *The Human Fantasy*. Then she wrote me an equally overwhelming letter—No, she didn't write me the letter about *The Belovèd Adventure*. It was Orrick Johns, whom I'd never met, a great friend of Sara's in St. Louis, who sent me a letter which Sara had written to him about the book. It was so extreme, an almost incredible letter. There was a group of poets out there who were very excited about me as the—Well, they regarded me as the coming poet. Then Sara came to New York one winter. She was an excruciatingly shy, oversensitive human being, so excruciatingly sensitive that she couldn't read any poem of her own aloud—not even to one person. Never did read them. She would hand me a new poem she'd just written, and I used to amuse her very much by doing the following: I would take a look at a sonnet she'd handed me, and I would tell her what I thought of it. Then I'd say, "Just let me read it aloud to you," and

I could read it aloud to her once. She would often be absolutely thrilled because it sounded so well when read aloud, and perhaps she'd been in doubt about that particular poem. Then I would hand it back to her. We'd have dinner together. After dinner I would recite it to her from memory. I'd have memorized the sonnet in that one reading. This made a deep impression on her.

Well, anyway, she regarded me as the greatest living poet, and of course I was tremendously set up. You can't please anyone more, who's a poet, than by saying that. And we became fast friends. I think that, at her best, she's a magnificent lyric poet. She's very much out of fashion now, but I'm glad to say that recently a poet who has some influence with the younger crowd, Marya Zaturenska, the wife of Horace Gregory, has written an essay on Sara Teasdale that she sent me. I was named literary executor by Sara, together with a woman friend of hers, and Sara left it to us to choose, after her death, the poems that were to go into the final collected edition of her work. Sara Teasdale committed suicide when she was forty-nine.

Marya Zaturenska had written this essay and sent it to me, and I wrote back and told her that I thought it was the finest thing that had been written about Sara Teasdale. It's a complete revelation, a discovery, by this younger poet who's in touch with the movement, that Sara Teasdale was the greatest lyric poet of her time. As Sara's literary executor, I was able, together with Margaret Conklin, the co-executor, to persuade Sara's publishers to include this essay as an introduction to the twenty-ninth edition of the *Collected Poems*.[14]

Sara was always, in a way, in love with death. And then she was very shy, and I suppose really a neurotic; she got exhausted so easily. For instance, if she was going to go out to dinner with friends, she would go to bed the day before in preparation for it; then she'd go to bed the day after to get rested from it. She really felt this was necessary. She never could walk more than a block. She seemed like a perfectly normal woman; she didn't appear to have anything wrong with her.

Sara wanted terribly to be married to someone with whom she could be madly in love, and I don't think she succeeded in this. She was not a beautiful woman. She was a fascinating woman, one that would have rewarded, but wouldn't attract, the attention of men. I think she was rather averse to marriage anyway, because of her semi-invalidism. Vachel Lindsay, the poet, fell in love with Sara and wanted to marry her. But Sara, who came from a well-to-do St. Louis family and had been rather spoilt all her life, couldn't face the thought of marrying a poet who was making his living by selling his rhymes for bread as he tramped around the country and who had no prospects whatever.

There was a young man named Ernst Filsinger in St. Louis who had known Sara for several years. He was the head of a shoe factory out there and was very much in love with her and with her poetry. He was of German descent and had all the German romantic feeling for poetry. Finally Sara came to me and said, "You know Vachel. I want you to meet Ernst. And I want you to tell me what to do. Which of these two men should I marry? Should I marry Vachel Lindsay, who's a genius and whose poetry I love? Or should I marry this very fine, tall, dark, good-looking business-man who seems to care for my poetry?"

I met Ernst Filsinger and talked to him, and I liked him very much. First I took the position that I couldn't possibly decide; it was too much responsibility. "You have to decide yourself." But that upset her very much, and she said, "No, I've asked you to decide, and I won't ever blame you if anything goes wrong." I said, "Well, knowing you as well as I do, I don't think a marriage with Vachel Lindsay would last, because I don't think you are one who could live in the kitchen doing all the housework and scrub-bing the floors, and he'd want to have children. I think Filsinger, from what talk I've had with him, is the man for you."

So she married him. And I think it was a very happy marriage. I've written all about this in the article they asked me to do for this dictionary that Radcliffe College is issuing of biographies of women.[15] A very happy marriage. They had no children, and Sara couldn't have had any. She was so preoccupied with her work and so delicate anyway. Half the time she wasn't even at home. Every now and then she'd get exhausted, and she'd have to go up to a place called Cromwell, a sanitarium. She wasn't really exhausted at all, but she found it hard to write her poems with a husband around. He was a gay young businessman and wanted to bring his business friends home and have an attractive, intelligent wife to entertain for him and act as hostess. But he was a patient man and so devoted that he put up with all these things. They drifted further and further apart. He was always being promoted—he became vice-president of Standard Brands and was sent abroad a great deal. Finally Sara decided that much as he loved her, she would have to divorce him. She talked to me a great deal about it, and I said, "I think it's a mistake. Don't do it, Sara, don't do it." "Well," she said—they slept in separate rooms apparently—"sometimes in the morn-ing when I go in to wake Ernst, he mutters under his breath, 'She'll never die, she'll never die.' I think he wants me to die. I think he's tired of me."

I said, "I can assure you he is not, because I've talked to him. He loves you deeply. It would be a terrible thing for you to divorce him, and I don't think it's necessary. He gives you all this freedom, something very few men would be willing to do."

Finally Sara told me, "I am going. I am going out West to get a divorce. I have only told two people, you and"—this same woman friend, Margaret Conklin. She went out, and it almost killed her; she felt she was doing such a terrible thing. Ernst got a cablegram in China, where he was on business, that she was divorcing him. He sent back the most vehement, dreadful message saying, "This will kill me if you do it. Don't. I'll do anything, anything. I'm coming back from China immediately. I'll give up my job if necessary. I'll do anything you want me to do, but don't leave me." But she then telegraphed back to him, "You are killing *me*. I can't stand it. I'm being torn to pieces by your suffering and by my knowledge that I have to do this thing. Be merciful and don't telegraph me any more. Help me."

So, because he loved her, he appointed an attorney to represent him, and they were divorced. Then she came back to New York. It was at the peak of the Depression, 1932. She found she was lonely. She couldn't go out to dine with friends because she didn't have the strength. She asked me to telephone her every day. It was hard for me to do this because I only had an hour for lunch, and I usually had authors to take out. But I tried to telephone her every day. I couldn't telephone her from the office. It was very burdensome, but I did my best. In the end, she was reduced—imagine, this woman, who was then considered one of the best living poets—to paying a woman to come in for an hour a day so as to have somebody to talk to. Her income fell off, was cut in half. She'd made bad investments, or her family had.

In the meantime, Vachel Lindsay was beating upon her all the time. He was desperately unhappy. He'd married. He'd married one of his pupils, a young girl he'd met when he was teaching in New Mexico, and they had two children. His vogue had passed, and he couldn't make a living any more with his readings. He had read at Oxford, Cambridge, all around the world. He and his wife were unhappy, and he wanted to get divorced and marry Sara. She got a certain amount of comfort out of seeing him whenever he came to New York. Two unhappy people, they clung together. She then made up her mind—I persuaded her, I said, "The thing for you to do is to go ahead with your work." "I can't write poems any more," she said. "Well, don't write poems," I said, "but you've always wanted to do a book on Christina Rossetti. Now, go over to England and get in touch with the

Sara Teasdale
(courtesy of
*Dictionary of
Literary
Biography*)

Rossetti family; you are the one who could do such a book better than anyone else."

Oh, I forgot one thing that I should have put in earlier, and that is that
Vachel Lindsay had committed suicide. And Sara had called me up—this
is before I had the pep talk with her—she'd called me up on the telephone,
at the office, and I could just barely hear her. She said: "Vachel has killed
himself." I said, "Oh, Sara!" Then I went on talking to her, but she was sobbing on the telephone, and I kept saying, "You must pull yourself together."
She just went on sobbing on the telephone. She couldn't speak. Finally I
just hung up. I think that was the mortal blow, the thing that really did her
in—when Vachel committed suicide. I think she'd always toyed with the
idea of suicide, and this, I think, just shook the underpinnings.

But she took heart, and she went over to England. And while she was
there everyone, many writers—Arthur Symons and all the rest of them
who were admirers of hers because her books were published in England,

too—were very kind to her. But she got bronchial pneumonia and became so homesick and frightened with bad news about money and mounting bills of doctors in England that she insisted upon coming home. The doctor said it was very, very dangerous for her to travel in her condition, but she came home, in the midst of this bronchial pneumonia, exhausted.

She came back, and the doctors got more assiduous than ever. They were all so sorry for her: "How awful" and "Oh, you mustn't be so depressed. You mustn't worry so much about money." And the next day a big bill would arrive. Sara got frightened. She was under sedation—I think very ill-advised sedation. It seemed stupid, because they were giving her bromides—bromides are hideously depressing—when there were so much better sedatives to be had, the barbiturates. Today, of course, we have tranquillizers, which they didn't have then. So when I went to see her at the hospital, her whole face was a mass of pustules from bromide poisoning. It didn't look like a face at all.

So one night, without writing a letter—but she'd indicated in several poems what she was going to do (she had been saving up the barbiturate pills they were now giving her, hiding them)—Sara got up. She had a nurse who was asleep in the next room. She drew a hot bath. She took an overdose of sleeping pills and lay down in the hot water, so that her face was just barely over the rim of the water. And when the deep unconsciousness from the barbiturates came over her, she slipped under the water and drowned while she was unconscious. She was discovered there, dead, in the morning, by the nurse. Then Miss Conklin was sent for, and later I was sent for, and her body lay in the morgue for three days, as it always does when there's suicide. She'd just been driven to it step by step, almost as in a Greek tragedy. Her husband killed himself in China where he had been sent again on business—or so I was told—after he had the news of her death.

It's one of the most extraordinary things that in spite of the terrific depression she'd been in which almost incapacitated her—she could hardly speak—she left behind her finest book under the title *Strange Victory*. This was found after her suicide. It's a small book, but her finest. Some day the poetry in those later books of hers—*Flame and Shadow, Dark of the Moon, Strange Victory*—is going to be recognized. She's an unfashionable figure just now. She's very much overlooked today partly because she's a poet of feeling and partly because she wrote in her youth some rather girlish, gushing poems. But her last books contain really magnificent work, wrought out of suffering. She had a hard, steely core of endurance and character underneath all the hypersensitivity of hers. The combination made her a great poet.

[27 February 1967]

I SHOULD SAY, TAKING THE TRADE department, the educational department, the religious literature department, and the subscription book department together, Scribners might have published, say, one hundred fifty titles a year in the Twenties.

There was William Crary Brownell, who was the senior editor; the son of Edward Burlingame, Roger Burlingame, who was next in seniority;[16] then there was a man named Fred Hoppin who was an assistant editor. He eventually became president of Duffield and Company, a firm that is out of existence now. These, in addition to Max and myself. Max Perkins became the senior editor and was probably the most outstanding editor of our time.

Then there was what was known as a first reader, who read all the manuscripts as they came in, and to whom I would like to pay tribute here. I knew him very slightly because he was a man whom no one knew very well. He was not married. He lived with his sister and brother-in-law in Jackson Heights and devoted himself to their daughter, who was a polio victim and bedridden. His name was Charles Dunn, and he was a most imaginative and perceptive man.[17] He read everything when it first came in. I think he was there for over fifty years. He never wanted a raise or a promotion. He had no ambitions. He always refused to write book jackets or advertising or to dictate mail. All he did was to sit at his desk, very often with his feet on it, smoking a terrible old pipe of his, reading one manuscript after another. He would pile on one side those that he rejected—many of them immediately, on opening and reading ten pages—and on the rare occasion when anything he thought worth considering turned up, he'd put it on the other side. That was all, and he did that every day, except for two weeks' vacation in the summer. He was a very New England type, very reserved, and one of the most extraordinarily talented men, actually. He never missed any really good thing. For instance, he was the first to read Thomas Wolfe and Scott Fitzgerald and Ernest Hemingway and others. Any good thing he never passed up, and I don't think he ever recommended anything that was bad, except in one case, a book written by a young actress who made a special appeal to him because she was very pretty. That was the only case I know of.

I forget who the receptionist was at that time. She'd take an unsolicited submission, enter it in a book with a number, and paste the number on the manuscript to identify it. Then it would go to Dunn. He would come in the morning, and there'd be a pile of manuscripts that high, and he'd work through it during the day, and that's all he ever did. He was a completely "unspotted-of-the-world" man. I've seen him blush like a young girl if anyone praised him or if anyone told a story that he didn't approve of. Really, an extraordinary person. They wanted him to sit in on meetings, but he always refused. He would never take on any responsibility, and he would never ask for more money. He was not a rich man—he had only what he earned—but he was very proud, and he was very aloof, and he didn't want to be drawn into things. He was timid in that way. Some people are afraid of responsibility.

Then a manuscript would go to the junior editor, which I was at the beginning. Then, if I passed it, it would probably go to Max Perkins. He was at first, of course, not the head editor. He had been head of the promotion department and then moved into an editorial post that made him junior editor, and by the time I came in, he was—well, next in rank to Roger Burlingame, who left very shortly after I came to the editorial department.

I'm probably getting all this mixed up, because I seem to remember now that I came in at the time of the retirement, not death, of Brownell.[18] What I'm mixing up is the fact that I used to go up to the editorial department, and I'd see all these people there. When Brownell retired as editor, everyone was moved up, and that left a job for me as junior editor. When I actually came in in 1926—I'm not sure of this—I think Hoppin was still there. Roger Burlingame was leaving. Max was there and was by this time senior editor. So there really were just Hoppin, Max, Mr. Dunn, and, of course, myself. Oh, and later, not at that time but a little later, a woman editor was added, Bernice Kenyon. Her full name was Bernice Lesbia Kenyon—an odd name that would be rather avoided today—and she stayed for quite a long time. She was moved up from the magazine. She'd been editor on *Scribner's Magazine,* or, rather, a combination secretary and assistant editor, and she was moved up to be an editor in the trade department, in other words the general book publishing department. She was a poet and published four or five books. The first one was *Songs of Unrest*. She was a very good poet.

When I left in 1957, Dunn was still there. He retired and died not long after. Max, of course, had died, I can't remember just when, but on his death I had become senior editor.[19] Another man had long before that taken the office occupied at one time by Mr. Hoppin—a man named Wallace Meyer, a very able editor. I don't remember whether Elinor Parker had joined the editorial staff at that time or not. They always wanted a woman on the staff. I think Elinor Parker came in a little later. She was manager of the Scribner Bookstore for some years. She's now an editor in the trade department. But I don't think she was there when I retired. I think when I retired there were Dunn; Burroughs Mitchell; Wallace Meyer, who succeeded me as senior editor; and myself. Nobody has taken Dunn's place. It's not done that way now. Frankly, a great deal of the first reading is done by some of the secretaries who play the role of being semi-editors, and in their spare time manuscripts are passed around. They're able to eliminate a great many manuscripts that are obviously hopeless. Then the ones that go through are distributed among the various editors. They have there today a young man—I think his name is Donald Hutter—and then they have a man named Harry Brague, a very able editor who I think might be the next senior editor, perhaps, unless it's Elinor Parker, who is also a very important member of the editorial staff, and then Burroughs Mitchell, who is now senior editor. But Mr. Dunn's job has not been continued, and his desk and the chair he sat in, all that, are gone.

Scribners had made its great success, originally, when it was founded in 1846, in the field of theology. It published books of sermons. A book of sermons had the popularity in those days that perhaps a mystery would have today. My grandfather's sermons were published by Scribners. The fashionable preachers of the day almost always had books of their sermons published, and the Scribners firm began in 1846 on Broadway in a basement store, where the original Mr. Charles Scribner sold these theological works and books of sermons.

But as the firm went on, they became interested in fiction—and in what you might call belles lettres—and they had many of the important authors of the day, writers that had a big sale in that time, such as J. G. Holland, George Washington Cable, Thomas Nelson Page, Richard Harding Davis, and authors like Theodore Roosevelt and Henry Van Dyke, and still later John Galsworthy, and so on. They have always continued to publish religious literature, as they later called it, rather than theological—there was a religious literature department. So that today Scribners has probably the best religious literature list of any publisher: it is the field in which they made their first success. They publish Paul Tillich and Reinhold Niebuhr and Jacques Maritain and many important writers in that field whose names I don't know because I never worked in that field.

Then it was later in the game that they added an educational department. It was before my time. There was a man—his name was Edward Lord—who had a business of his own, and Scribners bought him out, and he joined the firm. His business was a textbook business, mostly for schools. Scribners went into that, and they published a great many school textbooks very successfully. There was another man who later joined the Scribners educational department, Will D. Howe. He had a line of textbooks that he edited, the Howe Readers. He was taken on largely for that reason. He had originally been one of the founders of Harcourt, Brace and Howe. It became Harcourt, Brace when he went to Scribners. Scribners built up a very successful school textbook department, and then they tried to go into the college textbook field, which is the most profitable one, but they never were able to make a real success of it—I think partly because of the terrific competition from Harcourt, Brace, who have a very fine college department. And then of course houses like Ginn and Company, D. C. Heath and Company, Von Nostrand, and others were formidable competitors. But Scribners did have a great success in the school textbook field. They also had what's known as a subscription book department, which publishes sets of books in handsome, often autographed, limited editions. They had the authors, you see, with which to do it. They would have a set of Thomas Nelson Page, a set of Henry Van Dyke, a set of J. G. Holland, a set of George Washington Cable, a set of George Santayana, and so on, perhaps in eighteen volumes, autographed by the author, in a beautiful binding, and selling at $200 a set—and these were sold mostly by book agents from house to house, very often sold to people who could no more have read and understood the books than they could have walked on water.

The trade book department is the department that publishes the general run books, sold to the trade, that is to bookstores, and that went on developing very strongly in the field of fiction. They already had a very fine backlist, as I've just said, of these older authors. Van Dyke had an enormous sale; so did Cable and Holland; so did Page. Theodore Roosevelt, too, with his books—not fiction but travel and outdoors—had big sales. Then these authors, in turn, often ended up in a subscription book edition, and Scribners made additional money in that way, because if you issue a thousand sets at $200 a set, and you sell them all, as they usually did, you can be sure that there was a good profit tucked away in that price of $200.

In the trade book department, the greatest advance was made along the lines that Scribners was already famous for—namely, publication of fiction by American writers. Well, nonfiction, too, but I'd say that we had been rather weak in the field of science, for instance. That has been made up in recent years. Of course, in the years of the regime of Maxwell Perkins, the Scribners list reflected his own tastes. He was not at all interested in books translated from the French or the German or the Italian or what have you. He was interested in our native literature. It was under his aegis that they published Scott Fitzgerald and Ernest Hemingway and Thomas Wolfe and Vance Bourjaily and Marjorie Rawlings.

The advance would depend on the author's previous sale. Scribners had not been famous for liberal advances. The prestige of the house made up in author satisfaction, somewhat, although of course that wouldn't pay the grocer. But when they had an author who seemed important enough, they would be liberal because Max Perkins was always on the side of the author. Some people think he was a little bit too much on the side of the author. Scribners were sometimes very liberal with their advances, especially at the time when Charles Scribner III, the son of Charles Scribner II, was president. After the two brothers, Charles II and Arthur, had died, Charles Scribner III took over, and he was a genial, charming, fox-hunting, outdoor-loving man who didn't pretend to know much about books and leaned very heavily on Max and on me. Max could almost always persuade Charlie to a liberal advance.

I know that Scribners made a great deal during the years from 1920 to 1930. But the house, under Charles Scribner III, frankly, was depleting its resources. The two brothers, Charles II and Arthur Scribner—for them publishing had been an extremely successful business—had put by a capital surplus, which was drawn on heavily by these sometimes overgenerous and rather risky advances. Not all of them turned out to pay for themselves. I think when the present Charles Scribner took over, Charles Scribner IV, things were not in too good shape. He's a most remarkable man, you know. He graduated from Princeton summa cum laude in three years. His great passion is mathematics, and he's the sort of man who would normally have been a professor at the Princeton Institute for Advanced Studies. He became a cryptanalyst in Washington during World War II. I think he was decoding Japanese when his father died and Charlie was called to the presidency and leadership of the firm. The family fortunes are involved in this business, and Charlie had to leave Washington and become the chief of a big firm—the chief over men who were old enough to be his grandfather and who had been in the business for years. He was a very shy, intellectual young man. I must say I admired the way he did it. He just gritted his teeth

John Hall Wheelock at the time he was a junior employee at Scribners
(photograph by Danford Barney)

and put his shoulder to the wheel. He took that great intellectual ability of
his and applied it to publishing, and he has made a tremendous success.
Not only has he made a tremendous success, but in the process of dealing
with human beings, he's become mellowed. I've heard some of the firm's
travelers—men not overly emotional—speak about this almost with tears
in their eyes. They found it a very moving thing to watch the unfolding of

that severe, austere, difficult, critical, suspicious, playing-close-to-the-chest man, Charlie, into a fully grown, generous, wise human being.

I didn't see much that has taken place in the years since I left.[20] I saw a good deal of the other side. I've been bawled out by Charlie in a way that, if I hadn't had the greatest respect for him and also the greatest desire to hold on to my job, I would have resigned immediately. I remember one time when I had agreed to do something for Oscar Williams, the anthologist—namely, that Scribners should bear the full cost of changes made in the page proof of an anthology because we had not secured from one of the poets who was included his permission to be included. This poet had said, "Take me out." We said, "You're there and your picture is in there." "Take me out. I don't care what it costs. I won't pay for it either; you'll have to pay for it. I won't consent to be in any anthology by Oscar Williams." So we had to take out the poems and reset some of the page proof, and it cost about six hundred dollars, and I had to say to Mr. Scribner, "Mr. Oscar Williams doesn't think this is a proper charge against him." He should have been responsible for clearing permissions. But he couldn't well afford the expense. And besides that, he was an impossible man. Mr. Scribner finally, grudgingly, said, "All right, all right, all right, we'll pay it." But then Oscar came to me and said, "Will you let me have it in writing?" I said, "You have our word." He said, "You might die; Mr. Scribner might die"—he was right—"I'd have nothing to show." So I said, "All right, I'll give it to you in writing." And I did.

Then somehow or other, this was brought to the attention of Mr. Scribner. And he came into my office one day waving this paper, and said, "Did you sign this?" I said, "Yes, that's my signature." "Why did you do such a stupid thing?" he shouted. "How could you be so stupid?" Right in front of everyone, storming up and down the editorial department. I could have knocked him down, I was so angry. But I thought of my job and of my pension, and also I know that this wasn't the real Charlie. He went on and on, ranting and raving. I said, "I'm terribly sorry, Mr. Scribner, but you did give your word, you know." "I know I gave my word, but isn't my word any good? Do I have to put everything in writing for this man?"—whom he hated intensely. "Tell him never to come to this floor again." I said, "I can't say that, Mr. Scribner. We have business to transact." "I don't care! Get rid of him!" That's the way he was. Then in half an hour, or an hour, he came into my office and said, "Will you ever forgive me? I'm so sorry. How could I have spoken like that to you? I don't suppose you'll ever forgive me." I said, "Forget about it. You were just a little upset." He's a very fine person, very fine, but over-keyed, and he never wanted to be the head of a big commercial establishment. Now he's done wonders with it.*

I know very well how the Depression affected Scribners. There were some tragic things happened. One of the most tragic was the fact that Mr. Arthur Scribner, who was president for the two years between the death of Charles Scribner II and his own death, had put everything he had into Scribners stock. It seems incredible: A man who had this great big house in New York and a big estate in Mount Kisco and a most beautiful wife who loved to entertain but had no means of her own. I think she'd been a schoolteacher. It was a very happy marriage. Anyway, when the Crash came, Scribners stock didn't pay a nickel for I don't know how long. Mr. Arthur Scribner had died after the Depression began, and Mrs. Scribner found herself with a New York house on which the taxes were probably seventeen or eighteen thousand dollars a year, a country place with very heavy taxes, and several thousand shares of stock that no longer paid dividends.

Charlie Scribner III was then president. Mrs. Scribner went directly to him and said, "I've inherited all this stock from Arthur, but I have no money to live on. I'll just have to sell the stock." Well, the family has never allowed the stock to go out of the hands of the family. All the editors were allowed to buy a few shares, but they never saw the certificates. They paid in the money, and they received their dividends, and then when they retired, the stock reverted to the family. They paid it off. So Charlie Scribner held a meeting of the board of directors, and the business was not in too good shape at the time, but Charlie said, "What we'll have to do is to put a mortgage on this building, here on Fifth Avenue, so as to raise the money to buy the stock from my aunt, Mrs. Arthur Scribner." He said, "I'm very jealous of the rights to this stock. I can't allow any of the stock to go—we don't know whom it might go to. It might eventually go to some undesirable holder who would then be partly in control of the business. I can't let the stock pass out of the family hands." So that was done. That shows the condition the firm was in at the time. No dividends on the stock, and it used to pay ten percent.

The first thing that Mr. Arthur Scribner, one of the two brothers, did when he came in two years before his death was to announce that he wanted a week away from the office to think out his policy. He was a very sweet man, a lovable man, an attractive man, but very timid. He'd always been overawed by his much abler older brother. When he returned to his

*This crisis is reported again with a different emphasis on pp. 206–7.

office, he called a board meeting and, to the astonishment of us all, he announced his policy. His policy was going to be economy. Did you ever hear of such a negative policy? We were all asked—a purely rhetorical question—would we be willing to accept a ten percent cut in our salaries? Because of the Depression. And what could we do but say yes? And our salaries were not big. I remember that my salary at that time was five thousand dollars a year.

We took fewer chances during the Depression. We went in more for the things that we knew would pay off, which of course is fatal to a publishing house in the long run, because if you don't have enough imagination to take risks, you will never hold your own in the publishing world. It's a world where imagination pays off richly.

One of the standards maintained by the publishing house was a wonderful one, I think. I really think it was one of the few houses where the policy, the aim, was to publish the best books. By best I don't mean the best-selling books, but the books that were intrinsically the best work. Naturally, the house had to make money too. But at Scribners the sales department never overruled the editorial department, as it does in some houses. The editorial department often forced things that the sales department threw its hands in horror over. You know: "My God!" The sales people, of course, make their living from commissions on sales, and very often the rub would come when you'd published three books of an author, and they'd all be flops. Then when the salesmen heard that Scribners had taken on a fourth book by the same author, they would be pretty sore about it— and sometimes the fourth book was the one that rang the bell, because the editors knew they had a real talent there and it was just a question of time. The judgment of the sales department would have been very bad on those things.

When it came to poetry, I think the policy of Scribners was very much like that of any other house. Most publishers—I think this situation's improved now—but most publishers at that time would like to have on their list, as a matter of prestige, a very few books of poems of real distinction and quality, possibly one each season, two at the most. The reason for this was that as time went on, the sale of poetry became less and less. I don't know just what caused this. I think part of it may have been that the public was confused by the new movement in poetry. I mean the obscurity of many of the contemporary poets—the hermetic school of poetry written by poets for other poets, which has developed to an extreme degree today.

The older school of poetry, which was addressed more to the general reader, had had a better chance. The sale became so small that you would publish a book of poems of perhaps real quality, and the sale would be three hundred fifty copies. There's no use in putting printers and binders to work to get out something that doesn't do better than that. So the tendency was to publish less and less poetry. But we managed to take on, during the years that I was at Scribners, some very good poets. Some of them have been entirely forgotten today, but they are nevertheless quite remarkable. One, for instance, was Phelps Putnam, whom you never hear of now. Another one some people have heard of was John Peale Bishop, a remarkably fine poet. But he's been lost in the shuffle now.

When I came in, I wasn't allowed to publish more than, say, two poets a year. We took on Conrad Aiken. That was a success. And Louise Bogan and Peter Viereck and Rolfe Humphries, who later gave us his translation of the *Aeneid,* which has been a real money-maker. I solicited some of them. For instance, I knew that Louise Bogan had had one book published by McBride and that they didn't want to do her next book, and I got in touch with her. I got her for Scribners. She never made much money, but she's perhaps one of the outstanding lyric poets of our time.

The *Poets of Today* series was not my idea. I must give the credit for this series to Mr. Charles Scribner IV, the present head of the firm. He had a brilliant idea. I was always saying, "We must publish more poetry. There's so much good work being done. Can't we introduce some new talents?" And Charlie always said, "It won't sell. What's the use of publishing a book that sells only three hundred fifty copies?" We'd taken on some of the younger poets, like Howard Moss, and had no success. He edits poetry for *The New Yorker* and is one of the best living poets. We thought that because of his connection with *The New Yorker*—the fact that all the poets in the world, or all the English-writing poets, aim to please Howard Moss to get into *The New Yorker*—his books might have some distribution. But his books have never had any distribution to speak of.

So finally Mr. Scribner came up with the idea. He said, "I have a notion that if we could take three books and put them into one volume, so that you could say to readers, you are getting here, for a little bit more than the price of one book, three first books by three men of real talent, attested to by a poet who's on our staff, you might have a salable volume." It was my job to discover these new talents. So that's how we started *Poets of Today.* There were eight volumes, and each volume contained three complete books, by three poets who had never been published before. I found them by reading magazines and talking to other poets, particularly by reading periodicals and coming across poems by these people. Then I'd get tips occasionally from someone who perhaps lived in California: "There's a wonderful young poet in San Francisco who I think might interest you. May I ask him to send you a manuscript?" That's how we started, and in the first volume we had three remarkable poets that I had discovered. One was May Swenson who has since been issued in hard cover and paperback and everything else, doing extremely well. She was one of the ones that I discovered for the first volume. A volume came out each year.

I went on with it after I retired. I retired in 1957, and I think it went on—it must have started in 1954 and went on through 1961. After my retirement, Scribners continued to pay me a fee to go on with this. Of the twenty-four poets I published, about half of them have been successes. Some of that half have become outstanding poets, like May Swenson; James Dickey, who won the National Book Award; Louis Simpson, who's taken the Pulitzer Prize and National Book Award; and Joseph Langland; and—oh, I could go on with the names of many others. The books themselves, the volumes with the three complete books, sold well enough to pay for themselves. I think an edition was something like two thousand copies.

Charlie, the present president of the firm, got up a much more elaborate system of approving books. He thought we'd all been having too easy a time of it. After that, whenever you wanted to publish a book and made a case for it at an editorial conference, you would also have to submit an elaborate brief in which you told about the book, what it was, why you thought it would sell, how you could promote it, how much money you could afford to spend on it, a rough estimate of the cost of manufacture— the editor had to do all this for every book that he recommended, if he really believed strongly in the book. That discouraged many editors from recommending a thing that they were only half-hearted about.

I think a rough way of estimating the economics of a book would be like this. You know, the author's usual royalty is ten percent of the full retail price. Well, the publisher makes just about what the author makes. Take a five-dollar book. The author gets fifty cents a copy. That book will be sold to the trade at not less than forty percent off, which means it will be sold to the trade at three dollars, and if you get a quantity order, it will be sold to the trade at fifty percent off. So out of that three dollars, or let's call it two dollars fifty cents, the publisher would have to take his cost of manufacture, his cost of advertising, his income taxes, his rent, his light, heating,

POETS OF TODAY SERIES

Selected and edited, with Introductory Essays,
by John Hall Wheelock

POETS OF TODAY I

A Critical Introduction
Harry Duncan Poems and Translations
Murray Noss Samurai and Serpent Poems
May Swenson Another Animal: Poems

POETS OF TODAY II

Introductory Essay: The Fourth Voice of Poetry
Norma Farber The Hatch: Poems
Robert Pack The Irony of Joy: Poems
Louis Simpson Good News of Death and Other Poems

POETS OF TODAY III

Introductory Essay: The Poem in the Atomic Age
Lee Anderson The Floating World and Other Poems
Spencer Brown My Father's Business and Other Poems
Joseph Langland The Green Town: Poems

POETS OF TODAY IV

Introductory Essay: To Recapture Delight
George Garrett The Reverend Ghost: Poems
Theodore Holmes The Harvest and the Scythe: Poems
Robert Wallace This Various World and Other Poems

POETS OF TODAY V

Introductory Essay: On a Certain Resistance
O. B. Hardison, Jr. Lyrics and Elegies
Kenneth Pitchford The Blizzard Ape: Poems
Sheila Pritchard In Rainwater Evening: Poems

POETS OF TODAY VI

Introductory Essay: The Process and the Poem
Gene Baro Northwind and Other Poems
Donald Finkel The Clothing's New Emperor and Other Poems
Walter Stone Poems, 1955–1958

POETS OF TODAY VII

Introductory Essay: Some Thoughts On Poetry
James Dickey Into the Stone and Other Poems
Paris Leary Views of the Oxford Colleges and Other Poems
Jon Swan Journeys and Return: Poems

POETS OF TODAY VIII

Introductory Essay: Man's Struggle To Understand
Albert Herzing The Mother of the Amazons and Other Poems
John M. Ridland Fires of Home: Poems
David R. Slavitt Suits for the Dead: Poems

Wheelock published the first collections of twenty-four poets
in this Scribners series.

and telephone charges, not to mention the royalty of fifty cents—you know, all these things, wages and so on, and it would usually work out the publisher will be getting fifty cents a copy, too. Now, if a book of poems, which sold at three dollars, sold one thousand copies, the author would only be making three hundred dollars and the publisher would only be making three hundred dollars, which would not be enough to cover the cost of composition.

I think the biggest factor in sales is word-of-mouth enthusiasm. I never have been able to find out how much reviews count. Of course, the more a book is talked about and written about, the more people hear about it, the more they are exposed to it. But I know that my only prose book, *What Is Poetry?*, was never reviewed because it was made up, largely, of the introductions that I wrote for the *Poets of Today*. For each book I had written a long introduction on some general theme with regard to poetry and then applied it to the work of the three poets included. I took out the parts of these introductions that applied to the work of the three poets and published the rest of those introductions in this book called *What Is Poetry?* Since they had appeared previously in books that were reviewed at the time, my book was not considered to be subject to review. That book was never reviewed, and Scribners never advertised it. It immediately sold about ten thousand copies, went into paperback, and has sold over twenty thousand in all. Whereas my books of poems, which are so immeasurably better in every way than my prose and more original and more important: no one of them has ever sold more than four thousand copies.

You launch a prose book without any reviews or any advertising, and it just spreads by word of mouth. *What Is Poetry?* happened to hit some—I think—schools where there was somebody teaching a terrible thing called "Creative Writing," and the book just seemed to fit in. People today prefer to read about things rather than to read the thing itself. We're living in an Alexandrian age.

I am a great believer in all the freedoms. The thing I object to about the pornography in books today is not so much the pornography as the fact that the only reason it's used, in most cases, is for shock value and because it's the fashion. I feel that just to be doing what everyone else is doing, for everyone to try to be original in exactly the same way, is a contradiction in terms. I think we are passing through a phase that we have passed through before, in the time of Henry Fielding, for instance. The world has been through many periods when the sky was the limit as regards language and the subjects that you write about. We're going through one of those periods now, and I suppose perhaps one hundred years from now, or fifty years from now, we'll swing to the opposite extreme, and everything will be taboo again. I'm not in sympathy with it, myself. I just had occasion to write to a poet who has, I think, very real talent. She's a young woman, a friend of ours, and she has written some beautiful poems. Now she publishes a book in paperback containing ten poems at the book's beginning in which every four-letter word is used. She sent me a copy inscribed to me and asked me what I thought of it, and I wrote and said, "I much prefer your other poems because they are more original; now you're just trying to do what everyone else is doing, and I think that's a mistake." Of course, she didn't like that.

Scribners has always been fortunate in having a backlist that remained very much alive. For instance, today there is a book of Thomas Nelson Page's called *Two Little Confederates,* I think, which sells regularly every year about five hundred or six hundred copies, although it was published perhaps one hundred years ago. There are a lot of books like that on the Scribners list. There's a book by Stark Young, who was a friend of mine, a Southerner from Mississippi, and the greatest dramatic critic, so the *London Times* said, that ever appeared on either side of the water. Well, he wrote a novel called *So Red the Rose,* and that novel must have been published, oh, fifty or sixty years ago. It still sells, every year, seven hundred or eight hundred copies. Then you have the books of these theological writers, and books by Galsworthy, by Thomas Wolfe, by Hemingway, by Scott Fitzgerald, by Marjorie Rawlings, by Niebuhr, by Tillich—they go on selling and selling and selling.

It's due to the strong backlist that Scribners was able to publish what it felt was good and to the wisdom and courage of young Charlie. Because the first thing he did when he came in was to cut to the bone. We had a London office and published books over there, and in New York our own press in another building. He did away with all these. *Scribner's Magazine* had been discontinued, but there was some remnant of it left, and that was cut out.

Scribner's Magazine, when I joined the firm, was edited by a man named Robert Bridges—the same name as that of the then poet laureate of England. Bridges as he got older became senile and had to be retired. But he was so unhappy about it that Scribners gave him a job in the trade publishing department. They put him up on the sixth floor, where he was all alone in a big room, and all the manuscripts that had been rejected by Mr. Dunn were turned over to him, and he read them and wrote out his opinions of them. It was just to give him something to do, and it was safe, because they had all been rejected already, and nothing more could be done about them.*

The magazine was running downhill. We struck a very difficult time, of course, when the new magazines came in. *Scribner's* and *The Century* and one or two other magazines, known as the old family magazines, all were going into bankruptcy, when magazines like *The Saturday Evening Post, Cosmopolitan, McCall's,* and *The New Yorker* came along. *Harper's Magazine* was the only one of the old family magazines that survived,† and that survived because it, I understand, was subsidized by the Morgan family. *Scribner's* tried to change over into a modern magazine, and Max Perkins and I were given the job of achieving this. We employed a managing editor, and we devised a different format and made it a bigger size, like *The New Yorker.* We gave some of the new younger writers who were coming to us to be published a chance to be published serially in the pages of the magazine. It went along for a while, but it didn't succeed, and finally the whole thing folded in 1939. We couldn't get the advertising.

The book clubs, of course, were one of the things the Scribners were always very much against. Mr. Charles Scribner II, who was still alive and at the helm when this began, was very averse to having any book of his —— He didn't see why a book club should make a lot of money out of a book he had published. Why couldn't *he* make that money out of it? But I don't know; I really don't feel wise enough to pass on this question. For instance, I think the paperbacks have been a wonderful thing for publishing because they have created new readers and continue to do so. More and more people read good books because they get them cheap in paperbacks, just as in painting, more and more people know about painting now, and about music, than they used to because they are exposed to them more.

I don't know about the book clubs. I think one of the evil things about them is that in one season perhaps five really good novels are published, and each of them is deserving of some success—artistically and commercially. Then the Book-of-the-Month Club picks out one of them, and that book goes zooming on to a tremendous sale. The other four are neglected. That's bad. It does away with the normal competition of talent. On the other hand, I suppose perhaps the book clubs have made readers of some people that ordinarily wouldn't have become readers. I don't know.

---

*Thomas Wolfe's story about Bridges, "Old Man Rivers," was published in *The Atlantic,* 180 (December 1947), 92–104.

†*The Atlantic* was another "quality" magazine that survived.

■ ■ ■ ■

Alfred Knopf was one of the competing publishers in 1926. They were the first firm to make really good-looking books in this country. And it was a great team, wasn't it? Alfred Knopf was a born publisher, and Blanche Knopf had so much taste about design and about books. Then the growing house of Harcourt, Brace was a tremendous rival in the educational field. Doubleday—— Frank N. Doubleday had been a salesman in the Scribner Bookstore at one time. A lot of people started there. Joyce Kilmer also was a salesman there.

I knew Joyce Kilmer well and Aline Kilmer, his wife. Joyce was a most attractive man, and she was a very attractive woman. They were not very—what shall we say—they were very naive intellectually. They were warmhearted, fine people. I never quite forgave Joyce for going into the war when he didn't have to and leaving a wife with four children and practically nothing to live on. But he was hell bent to get into the war. He was like Alan Seeger, you know, but Alan was a bachelor. Then, some of Kilmer's poems—"I think that I shall never see, / A poem lovely as a tree"—that awful stuff that he wrote became so popular. He was idolized by many people and especially by his wife, who had a very tough time.

There were still other writers who worked in the bookstore. There was Robert Cortes Holliday, who made a great success with a series of volumes called *Walking Stick Papers,* essays, a little bit along the line of Hilaire Belloc. Holliday was a dipsomaniac, one of these cyclical drinkers who had spells of drinking and all the rest of the time were all right. I can't remember all the writers who made their beginnings in the Scribner Bookstore.

In some ways, of course, I feel proudest of the poets I discovered. You see, it's a very complex thing. You don't know just exactly. Some books you discovered by reading the manuscript and being very much for it, and then it was handed over to some other editor to see through. Sometimes you as an editor saw things through that somebody else had originally taken on. I found some remarkable writers who have not come to much. One was Erskine Caldwell. I first read a story of his in one of these little magazines—I don't remember the name of it—and wrote to him, and we got his first book, which was one of the most beautiful and truly poetic books I've read, called *American Earth,* which was published in 1931. It was more like poetry, though it was written in prose. Then the next one that came along was *Tobacco Road* in 1932. We could have made a million dollars out of that book. That was one I discovered. Mr. Arthur Scribner was president then, and I had his permission to publish this book, and it was published. Then he took it home one night and started to read it, and he came around to me the next day and said, "Is this the book that you——?" I said, "Yes." "Oh, I'm so sorry we published it," he said. "That's a terrible blunder. It's going to cost us a great deal of money. It's a disaster for the house, absolute disaster." I said, "Why, Mr. Scribner?" "Well," he said, "in the South we have our chief educational sale, in the schools there. They probably will ban Scribner books after our publishing a thing like Erskine Caldwell's *Tobacco Road*. It's a dirty book," he added. "It soils the Scribners imprint." I said, "You agreed to it, you know, Mr. Scribner." "I know. I didn't understand what I was agreeing to at the time of that editorial conference."

Then Will Howe, head of the Scribners school department, came to me, spurred on by Mr. Scribner, with the same feeling. I thought I'd probably lose my job. They didn't advertise the book, and the salesmen in the Scribner Bookstore were told that, under the law, they had to sell it if anyone asked for it, but to keep it under the counter where no one would see it. The book sold about one thousand copies. Caldwell was very hot under the collar, naturally. He said, "You're not advertising my book, and I can't find it in the bookstore." So we lost him. Caldwell left Scribners and went to the Viking Press, and that house took over *Tobacco Road*. Mr. Scribner was glad to get rid of it. It then sold by the millions, as you know, both in hardcover and paperback.

There were some other authors that I was very proud of. Thomas Wolfe was an author that Dunn and Max and I were all responsible for. Dunn was the man who had the imagination and enterprise in the beginning when a suitcase came in crammed with this confused mass of typescript. Tom had given up all hope. He'd been turned down by a number of publishers; he'd gone abroad. He was over there getting drunk when this thing came in from his agent, a French woman, Madeleine Boyd. Dunn opened the huge suitcase.* Most first readers would have looked at this mass of stuff and thought, "It's impossible. Anyway, you could never publish anything of that length." Dunn started to read it, and he got terribly excited and came to me and said, "Read a few pages, read some of this." I did, and I thought it was simply magnificent. Max saw it, and we cabled to Tom—found out his address from his agent and cabled him to come back

*The typescript of *O Lost* had 1,110 pages and was about six inches in bulk.

Charles F. Dunn, the Scribners first reader for fifty years (courtesy of
Princeton University Libraries)

to this country immediately for a conference, and that we wanted the book. That's how it all started. I was just as responsible for it as anyone. So was Dunn. So was Max. A lot of books are like that.

Mussolini's autobiography was offered to Scribners, and for some reason or other Scribners was not willing to pay the advance. That was what I heard. His agent had big ideas on advances, and Scribners was canny enough to know that that book would not have a big sale. Mussolini was an unpopular figure. The autobiography was declined. On the other hand, Scribners has sometimes declined very successful books of that kind. We have been very weak on getting books by great figures. Harper's does most of them—lives of the presidents, lives of Eisenhower—because it's done by competitive bidding, and Scribners has never wanted to go in for that. Sometimes Harpers has won out, and often I think they've lost, because by the time you make the winning bid, you may have bid more than the book will bring in.

I was Vachel Lindsay's friend, but he never published with Scribners. Macmillan was his publisher. First he was published by Mitchell Kennerley, the publisher who disappeared as a firm some time ago; of course, he's been dead now for some years. He was the man who got so many good authors. He had a real literary flair. He got Edna Millay's first books; he got Vachel Lindsay's first books. A number of writers who have gone on to become well-known figures were first launched by Kennerley. The only trouble was he never paid any royalties. He signed contracts, but he never paid anything, and Edna Millay had to sue him to get her money, and so did Vachel Lindsay. Kennerley published Vachel Lindsay's first trade book, *General William Booth Enters into Heaven*.[21]

I knew Vachel very well, and I was one of those who first heard him read. This was at the house of a woman whose name has been forgotten now but who was very well known in that day as an anthologist and a small poet, Jessie B. Rittenhouse. At her party, given at her apartment here in New York—or perhaps at some other place, because it was quite a big room—Vachel, who was there, was asked to recite, and he got up and recited "General William Booth" and "The Santa-Fé Trail" in that way of his that no other poet has ever used and that he made such a huge success with, not only here but in England, at Oxford and Cambridge. For instance, when he was reading "The Santa-Fé Trail," he would use his voice as a musical instrument—"Hark to the faint-horn, quaint-horn, saint-horn / Hark to the calm-horn, balm-horn, psalm-horn"—with all the sounds of crossing the prairie. He would close his eyes, screw up his face, and throw back his head so that it really was embarrassing. But he got his audience with this extraordinary way of reading.

He was very young. Very many things happened at that party. That was the beginning of Vachel's career. It was at that party that William Rose Benét, the poet, who had lost his first wife some ten years before, fell desperately in love with probably the most beautiful woman of her time, or one of the most beautiful, Elinor Wylie. I saw it all happening. He had never met Elinor before. She was on the other side of the room standing, and Bill came in at the side and stood there, and all the time Vachel was reading he wasn't hearing a word. He was just looking at Elinor Wylie. Bill managed, somehow or other after it was over, to take Elinor out to dinner. She was divorced at that time from Wylie. Her first husband had committed suicide; she made him so unhappy.* Then she married Horace Wylie, a man old enough to be her father, who was the first person to cultivate her taste in books and who made a poet of her. She was the strikingly good-looking, disdainful type, and Bill fell for her like a ton of bricks. He was just done for. They were married much later, but I think that——
Oh, she was very fond of him; no one could fail to be fond of Bill Benét. Also he was a refuge for her; she was on the rocks financially. He was the perfect husband for Elinor in that he allowed her every freedom, cherished her, and adored her, encouraged her in her writing, even typed out her poems for her. He was an abject husband, in a way, and I think the more unselfish he became, the more Elinor took advantage of it. Eventually, she used to spend her summers abroad in England, where she was supposed to be having a very romantic affair with an Englishman. She dedicated her best book that came out shortly after those years, *Angels and Earthly Creatures,* to "MM," and everyone thought this was Middleton Murry. It wasn't. She had fallen in love with an Englishman, a married man who was very happily married and hadn't the faintest intention of falling in love with anybody else. He had three or four children to whom he was devoted; but he admired Elinor Wylie, and they had much in common intellectually. They used to recite poetry to each other when they went out canoeing. It was a perfectly innocent thing, and it gave Elinor great happiness. While she was sitting in the canoe and reciting, talking to this attractive man, poor Bill was over here just eating his heart out but feeling he mustn't complain because she was a genius, and you must allow every freedom to

*Wylie left her first husband, Philip Hichborn, who some years later committed suicide.

a woman of genius. In the meantime he was doing everything he could to promote her work. She came back to him and died almost within a month after she had come back, very suddenly.

I think that Vachel Lindsay was one of the best poets we've had, and I know that if I were to say this at any literary gathering today among the members of the "Establishment," if you want to call them that, or the elite, they would write me down a peg or two for saying it; but I would say it just the same. I think in "The Chinese Nightingale" and "General William Booth" and "Bryan, Bryan, Bryan" and—oh, a great number of his poems— Vachel sounded an entirely original note in American literature. He was uncouth. He was a provincial. He came from Springfield, Illinois. He had not been to college.* He was a natural talent, but a great talent, I think, and a very brave man. He was an epileptic. Most people don't know that, but he was epileptic all his life. As he made his living eventually by reading from the platform, giving readings all over the country, this was a terrible handicap. Vachel was always an idealist, but as a young man he was so idealistic that he expected to make a living traveling around the country, trading his rhymes for bread. He would take a package of his poems with him, stop off at a farmhouse and knock at the door, and they'd let him in. Then he would announce that he would give them a reading of his poems if they would put him up for the night and feed him. He'd travel all over the country that way, and he wrote a book about it, *Rhymes to Be Traded for Bread*.

The tragedy in Vachel's life was that he had had this great success— that is, for a poet a very great success. He made a living out of his read-ings, and a good one, and he taught also. While he was teaching at the University of New Mexico, he met a young woman—oh, very much younger than he was—whom he fell in love with, and Vachel was a man who was intensely religious and intensely idealistic. I think he was late in his thirties when he married, and he was an absolute virgin. He had never taken a drink or smoked tobacco. He had kept himself, you know, a Sir Galahad, and he believed in this. He fell head over heels for this young woman, and they were married and proceeded to have a family.

Then, unfortunately, Vachel's vogue began to wane. His antics on the platform had enchanted people, and they'd laughed at the right places in his poems. Well, now they just thought he was a clown, and the audience, the young students, boys and girls, would jeer at him. Then, finally, they

---

*Lindsay attended, but did not graduate from, Hiram College in Ohio.

Vachel Lindsay declaiming his verse (courtesy of *Dictionary of Literary Biography*)

got so they wouldn't come to his performances, and he lost his living. He lived in Springfield where he was born, and he turned to the authorities there to find out if they couldn't help him to get a job. No one was able to do anything for him. In the meantime, his epilepsy got worse. So he was put on a very, very heavy dosage of a thing called Luminal, which was the best remedy they had for epilepsy in those days. Luminal is simply phenobarbital. He was given a very heavy dose, I've learned since from a friend who knew him at the time, two grains a day of Luminal. Luminal, unlike the other barbiturates, is very depressing psychologically, and it is cumulative. This would have been enough to upset any man. Well, he got into a psychosis of depression about his inability to support his wife and children. The young wife was, I think, getting a little tired of Vachel, anyway. He was much too old for her. So that one unhappiness piled on top of the other, and he couldn't get any help from anyone in Springfield.

Finally, one night—— He had downstairs a little shrine, with a picture of his mother, where he sometimes used to pray. Vachel had been rather over-mothered. He asked his wife to go upstairs and said, "I'll come in just a few moments. I just want to say a little prayer here." The next thing she heard was these animal sounds, and Vachel was coming up the stairs on his hands and knees, making inarticulate cries and moans. He had drunk a bottle of Lysol and, of course, died within an hour in extreme agony.

Now, in his home in Springfield, Illinois, the city charges a dollar to show you the room Vachel worked in and so on. But when he was alive, nobody would do anything for him. Edgar Lee Masters wrote the best book he ever wrote, apart from his famous *Spoon River Anthology,* when he wrote *Vachel Lindsay: A Poet in America,*[22] showing the treatment that Lindsay had received while he was alive. Now the city makes money out of his home.

I want to say one thing more about Vachel. The most touching thing happened. When I was at Scribners, whenever Vachel was in town he would look me up, and we would quite often have dinner together. I would take him home. I was still unmarried and living at home. We'd go out to lunch together, and in the evening we'd make an evening of it. He never drank anything. One day Vachel visited me, and I thought there was something strange about him. It bothered me, but I didn't know what it was. He said, "Look, Jack, you and I are failures. Other people have gone on and achieved great reputations. You and I have not. We're failures. Let's just accept it. I just wanted to see you. Haven't seen you for some time." I assured him he was talking nonsense. I refused to take him seriously, and we got onto other subjects. Yet he didn't seem himself, and when it came time to go, he shook hands and hung on to my hand for a long time, and after he was gone I felt uncomfortable. I didn't know—it never occurred to me—that he was going to kill himself. But I had that feeling, when some part of you tells you, some part of yourself that you don't know much about, some strange foreboding feeling. It was within a week of this that Vachel killed himself. This was his farewell. I have often worried about it.

Vachel used to recite his new poems, and I would recite mine. He liked my work. I had had some fine letters from him, before I knew him, about my first book. He was one of those people out west that liked it so much. I have wonderful letters from all that group in St. Louis, and from people like Richard Le Gallienne and old Weir Mitchell, the novelist doctor, and from Barrett Wendell, who was a professor at Harvard, and from John Masefield, who was not yet the poet laureate. We never criticized each other's work. It would have been a good thing for me if Sara Teasdale had been more critical, but Sara thought I was the greatest living poet. Of course, I accepted this as no more than my due, being young and unself-critical. Sara really did have a very special liking for my poems. I liked hers, too, but not perhaps to that extreme extent. It was bad for me, I think, to have as a friend anyone so uncritical of my work.

If they are poets, they are pure originators on their own. You could suggest ideas to a playwright or to a novelist, for instance, or even whole scenes and situations; but never to a poet, unless he was a narrative poet or an epic poet. I suppose I may have suggested some ideas to Marjorie Rawlings about the relations between human beings and animals, and she wrote that book *The Yearling*, which I think may have been slightly affected by that.

I did suggest to a man named—he's been forgotten now—Edwin Franden Dakin that somebody ought to write a book against Christian Science. He did write such a book,[23] and it was extremely successful. There's a long, quite exciting story about that, because the church threatened the firm. First, they sent a very friendly delegation to call on Mr. Charles Scribner to say that they were intensely interested in this book; they'd heard about it, and they would like to buy the plates. They felt that they would have opportunities for distribution that Scribners perhaps wouldn't have. Mr. Scribner of course refused.

Then, after that, came another delegation. They said that they didn't approve of this book and were willing to pay a good price to have it turned over to them with the promise that Scribners would not publish. That didn't work. Then the third time they came they used another method, a threat: foreclosure of mortgages. It's a very rich church, and apparently they held mortgages on a great many bookstores. They said they could close them out, and many of the channels of the book trade would be affected. Mr. Scribner told them to get out, or he would bring suit against them for blackmail. Then I was told by a woman who came to see me, one of the officers of the First Church of Christ Scientist, that they were going to use "malicious animal magnetism" against the heads of the firm of Scribners. She said, "We have powers that you know nothing of. You might mention this to the Messrs. Scribner sometime." I never did—but it is a fact that within three years Mr. Charles and Mr. Arthur Scribner were dead. Considering that one died at the age of seventy-four and the other at very nearly the same age, it's not so extraordinary.

It sold very well. It was the book, you know, that first revealed the fact Mary Baker Eddy was a morphinist. It also showed that she got her principal ideas from Phineas Parkhurst Quimby, a New England philosopher. That fact had been known, but it had never before been publicized. The morphine thing Dakin came across in the course of his research.

I knew Edna Millay, and I had some letters from her about my poems. I came into collision with her once or twice. I called my book, published in 1922, *The Black Panther*, and led off with a poem called "The Black Panther," the last two lines of which read: "The eternal passion stretches me apart, / And I lie silent—but my body shakes." Edna Millay called my attention to the fact that she had written in a poem about autumn: "Here such a passion is / As stretcheth me apart,—." I was able to show her that my poem, "The Black Panther," had appeared in *Scribner's Magazine* about a year before her book with the line in it appeared. So I said, "You must have got it from me."[24] She'd never seen that issue of *Scribner's*. It was just a coincidence.

I used to meet her sometimes with a mutual friend named Arthur Davidson Ficke, a well-known poet at the time who's now been forgotten. He and Witter Bynner, the poet, were friends, and they'd perpetuated a hoax. They started what they—— Oh, they'd got sick and tired of all these modern schools of poetry, and they started a fake school of their own called "Spectrism." They announced that every word throws a shadow and that if a poem is properly written, the shadows all lean in the same direction. Then they published this book. It was called *Spectra*,[25] and each poem, instead of having a title, was named as musical compositions often are: Opus 1, Opus 2. The two authors were given as Emanuel Morgan and Anne Knish. Those were their pen names. They got the most terrific reviews. Harriet Monroe in *Poetry* said this was one of the important movements of the period. It was going to influence poetry greatly. Then after a number of these reviews had appeared, the perpetrators stepped out from behind their masks and showed up the whole thing. Ficke and his wife lived near Austerlitz, New York, where Edna Millay and her husband lived, and where Louise Bogan and her husband, Raymond Holden, lived also.

Edna Millay died by falling downstairs in her house in Austerlitz. Her husband had died before her. They lived alone there. Her husband was a man named Eugene Boissevain. He was in a way of being a professional husband of prima donnas. Previously, he had married Inez Mulholland, the well-known feminist. Then he married Edna Millay and was the perfect husband for her because he secured for her the necessary solitude for her writing. Every evening—they were living in this lonely place—every evening, he put on full evening dress—not just black tie, but tails—and she wore her smartest evening low-neck gown, and they drank champagne and toasted each other and dined in grand style. Every evening, in that funny little rundown country house.

I had sent her the proof sheets of Rolfe Humphries's translation of *The Aeneid*. Edna was something of a classical scholar. Well, that day after she died, a telegram was delivered that she had sent me about Humphries's *Aeneid*. She was found dead at the foot of the stairs with the proof sheets in her hand. She had been drinking heavily during those widowed years, and she'd fallen. The telegram was an excited one about Rolfe's translation. Scribners wanted to use parts of it to advertise the book, but Rolfe, who was a man of very fine feeling, said we certainly must not, because it was not possible now to get Miss Millay's permission to use it, and he wouldn't allow any part of it used. It wasn't really necessary because the book went on to have a very fine sale on its merits.

Millay's vogue had passed. She was at one time considered the prima donna among American poetesses. But now her work is held in less esteem by the critical modern crowd. Edna Millay was one of the poets bred up in a time when poets were not all professors. Now all poets are professors in universities, and their critical standards are—— They're much more erudite and much more critical. Browning never went to college. Shelley was thrown out of college. Keats never went to college. Yeats never went to college. Swinburne was thrown out during his first year. Now, every poet is a Ph.D. teaching at some university.

■ ■ ■ ■

Henry Goddard Leach, the great Scandinavian scholar, said that he and Robert Frost were walking out from a Poetry Society of America dinner, the big annual dinner, and as they were walking out, Frost had taken him by the arm, turned him around, pointed at me, and said, "That man is a real poet." I was terribly pleased by that. I only heard of that recently. I got this letter just a few months ago from Leach.

I knew Frost quite well. As he got older, he got a little bit mixed up. The last time I saw him was at his daughter's house, Leslie Frost's house, and Frost was at the head of a long receiving line. He told me later, he'd thought that he'd been invited to meet just a small group and that they'd all sit on the floor and he would recite his poems. Instead of that, about two hundred people showed up, invited by Leslie Frost. As the line advanced, when I finally reached Frost, he took my hand and shook it and said, "Ah, yes, Van Wyck Brooks." I was pleased. I thought, he's thinking of the poem I wrote to Van Wyck Brooks. When I was at college I wrote a poem called "Sunday Evening in the Common"—the Boston Common, where Van Wyck and I as undergraduates used to walk on Sunday evenings and discuss all the problems of the world. We usually settled most of them before the evening was over. The last stanza begins with "Van Wyck, how often have we been together," and I thought, "Frost has this poem in mind—it has appeared in a number of anthologies—and he's paying me a compliment." But not at all. Two days after that, he called up my wife, terribly unhappy and contrite, and said, "Oh, do tell John," as he always called me, "that I recognized him perfectly. I don't know what happened to me. I guess I was just tired. But of course I knew it wasn't Van Wyck Brooks." He was worried.

We never recited poems together. Frost was, as you may know, rather cold toward other poets. He never gave a leg up to a younger man. He had many magnificent qualities, and I think he was a great lyric poet; but magnanimity, generosity toward other poets, was not among his virtues. In fact, I remember, whenever he came into a room where there were a number of poets, at the Academy or elsewhere, if some little-known poet came forward in a friendly way to greet him, he would be sort of restless, looking around the room, wondering, "How can I disengage myself from this man and be seen talking to some more important person?" It's an unattractive trait, but he had it very definitely.

I remember the evening—I think it was one of his birthday celebrations—that they had a Robert Frost Evening at the Poetry Society, and I was appointed to introduce him and to give a little talk about him. He was very gracious, but always as a superior to an inferior. He told me some amusing stories, though. He had a great sense of humor. He told me one time about traveling in a—not a Pullman sleeper car, but what they call a compartment, which you share for the night with somebody else. On this occasion his partner turned out to be a traveling salesman. They shared a bottle of bourbon and talked until late into the night. The salesman told Frost all about himself and his wife and her indigestion and the children and everything else. Toward the end of the evening—Frost hadn't said a word—the salesman suddenly turned to Frost and said, "By the way, what do you do?" And Frost said, "Well, you know, I'm a poet." The man looked at him in horror and said, "My God! My wife writes that stuff." That was his only comment. He lost all interest in Frost from then on. They went to bed in dead silence. I thought that was a good story.

[6 March 1967]

I HAVEN'T REALLY SAID MUCH ABOUT the time in Göttingen when I first came there. I moved later to Berlin but while in Göttingen for that one semester, I came to be friends with three people in particular. Two of them were Swiss, and they taught me a great deal—taught me, for one thing, how men can work and study, because they studied practically every hour of the day, except for six hours devoted to sleep. They were both working for the doctorate and got the highest possible degree, of course. But there was one man I came to be friends with who was a very different type. He belonged to one of the Hanoverian student corps—I forget just what you called them, not exactly clubs—where they had what was known as the Mensur. That is a German word for these student duels. I got dragged into this, out of vanity, and I had a duel with this man. It's all just in good sport, you know, but I got my chest pretty badly slashed up with this saber fighting. Not serious—they always have someone there to put on styptic or stitch up cuts if necessary. The scars remained for a long time, though. They were very shallow scars, but I had the greatest delight in showing them on my return to America to some of my friends on the beach at East Hampton, and they were very much impressed.

I suppose my use of barbiturates really isn't very interesting, unless it might be of interest to physicians that a man could take those drugs for so many years without harm, apparently. I began at the time when I was trying to work for my Ph.D. and to write poems. I had several poems under way, and others kept flooding in on me. I worked at night on my poems and couldn't get to sleep. You could get, in those days, two drugs, one called Sulfonal and the other called Trional, both of them sleep-producing drugs, without any prescription. They had their drawbacks because they did give you a headache the next day; but at least they made you unconscious for five or six hours, and I came to take them fairly steadily to get to sleep. If you work at night, say, until one o'clock in the morning, and your mind gets stretched very wide open, it's almost impossible to close it down. It's wonderfully convenient then just to be able to turn it off with a drug. Sleep is partly a matter of will-power, and the bad thing about drugs is that you give up your will-power and depend on the drug.

When I moved to Berlin and entered the university there, it was even worse. I was having this entanglement with a young woman who was older than I was, actually, but anyway, in trying to work at my studies and trying to write poetry, too, at night—most of it very bad—I became more sleepless than ever. Then I found a new drug with much less unpleasant aftereffects. It was called Veronal. It came in five-grain tablets and was also available without prescription. I took them quite steadily, and not only for sleep, for I discovered that the next day, after a sleep from this drug, you enjoyed a definite euphoria. It speeded you up. Your cheeks felt hot and burning. I was, like most young people, rather shy, and I found it did away with my shyness completely. The thing I had to look out for was not to take a drink when I was in this barbiturate euphoria. It seemed to heighten the effect of alcohol very much.

I took it pretty steadily all through the time I was in Berlin, and the only time I dropped it was when I went with these two friends of mine down the Adriatic coast to Montenegro and up through Corfu and back through Italy. When we were traveling and taking long walks and living outdoors, I didn't need it because I wasn't working. But as soon as I got back to Berlin, I started taking it again. I've already explained about coming back to America, how I tried to stay on in Berlin but unsuccessfully.

When I got back to this country, I needed them even worse than ever. It was a long time before you had to have a prescription in order to get them. I had come back with the conviction—this shows how immature I was, childish, really—that I could persuade my father to let me marry this young German woman and that he would support us till I got a job and got started. When I broached the subject to my father, I was amazed to find how hard-hearted he was! We have been all through that. So I did continue taking these drugs.

When the time came when it was necessary to get a prescription, I was going to a doctor who was very broad-minded about these things. He would give me what I needed. Later, better things came in—Medinal, Nembutal, Seconal, phenobarbital, and then still later the tranquillizers, Miltown and Equanil, Librium, and so on.

Before the prescriptions were required, I would just go to a drugstore and say, "I'd like———." When the better things came in, they were procurable by prescription only, and my doctor, who was a very reputable, very fine physician, understood the situation I was in and saw to it that I was supplied with these barbiturates. I've been taking them ever since. As you get older, you do have to step up the dose a little bit. Nothing like narcotics, though—then you're really in a bad way. I take perhaps half again as much as I did when I began, and I always try to hold it down as much as I can.

■ ■ ■ ■

My wife and I had met——— Let's see, how old was I when I first met Phyllis de Kay? I think I must have been seventeen, and she fourteen or younger. She was the oldest of a family of eight children. I remember seeing some of them go by on bicycles, wearing the very attractive costumes their mother put them in, red sweaters with little green corduroy trousers. I think the first time I saw Phyllis de Kay was when she went by on a bicycle in that costume, and I was instantly struck. I was in that state of mind, quite usual in youth, when you don't particularly want to meet the person you admire, because you're a little afraid. But you want to think about her a great deal. I wrote a sonnet to Phyllis. I was writing verse all the time, and I wrote this sonnet, which I thought fairly good. Phyllis had a bathing-box in the beach pavilion at East Hampton where we all bathed, and I dropped this sonnet down over the top of the bathing-box while she was in it. And she was furious. This was an invasion of privacy. I really didn't make a hit with my poem.

Then later I met her family and was invited to the house and saw her with her father and mother and some of the other children, and I wrote another sonnet. This was a poem about a painting of Phyllis by an artist named Whittemore,[26] a very good artist who lived in East Hampton. By this time I was accepted a little bit more. Phyllis's father, Charles de Kay, thought my sonnet wasn't too bad. He was the art critic for *The New York Times* and a poet himself. Curiously enough, Scribners had published two of his books.[27] His approval meant a great deal to me; I remember being thrilled by this.

Phyllis's uncle was Richard Watson Gilder, who was the editor of *The Century,* the head of the Century company, and a poet, a very well-known poet at that time. In fact, his *Collected Poems* was published in the Houghton Mifflin edition of "Household Poets" with Longfellow, Lowell, Whittier, Holmes, all the rest of them. Gilder was shown some of my poems and liked one of them. This, of course, was reassuring to a boy.

Then I started work on a long poem in which Phyllis was the central figure. It was a dirge on the death of Urania, whom I pictured as destroyed by the materialism of the ages. The only person who remained a defender, one of the chief defenders and appreciators and sympathizers with the poetic side of life, was of course Phyllis. She was the center of the poem. It was a long poem, and she still has a copy of it. One or two people who collect my books and papers fortunately do not know this because, if they did, they would pester me to let them have it. They have many things of mine much less valuable than this. It's called "A Dirge on the Death of Urania," and it is written in the stanza form of Shelley's *Adonais,* the great elegy on Keats. At this stage of the game, my work was very imitative of other poets. You know, you start by imitating Walter Scott, and you end up by imitating—— You go along being intoxicated with one poet after another until you come to the most modern ones. At least, that's the way I progressed. I think the poem had some fairly good things in it. Some parts of it were published in the *Verses by Two Under-graduates* that Van Wyck Brooks and I issued in 1905 while we were freshman at Harvard.

Phyllis and I used to see each other a good deal during the summers at East Hampton particularly. Her family's house was in the country some distance from ours. Both our houses were in deep country, and I used to walk over after supper to call on her. It took a good deal of courage, too, for a young shy man to enter a house where there were eight children, girls and boys, who were intensely amused at the arrival of the suitor, and didn't hesitate to—— You could hear all sorts of giggles and squeals. It was a real test.

We used to have wonderful talks about poetry, up on the loggia of the house, eaten alive by mosquitoes. Phyllis was much better read than I was. She was and is the most tremendous reader I've ever known and remarkably interesting to listen to. Also, she had the feminine tact to let me do a lot of the talking while she listened respectfully. I fell very much in love. In New York I used to go and see Phyllis at her family's house in what was then called London Terrace, on Twenty-third Street, nearly opposite where the old Hotel Chelsea is. It was a row of old-fashioned, very attractive houses with gardens in front.

Well, it would take too long to go into it very much. I wrote a great many poems that I showed to Phyllis. She was quite a stern critic, which was very good for me. As the years went by, I went to Germany and was away for over two years, and Phyllis in the meantime lived a great deal in Italy and in England. She had cousins in Italy, the Rucellais, one of the old Florentine families. She had relatives in Ireland and in England. And there she met the son of John Bury, the great Greek historian. I was not in a position to be able even to think of marriage at that time. In the first place, I didn't have the money. I didn't have an adequate job. This thing came as a stunning blow, the knowledge that Phyllis was engaged.

I met Basil Bury. He came over from England and visited the de Kays at East Hampton that summer, a very attractive man, the intellectual type, an Oxford man. His father had been Balliol Professor of History at Oxford. So almost before I knew it, Phyllis went to England in 1914 and was married. I remember that very strained evening when we three sat on the balcony of the house at East Hampton and made conversation with a good deal of tension. However, we were all civilized people. Phyllis and Basil talked about meter in Greek poetry. He was very much interested in Greek meters.

She went back to England in 1914 and was married there and had three sons. I settled down to my work at Scribners, and we didn't see each other any more; for a long time I remained in this state of being very unhappy about it all. But eventually I did form an attachment to someone else, a woman who was a widow and ten years younger than myself. This lasted from 1918 until 1939—that's twenty-one years, isn't it?—at which time Phyllis came back from England. Her husband had had a complete mental breakdown. This had been coming on gradually for some years. Finally he had to be certified, and they were separated, though not yet divorced, and Phyllis came over to this country on a visit.

In the meantime I had really formed a very great emotional attachment to this other woman. We were not married, but after twenty-one years it was virtually as if we were. I was put in a position where I was torn in two directions. I wanted to be free to marry Phyllis when she got her divorce, or at least to try to get her consent, and yet I felt that I couldn't bear to desert this loyal woman. I just didn't know what to do, and I broke down and had to go away for a while—for about a year. Then I slowly got well and went right back to this attachment. There didn't seem to be anything else to do. Phyllis, after some months in New York, had returned to England. Eventually I was able to summon the force, or whatever you call it—something I've never quite been able to forgive myself for—Anyway, I left Harriet, and Phyllis and I were married. By that time I had put by some money, and I took it all and set up a trust fund for Harriet so that she would be taken care of. I had been supporting her. She didn't lose anything financially, but you can imagine that it was rather bitter thing, after twenty-one years of devotion.

Then Phyllis and I were married in 1940. She had come over again and was very wonderful and broad-minded about the whole thing. She knew all about it, of course, and she had said, "It's a decision you have to make. I can't make it for you." So I had had to work it out, and I finally did, but it was a nearly mortal experience, and, as I say, I have never quite been able to forgive myself. After all, I had let Harriet feel that I cared very deeply for her. And I did, too. Yet when it came to this choice, there was no question in my mind as to what I wanted.

Well, anyway, I had gone to England in 1939, partly because the doctors said it would be good for me to get away. My sister's mental illness was weighing on me. She was in the hospital known as Bloomingdale then, and I went up to see her once a week, and it was excruciating. She was so desperate to get out. It was wearing me down. The doctors said, "You don't do her any good by going to see her. Can't you get away for a while, go to Europe or something?" Phyllis suggested that I come to England for a visit, and I did, and while I was there, toward the end of the visit, two things happened. One was the news of my sister's suicide, which Mr. Scribner telephoned to me in London. The other was the outbreak of World War II. I was in London when war was finally declared. Of course, we knew it was coming. One afternoon when Phyllis and I were walking down the Strand together the papers came out with huge headlines about the pact between Stalin and Hitler, and everyone knew the fat was in the fire.

My sailing home on the French Line was canceled. I was living in an apartment in Mayfair and had to have it blacked out because they expected the Germans would bomb London any minute. I hated the thought of leaving Phyllis there in London. In fact, it was a most agonizing period. But I had to get back to my job, and I finally secured passage on the Canadian Pacific line. I shared a cabin with two other people. How crowded it was! We were blacked out all the way over, and we zigzagged all the way over, and as you know, the Canadian Pacific takes ten days on those boats. They go in up at Montreal, go in through the mouth of the St. Lawrence River. When we were in mid-ocean, we were turned around and ordered back to the United Kingdom by the Admiralty. We weren't told about this, but some observant passenger noticed that the moon was on the wrong side of the ship, and a committee was formed to call upon the captain. He said the Admiralty had ordered us back because the *Deutschland* and another German ship had not berthed at New York, and it was thought they might be hiding in the waters outside New York, armed and lying in wait for us. Because of what the Germans had done in the past along these lines, we were ordered back.

Then, after we'd been ordered back, we were ordered to proceed again to America. So we were at sea for about fifteen days without any means of communication. I had expected, when I got on the ship, that I'd be able to radio to Phyllis, but no radio messages could be sent or received. For half an hour a day we were herded into the ship's library and allowed to listen to an official broadcast bringing us the news of the bloodbath Hitler was threatening to give London and what he was doing to Poland, and I pictured Phyllis over there in the midst of it all. Her main concern, quite naturally, was her boys. She knew all three of them would have to go into the service. She was going to stay to see them properly placed and to be with them right up to the last moment when they had to go, and especially with her youngest son, Patrick, who was not yet of age. And there were financial problems. She was his guardian, as well as being his mother, and she had to be there.

I came back to New York. My mother had died the year before. I came back to the apartment that my mother had lived in, over here on Fifty-eighth Street just west of Lexington Avenue, where my sister also had had her apartment. Now both of them were gone, and Phyllis was over there in the midst of the war, and I had broken with Harriet, who kept bombarding me, now that she knew I was back, with the most wonderful gifts and letters day after day. I had to just not even acknowledge them, send them all back, and it was a tough time. Also I had on my hands the little six-year-old daughter of my sister. Fortunately, she was at camp that summer, but of course in the autumn she came back and had to live with me, and I had to take her to school every morning. The little girl—her name was Sally—was bewildered and upset. She became very difficult.

This went on. I got back in September, and I had to wait through September, October, November, December, January, February, March, April, and May. All this time I'd seen one means of returning to America cut off after the other. There didn't seem to be any way that Phyllis could possibly get here. She finally arrived on the last ship from Italy, the *Rex*. Those were very bad months. Very bad. Everything was taken away, and there didn't seem to be any certainty about anything.

Phyllis went out to Nevada and got her divorce, and in August 1940 I went out, and we were married in Carson City and took a month's vacation in California, at Lake Tahoe, and in New Mexico, and then came back to New York to live.

■ ■ ■ ■

The Scribners were most generous. They always have been—to me and, I think, to everyone else. It's a wonderful house. In the old days, like all other publishing houses, they used to have to—well, I don't know whether they had to or not—it was the custom not to pay very large salaries. But they went along with the times on that and were most generous. And I think it's a place that anyone who has worked there gets attached to. They couldn't have treated me better. I know Max Perkins, who was my immediate superior, liked to have a man who wasn't married working with him because a man who isn't married (at least, so Max thought) gets more work done, and we all worked—I worked— terribly hard. So that for a long time I couldn't get up the courage to tell Max I was going to get married. We used often to have lunch together, and day after day I nerved myself— I even took a drink—but I couldn't bring it across my lips. It seemed so silly, a man of fifty-four announcing he was getting married!

Finally, one day, when we were walking back to the office past St. Patrick's Cathedral on Fifth Avenue, I thought this would be the easiest time. I turned to Max and I said, "You know, Max, I'll have to have a month's vacation this summer. I'm getting married." Max just turned and looked at me once and never said a word. He never said a word. He didn't say, "Congratulations" or "I'm so glad." He said nothing. We went back to the office in dead silence. I knew I'd have to know about this, so I followed him into his office and said, "You know, Max, I have to know. Can I take it and when can I take it?" Max didn't say anything, so I added, "Can I have the month off?" "Yes!" he said in a very irritated tone. That's the only interest he showed in it.

The first time my wife and I were visiting with the Van Wyck Brookses in Bridgewater, Connecticut, they suggested, "Let's all drive over to New Canaan and visit Max and Louise Perkins." We called up, and Louise, who always loved people and parties, said, "Oh, how wonderful! Yes, come. Max will be thrilled to see you." Max never came downstairs. He stayed upstairs reading manuscripts all the time we were there, and Phyllis's feelings were hurt. She thought it very rude. Max had known all the de Kay family. He was very eccentric in his behavior. It didn't mean anything. I didn't hold it against him. I knew just what had probably happened. Louise was very sociable. Every weekend Max had some big manuscript that had to be read or edited, and he'd come home, and he'd say to Louise, "Don't make any engagements this weekend the way you did last weekend and the time before that because I'm going to get this work done." Then, when she'd announced that we were coming over, and he'd just blown up and said, "I don't care if God Himself is coming over. I'm going to sit right here and do my work!"

■ ■ ■ ■

Harriet Monroe I met quite early—that is, from my point of view. I think it was in 1911, and I can't remember at the moment whether she had yet started *Poetry* or not.[*] That magazine first took on importance in 1915, I think, when it became the organ of so much of the new work. They published those three sonnets of Rupert Brooke's that made him famous. They were the first to publish, in this country, T. S. Eliot's "Prufrock," which was his first major poem. All this had come about—not the Rupert Brooke poems but the Eliot and many other innovators' poems—under the influence of Ezra Pound, who kept hammering on Harriet Monroe, "Don't miss this. Don't miss this. This is more important than any of the poems you're publishing." Partly guided by Pound and partly by her own great talent as an editor, Miss Monroe was responsible for the first appearances of many of the important poets, and the magazine became very well known.

Poetry: A Magazine of Verse, as you know, was in Chicago, and Miss Monroe lived there. She seemed, of course, to me, an elderly woman. Actually, I think she probably was in her middle forties. Whenever she came to town, she always looked me up, partly because she was a great friend of Sara Teasdale. Miss Monroe would come partly for that reason and partly because I could keep her in touch with various poets whom I knew and with what they were doing. But she never approved of me. I always knew that.

[*]*Poetry: A Magazine of Verse* was founded by Monroe in 1912. She edited it until her death in 1936.

I liked Harriet Monroe, with reservations. She had a curious dead quality. They used to say of her that she could kill any party just by going to it. I put it to the test. We had a little party at my mother's house. Various poets and friends came, and I invited Harriet Monroe. She was a small, grey, very silent woman. She came in, and the party sort of—everything stopped. It really did work—partly because she was a celebrity and partly because she was so critical. She was the opposite of genial, you know. Would never take a drink.

Harriet Monroe didn't approve of me because she didn't like my work. She hadn't seen very much of it. Most of the things I sent her that she published in her magazine were very early poems. She later changed her opinion somewhat. When she came to town, I used to take her to the theater when I could afford it, which wasn't very often. It cost a good deal to get good seats in the orchestra and take her out to dinner first. All she would talk about, on one of these occasions, was the marvelous evening that Wallace Stevens had given her in Chicago when he took her to a much better play or when he had shown her this or that or the other thing. She said, "I like him especially because he's so forthright. He doesn't hesitate to use four-letter words or profanities when he feels like it." I could sense that this was one of the things she didn't like about me. She thought I was too genteel.

One day Miss Monroe attended a reading I gave at the Cosmopolitan Club here in New York, together with a young woman who was also at the time an editor at Scribners, the poet Bernice Lesbia Kenyon. We both read, and Harriet Monroe went back to Chicago and wrote the reading up in *Poetry.* I can't quote the article verbatim, of course, but I do remember one very strange thing she said there. She said, "John Hall Wheelock reads extremely well, but is so much the gentleman"—or "so genteel" or something of that sort—"that I fear some dreadful fate is in store for him." I have never understood why she said a thing as uncomfortable and as harsh as that.

That's the feeling, then, I came to have about Harriet Monroe, until I wrote a poem that happened to move her, and she changed her opinion of me a little bit. I think one trouble was that she'd heard too much from Sara Teasdale about how marvelous my poems were, and she thought this was very bad for me, and so it was. You should have a more critical friend, you know, to tell you where you're going wrong. Harriet Monroe thought she would take me down a peg or two, and she succeeded admirably in doing it. But later on we became friends.

I remember her coming to see me before she went on her trip to South America, talking with great excitement about this. She was going to meet all these South American poets whom she had published in translation. That was the trip on which she died, crossing the high Andes in a plane. Apparently, they didn't have pressurized cabins in those days, and the altitude may have been too much for her. And I always remember this strange intuition I had had—the tremendous enthusiasm with which she looked forward to this great adventure.

I had had other experiences with Harriet Monroe. When my fourth book, *Dust and Light,* came out, a woman who lived in Chicago reviewed it. She was a woman who wrote mysteries, a very able young writer, and the gist of her review was, "It's a pity when businessmen try to write poetry. Mr. Wheelock is a businessman who works in the Scribner Bookstore." She took that line. It just absolutely infuriated me. I'd been writing poetry, or writing verse, since I was nine. I sent a telegram to Harriet Monroe—the sort of thing you do when you're young, that you learn not to do when you're older, a very sarcastic telegram saying, "Still earning my living as a businessman. Sorry that so and so——" Then Miss Monroe showed how much feeling she really had. She wrote me a very beautiful letter. She said this was one of the things that took the heart out of her and made her feel that she'd better throw up her job, give up the magazine and retire. She said that this was one of the few issues that she hadn't proofread personally, that she never would have allowed a thing like that to go through. The telegram had evidently upset her. But it was a silly thing to do. If you get a bad review, the only thing to do is to do nothing.

Harriet Monroe never married, and I think that's one reason why a man like Wallace Stevens, who—— Well, he's a great poet, of course. He was the vice-president of the Hartford Insurance Company and one of the great poets of our time, a most extraordinary combination. I don't think he was a particularly masculine male—in fact, rather the contrary, I should think—and partly in compensation for this, he threw his weight around, using coarse language and so on. This deeply impressed Harriet Monroe because she was rather the spinster type. This, to her, was being "a real he-man." He took her in completely.

In this country the whole movement of the new poetry had its focus in *Poetry: A Magazine of Verse*, edited by Monroe. It has been edited ever since by well-known poets, such as Karl Shapiro, who was editor of it for a time, and George Dillon, and Morton Dauwen Zabel. It had a tremendous influence. Harriet Monroe and Alice Corbin Henderson got out an anthology called *The New Poetry*. It introduced Vachel Lindsay, for instance, and Edgar Lee Masters and all the people who were the innovators that were coming along in 1915. It was financed by a rich family in Chicago, whose name I do not remember. The subscription list was quite big, and the advertising was quite small. It was not self-sustaining, but it's continued ever since and is one of the most distinguished magazines there is devoted entirely to poetry and reviews of poetry.

I've never written a review in my life. I probably should have done so because it's a good way to keep yourself before readers of poetry. I have written a book about poetry, but I've never written a review. I have occasionally written an article about a poet, and I've written many letters to poets about their work, and I get a great many letters from poets that require an answer, but I've never written a review.

■ ■ ■ ■

George Santayana was a unique character. When I was one of his students at Harvard, I never thought that I would someday be his editor. He was a very fascinating man, I think, to all his students—in fact, to everybody. I don't believe he could have been cold because no cold man could have written some of the poems he wrote. He was extremely shy, but it was more than that; he was aloof. Although in class he never looked at his students, his lectures were beautiful, works of art. You saw a different side of him at the tea parties he gave in his rooms—I think Hollis Hall, anyway in the Yard. He would ask some of the students to come and read their poems or essays or whatever, and he would be very charming, though always a bit aloof. I used to go to those tea parties.

I came to be his editor, later in life. Of course, I was not his initial editor. Santayana's first book was taken on by Scribners in 1886, the year I was born, and that was *The Sense of Beauty*. It still sells regularly in moderate quantities. His editors had been Brownell, Burlingame, and others. But when I became an editor, after I'd served my junior year or so, Santayana was turned over to me. I never referred to the fact that I had been one of his students until I got to know him a little better. Whenever I brought this up, he never seemed to remember anything about it. It wasn't at all flattering.

Santayana lived to be very old. I think he was going on to eighty-seven when he died. When Mr. Scribner died—that was Charles Scribner III—Santayana wrote me a very beautiful letter, a very sympathetic letter, and said among other things, "It seems so strange to me, and I feel grateful when I think of it, that you and Mr. Scribner had the courage, as far back

George Santayana (courtesy of *Dictionary of Literary Biography*)

as 1886, to publish my——" So then I wrote him a desperate letter, and I said, "Look, Mr. Santayana, that was the year I was born. I was one of your students at Harvard from 1904 to 1908. I never got any answer to this. Oh, I got an answer to my letter, but he never referred to this part of it.

As you may imagine, there was practically no editing to be done. Before Santayana had put pen to paper, he had worked all the revisions and changes out in his mind, so that there was nothing to change, not even a semicolon. But he was courteous and always claimed that I helped him a great deal. I did have a chance to help him in various ways as life went on. I never had a chance to go over and see him. I sent him some of my poems, and I don't believe he liked them very well. He wrote and said, "Your poetry is far more tender and humane than mine." I would have liked to go over and see him. He lived at the Convent of the Blue Nuns in Rome. Toward the end of his life, he wrote a novel called *The Last Puritan.* He had finished this novel, and it was ready for delivery while World War II was in full blast, and there was no way of getting it out of Italy. It was a puzzle. Here was a novel which we were most anxious to publish and which he was most anxious to have published, and he just couldn't get it to us.

I finally managed, by pulling various wires, to get it over here, but this involved a great many people. First, I had to get Padraic Colum, who's a Catholic and an old friend of mine, interested, and to get the Spanish ambassador over here and our representative in Spain interested. Eventually the Vatican came into the picture. And somehow or other the manuscript was smuggled through by diplomatic pouch from Vatican City to my desk at Scribners. I don't know how many letters I wrote or conferences I had to bring this about. Yet I have seen a letter that Santayana had written to a friend. The letter was in a book of Santayana's letters published by some other house. Somebody had asked him, "What do you think of Scribners?" Santayana had written, "I have always found Scribners very civil." That's just like him, you know.

I remember Santayana wrote me, as he often did about his books, a very apologetic letter about *The Last Puritan.* He said, "I know it's going to fall flat because, after all, I'm not a novelist; yet I had to write it." I told him—of course, editors are supposed to tell authors this—to encourage him, "I think it's going to have a very good sale." Well, it went on to have a tremendous sale. I may be wrong, but I think it was taken by the Book-of-the-Month Club. The old *Sun,* I think it was, came out with a headline reading "Santayana Is Discovered By The Masses," and I sent him this to amuse him.

He was a strange figure in the world of letters. He was never quite accepted by philosophers, although he was a philosopher, because his system begged the point, some philosophers felt. Instead of being a perfect self-sustaining closed system, he begged the point here and there by using devices like, "This we accept through animal faith," or getting around it that way. He was never regarded as an important writer by writers because he was a professional philosopher. Among the finest things he did were his sonnets. I keep meeting people all the time who know his sonnets by heart. They're extremely moving, and they're extremely well made, and there's one that tells his whole story, how he began as a devout Catholic and ended as a pagan. Towards the close of that sonnet, he expresses it all in a few lines. He's talking about the figure of Christ: "And though his arms, outstretched upon the tree, / Were beautiful, and pleaded my embrace, / My sins were loth to look upon his face. / So came I down from Golgotha to thee, / Eternal Mother; let the sun and sea / Heal me, and keep me in thy dwelling-place." It was the change from Christian to pagan.

The nuns did have a very strong feeling. They were, up to the last minute and the last breath he drew, hoping Santayana would return to his original faith. As you know, he was regarded by many as a Fascist. He was a man who believed in aristocracy and in authoritarianism, and he had said that although he was a renegade Catholic, if ever he married he could never marry anyone but a Catholic. When Santayana was dying, there was always a priest just around the corner of the door, waiting for him to break down and express his willingness to come back to Mother Church. He never did.

Toward the end, he ran out of subjects for his books. He had published some twenty to thirty of them. I came up with several ideas for him. One was that he revise the four volumes of his *The Realms of Being* series. I said, "Why don't you condense these into one volume? You could cut and bind them together and give the whole thing more unity." He thought that was a good idea, and that kept him busy for almost two years. Then, when he had completed that project, I suggested that he revise his big five-volume *The Life of Reason,* condensing it into one volume. That kept him busy for a long time and gave him the greatest pleasure. Also he wrote his autobiography, *Persons and Places,* in three volumes, a beautiful work that did very well.

In the end, Santayana succumbed to cancer of the stomach, one of the most painful forms of cancer, and he had a dreadful time. He had a particularly bad time because in the convent there they disbelieved in the use of narcotics and pain-killers, on the theory that the more you suffer here the less you will suffer in the hereafter. So he sent for his young friend, himself a philosopher, Daniel Cory, a man who had been a disciple and an intimate of Santayana's. Cory has given me a description of those last days. Cory went to Rome and stayed nearby, and he saw to it that no priest or other person had access to Santayana so that it could be said that Santayana had broken down and returned to the Church. He told me a most moving thing. Santayana was in great pain. Cory had been able to see to it that he got morphine, which helped. But one day, after a particularly severe bout of pain, Santayana looked up at Cory—Santayana had become very thin and shrunken from this long ordeal—and said, "Oh, I wish I could just lay my head on Abraham's bosom and sleep away." As Santayana said this, the look on his face was so piteous that Cory broke down and wept. Santayana was deeply thrilled, touched to the core, to think that anyone cared enough for him to show that much feeling. It was a great moment. It brought the two men very close together. And Santayana died the next day.

■ ■ ■ ■

It must have been some time when I was in college, which would be between 1904 and 1908, that President Roosevelt came up to Harvard and spoke at the Harvard Union before a tremendous crowd of undergraduates in that big room. His theme was that Harvard was turning the undergraduates into mollycoddles. President Eliot had objected to the number of casualties incurred during recent football matches and had argued that it should be less rough. Roosevelt asked the men, in his magnificent voice, "Do you want to be a lot of mollycoddles, or do you want to go right in there and smash them?" And every man there gave a great shout and brandished his right arm in answer to Roosevelt's brandished right arm. Eliot was in the gallery. It was really very rude of Roosevelt, for this was a demonstration against the president of Harvard.

Well, the next day, I think it was, Roosevelt came to the office of *The Harvard Monthly,* and the editors, of which I was one, had invited a few friends in, and Roosevelt gave us a pep talk. The gist of his talk—he didn't seem to put much emphasis on the importance of writing poems, essays, and novels—but he said, "The thing to do is to become expert reporters and go out to the Philippines."

The last time I saw Theodore Roosevelt was when he came into Scribners and got into the elevator in which I also happened to be. Mike, the elevator operator, dropped the helm of the car, stopped, turned around, and grasped Roosevelt's hand: "How are you, Teddy?" And Roosevelt responded instantaneously. He beamed on Mike, "What is your name? You're married? How many children do you have?" Mike said he had five. "That's good, but you'd better do better," said Roosevelt. You know, he was very much for big families.

I remember seeing Roosevelt come into the offices from time to time when I was at Scribners. Robert Bridges, who was then editor of *Scribner's Magazine,* was one of Roosevelt's best friends. Bridges was an extraordinary man; he had as his closest friends two very opposite personalities: Theodore Roosevelt and Woodrow Wilson. Bridges lived at the University Club. He never married. Roosevelt, when he went to Africa hunting big game or to South America to explore the Amazon River, would send

Scribner Building, 597 Fifth Avenue, New York (Matthew J. and Arlyn
Bruccoli Collection of F. Scott Fitzgerald, Thomas Cooper Library,
University of South Carolina)

back the manuscripts he wrote every night on his typewriter in his tent at camp, by runner through the jungle, and they would eventually come to Bridges's desk and would be serialized in *Scribner's Magazine.*

I did a bibliography of Theodore Roosevelt, and it was published. That was while I was still a clerk in the Scribner Bookstore. Mr. Scribner, Charles Scribner II, a man then in his seventies, summoned me to his office one day and said, "Would you like to do a bibliography of Theodore Roosevelt?" and I said I should like to very much. He said, "I'll pay you $250 for it." I said, "Excellent. When must you have it?" and so on, and I made up my mind that I would do a good job.

So in my bibliography I included every book by Theodore Roosevelt, in all its various editions; every book of Roosevelt's translated into any language that could be traced, in all its editions; all the books about Roosevelt and his books, in English or in any other language; all the books and anthologies containing essays—and so on and so on and so on. When I presented this thing to Mr. Scribner, he was horrified. He said, "Why, Wheelock, this was supposed to be a bibliography at the end of Mr. Bishop's life of Roosevelt![28] You've made a separate book of it! What can we do?" I didn't know what to say. "We'll just have to publish it as a separate book, and we'll have to pay you a bit more." So it was published as a separate book in 1920. I still have a copy of it. A small edition, it didn't have much sale, mostly to libraries.

I didn't know Henry van Dyke until he was an old man. I think he must have been seventy-two or seventy-three when I first met him. He had read some of my poems, and I used to see him when he came in. He was a great friend of Mr. Arthur Scribner's and of Mr. Brownell's, and he was a very popular author. Some of his books sold in large editions, as Christmas gifts. Also, he wrote books on fishing that had a great vogue, and he wrote poems. He dedicated one of his books to me,* which flattered me very much, for he was a famous man at the time. He was also, I think, really a very modest man, but he gave the impression of being rather pompous, and as professor of English at Princeton, his students used to say of van Dyke that he was "The only man who could strut sitting down."

In his old age, he was a pathetic figure. I had done a bibliography of Tennyson for van Dyke's *Studies in Tennyson.* That was what first attracted his attention to me. Then he got me to read and make suggestions for his

*Van Dyke's *The Man Behind the Book: Essays in Understanding* (New York: Scribners, 1929) was dedicated to JHW.

last books, which frankly were potboilers. He was just looking for some subject that he could exploit and make a little money out of. I used to go out to Princeton to see van Dyke. He wasn't well enough to come in to New York then. He was an old broken man and very deeply wounded. He had been a favorite author, very much admired by a large number of people, and now he would take up a book by H. L. Mencken or somebody, or a review, and they'd say of some writer, "This man's writing is vile. It's almost as bad as Henry van Dyke's." Or some other reviewer would say, "I count him out as a pure sentimentalist of the Henry van Dyke type, a vulgarian of the first water," and so on. These cruel, cruel things hit this old man very hard. He asked me many times, "Wheelock, am I as bad as all that? Is my work as bad as all that?"

I would say, "Of course it isn't. It's just that fashions change. You belong to one period, and these men belong to another, that's all." But I know it broke his heart. It really did. He went out, not in honor and glory but in disgrace, almost as if he were a criminal. In our day, not to be up-to-date in matters of point of view, taste, and style, not to be "with it," is practically to be a criminal. He felt it very much. I used to go out to his house; he was a charming host, a very distinguished-looking man. He'd been Minister to the Netherlands, and he would give you a drink—he liked drinking, himself. He would make me comfortable and draw me out and flatter me, too. He was a charming man, I thought, but a deeply wounded one, in those last years. A good thing for him when he died.

Edwin Markham I used to see more of, because Edwin Markham lived on Staten Island, and we often met at the Poetry Society of America, where he was the "big shot." Whenever he came to a meeting, that was a very special occasion. He had become famous through his "The Man With the Hoe" poem and his "Lincoln" poem, although to a lesser degree with the latter. He did me the honor of inviting me out when William Watson, the great or then-great English poet, came to visit Markham and stayed with him for, I think, a week on Staten Island. William Watson was in all the anthologies, the *Oxford Book of English Verse*—I think he had three or four pages there. He was considered a very remarkable poet then, best known perhaps for his poem, "April, April, April, / Laugh your girlish laughter; / Then the moment after, / Weep your girlish tears." Now his name is mud because he was a rhetorical poet, and not a very good one.

But I can still see those two, Watson and Markham, talking about poetry as they stood in front of the fireplace in Markham's home. Edwin

Markham used to send me his own poems. We were both, at that time—or I was, in my youth—tremendous admirers of Swinburne. Markham was absolutely obsessed with the rhythms of Swinburne and wrote some of his worst poems in imitation of Swinburne—especially a longish poem about some obscure love affair. I know the whole poem by heart, and I try not to remember it; but I can't seem to forget it, it's so bad. Very unlike his best work. He called it "Virgilia," I remember.

Then, he got old and came into some money. He'd been very poor all his life. Markham had been a poet and made a living by doing editorial hack work. He'd never taught, as far as I know. I think his wife had a little money. He made a good deal of money with "The Man With the Hoe." It had a big sale, and he was invited to speak at Rotary clubs, one of the few poets who broke through into the business world. This poem was considered very revolutionary. But he got very tired of saying it over and over, again and again; wherever he went nobody wanted to hear anything except "The Man With the Hoe." He got very tired of it.

When Markham was very old and had come into some money, he became senile and foolish. It was a very tragic occasion when he read, at St. Mark's-in-the-Bowerie, that church down on Twelfth Street where Dr. Guthrie was rector. This was on the occasion of Markham's eighty something-or-other birthday. He got up, on the platform there, and I remember that it seemed to me that somebody should have stopped him because he sat with his mouth wide open—you could see the dark cavern where his mouth was, you know, poor old man—before this large audience. He would get up and recite a poem (he knew all his poems by heart), and after each poem he would make exactly the same comment— "Could have been a whole lot worse." Then he'd go on to another poem—"Could have been a whole lot worse"—just like a machine. He'd lost his memory completely, but he remembered all his poems. And he went on much too long. People got very restless, and the person who was presiding—Mr. Wheeler, president of the Poetry Society of America—got up and began to speak in order to give a hint to Markham that this was the end. Then Mr. Wheeler sat down, and Markham immediately put his hand on his shoulder and pushed himself up and began reciting another poem. And when he got to the end of it he said, "Could have been a whole lot worse."

It was a painful occasion. The poor old gentleman should not have been allowed to appear at that time. That's all I remember about Markham, except his many kindnesses to me. He was a very warm-hearted, generous man with a spark of genius. He read many of my poems and gave me suggestions about them. He was quite a severe critic, but a friendly one. I'm very grateful to Markham. He was not a distinguished poet and has been forgotten today, except for one or two poems.

■ ■ ■ ■

After I had been fired by the Funk & Wagnalls dictionary, Van Wyck Brooks remained doing this work. He was much more skillful at it than I was. He had been in love for years with a girl who lived in Plainfield, New Jersey, the town that he grew up in, Eleanor Stimson of the well-known Stimson family. She was a niece, I think, of Henry L. Stimson, who became secretary of state, and had been, before that, secretary of war. Anyway, it was to Eleanor that the poems in *Verses by Two Undergraduates*—the poems on the right-hand page, Van Wyck's poems—were addressed, at least those poems that were love poems. And the poems on the left-hand page (I think I've got that right) were mine and were addressed to Phyllis de Kay.

Van Wyck got word from California, where Eleanor was staying with her mother—the mother had a small competence which just barely enabled them to keep afloat—that there was a very attractive man on the scene, an architect of some substance, who had fallen in love with Eleanor and wanted to marry her. Eleanor was puzzled what to do. She wanted Van Wyck to know this, anyway. Van Wyck sensed the situation, took it in right away. He said, "If only I can get out there quickly, I'm sure everything's going to be all right."

But how to do it? He had no money. Van Wyck just managed along from week to week with what he earned. I was in the same situation. So he went to Edward Sheldon, our mutual friend, who was then a famous playwright. Ned had made hundreds of thousands of dollars with his *Romance* and *Salvation Nell,* with *The Boss* and with *The High Road.* Van Wyck went to Ned and borrowed a thousand dollars, bought a new necktie, jumped on a train, went to California, and married Eleanor on nothing a year. She had nothing a year. Neither of them had a job. They had to live with her mother at first.

He gave up his job. He did, later, get a job as an instructor at Leland Stanford University. As you know, an instructor isn't paid very well. And a hard struggle began, especially as they proceeded to have children, two boys. Van Wyck had begun his writing career very early. He was remarkably able, remarkably alert—I don't know if that's just the word I mean, but he managed to graduate from college in three years, to get his B.A. in three years with very high marks, just as Ned Sheldon graduated in three years summa cum laude. Then Van Wyck had gone to England and published a book over there called *The Wine of the Puritans,* his first book, on the same field—that is, literary history, history of American literature—to which he devoted the rest of his life.

After the year at Stanford, Van Wyck and his family came on to New York, and Van Wyck had various jobs. He was with *The Seven Arts,* an avant-garde, very brilliant magazine that other distinguished men were editing —Waldo Frank and James Oppenheim and Gilbert Seldes and others. He also edited an annual called *The American Caravan.* (My memory is bad about these things. I'll probably get some of these things all wrong. I shan't try to give any more names.) But I do know that eventually Van Wyck had a job with the Century Company, and during all this time he was writing books, or trying to, and he'd written some of his most outstanding books; *America's Coming of Age* and *Letters and Leadership* had, I think, been published around that time. But if I can't remember dates, at least I can remember the general situation, which was that Van Wyck discovered he could not go on working in a publishing house and do the research and the writing that his very good books required. They made no money as yet: a sale of perhaps one thousand copies, and the author gets three hundred dollars.

So there he was, and the impulse to write was extremely strong in him. In fact, in college Van Wyck thought of little else, even as a freshman. It was almost a form of mental derangement, his passion for it was so strong. The Stimson family couldn't understand why he didn't give up his writing and buckle down to his job at the Century Company. Van Wyck was under great pressure; he had a wife and two children, and of course that was his first obligation. Finally he just cracked up completely, and he really did a good job of it. He was out for about—oh, I think it must have been five or six years, going from one hospital to another, from one sanitarium to another. His illness took the form of extreme suicidal depression. His wife did everything she could. Eleanor was a wonderful person. So was Van Wyck—he just couldn't help what was happening to him. Eleanor got to work doing translations. You know how little they pay. If you could do two whole books a year it would bring in perhaps, at the very most, two thousand dollars. Fortunately, there were members of the family who were able to help.

I used to go and see Van Wyck at the hospital whenever I had a chance. He wouldn't speak to me, but he never lost his deep courtesy. When he first saw me, his face would light up for a minute, and he would take my hand. And when I came to go, he would come to life for a moment, but the rest of the time he just couldn't bring himself back from wherever he was, lost in some torment. It was dreadful. He seemed to be blazing inwardly with a terrific fury of some kind—moving on an entirely different plane from the one that we're moving on. However, I was allowed to take him out on walks. He was for a while at a sanitarium in the country called "Four Winds," and we would go out walking together. He was never told when I was coming, for fear it would get him excited, and sometimes I would have amusing experiences, as on the day when I went up there and was told by one of the nurses, "Oh, the boys are out berrying today." This was in the summertime. "They'll be back in a little while, with their pails full of berries, so you just wait here." I waited, and then the nurse introduced me to a man who was sitting there, "This is Dr. So-and-so." I sat down, and this hollow-faced, hollow-eyed man sat there and never said a word. I thought I'd have to be polite; I'd have to say something. I said, "Doctor, can you tell me, do you think there's any improvement in the condition of my friend, Mr. Van Wyck Brooks?" And he looked at me with those hollow eyes of his and he said, "We patients are not allowed to discuss one another's cases." Well, then, soon "the boys" came back from the woods, Van Wyck carrying his little pail of berries—it was so pathetic— and as soon as he saw me, he started running, and his face lit up for just a moment. Then I was allowed to take him out for a walk. This would depend upon the time of year. I would see him either indoors or out. But it was difficult, because he wouldn't talk.

The difficulty was dramatized on the occasion when I was sent out to the sanitarium by Max Perkins, who was Van Wyck's oldest friend. They'd grown up in Plainfield together. The Literary Guild had agreed to take one of Van Wyck Brooks's books. I think it was his book on Emerson,[29] one of the finest things he ever did. Of course, in the state of mind Van Wyck was in, he was convinced the book was absolutely worthless. And I was to go out and persuade him that here was a great opportunity—with money, prestige, a big sale! Van Wyck said, "No!" "But Van Wyck," I said. "The book is bad! Bad! Bad!" he shouted, as if in anger, breaking his long stubborn silence. I said, "It isn't, don't be foolish—the Literary Guild would not take it if it wasn't good. Everyone thinks it's wonderful. I do, Max does." "No good!" He wouldn't hear of it, wouldn't hear of it. Then, after a few weeks somebody succeeded in changing his mind. The Emerson was published, and that helped a little bit, because it had a great success.

When Van Wyck was getting ill, the real source of the illness, I always thought, was this conflict in him between his duty and his absolute need to go on with his writing. But in that state of mind, he got queer ideas. He was working on a book on Henry James,[30] and he began to feel that what he had said about Henry James was something that one gentleman should never say about another gentleman, that James would never forgive him, and that James annoyed him by haunting him at night so that he couldn't sleep. He got these queer ideas. He became afraid of James, and he became afraid of the book and couldn't go on with it. All these queer things happened to him.

Finally, one of the things that helped was the fact that his wife came into a little money through a relative, a small trust fund, enough to keep them going. It gradually percolated through Van Wyck's mind that he could come home and do his own work and not feel that he was being a scoundrel, a slacker. Very gradually he got better and better, and finally he occasionally came home. He used to be allowed home on weekends quite often, and I used to be invited by Eleanor to come up on those weekends. I think I've talked about that, too—how he always had to be kept busy every minute. We'd put these picture puzzles down on the table for him to work on. He always seemed to be out of breath and terribly agitated, and you'd put him down at the table and he'd work on these things, which he hated, but at least they took his mind off his troubles, and he became absorbed in them and less agitated.

Gradually, then, he became perfectly normal. And then, as good luck would have it, from that point on, his books began to make an impression and to sell. In 1936 *The Flowering of New England,* which sold several hundred thousand copies, took the Pulitzer Prize that year and was a Book-of-the-Month Club choice, and almost every one of that five-volume series took prizes and had a big sale. One year, he got the Gold Medal from the American Academy. Everything came his way. He made so much money that he and his wife very foolishly built a big house up on the hill above Westport, where they were living—most luxurious bathrooms, green marble, and everything else in the place equally luxurious, completely impractical. They couldn't get a maid or other service way out there, and poor Eleanor wore herself out scrubbing those marble floors.

From then on Van Wyck had this big success, and it seemed to heal him completely. It was just that it made it possible for him to do his own work. For the rest of his life he got up every morning at quarter of six or half past five and went to his desk, and he would work there every day

Van Wyck Brooks (photograph by Robert Gumpper)

until noon. He never wrote more than 300 words a day. Then the afternoon would be devoted to research. He had a very fine library of his own, but if necessary he would go to New Haven and work in the Yale library or to New York and work there. He had to go to bed early so as to be able to get up at five o'clock in the morning and be at his desk. He kept that up all the rest of his life. I don't know how many books he published—perhaps thirty or forty.

Van Wyck was my best friend, my closest friend, right up to the very end. As we used to agree—we always said, and we knew it was true—"Every life ends in tragedy." His certainly did, for he died of cancer, and it was a long, grueling illness, and he knew there was only one outcome, and it took months and months. Some day they won't permit that, I think. Some day people will be allowed to get out without going through all that. His first wife, Eleanor Stimson, had died of cancer. That ending also was tragic. Eleanor had complained of rheumatism; the doctor sent her to the great specialist, Dr. Boots, a great arthritis specialist. He neglected to take an X-ray. He treated her for arthritis. The pain got worse and worse, and finally she was X-rayed and found to have cancer of the bone. Now it was probably too late. However, they did amputate the leg, way up here in the thigh. Eleanor was one of those Spartan Stimson women, took everything in her stride, took it as a huge joke, almost. Her only concern was that Van Wyck shouldn't be depressed by it all. She succeeded in convincing him that she didn't mind losing her leg. In fact, she thought it would be rather jolly, having an artificial leg, they did such wonderful things now. That's the sort of a person she was.

Eleanor knew that she had about two or three months to go. The doctors told her. She insisted upon knowing. She asked me to come and see her. She told me what she knew, and said, "I can take it. I'm prepared to go. I have two wonderful sons, and the best husband in the world, and what I want to do is to shield them. I want you to see to it that Van Wyck doesn't know that it is hopeless. Let him think that there is a chance, and then it'll gradually come over him, and he'll be able to bear it. But he's very sensitive, and I don't think he could bear it now." I did the best I could, and Van Wyck was a man not at all observant of bodily symptoms. I don't think he knew whether his heart was on his right or his left side. There are people like that. But, of course, eventually, when Eleanor was dying, he knew.

Van Wyck was one of my two or three dearest friends. His death meant the end of a great deal for me. It's just like having part of yourself lopped off. But Van Wyck Brooks lives on in his books. He did a masterly piece of work—those books will never be out of fashion. His *Makers and Finders* is *the* one great history of American literature, by a man who is not merely an historian but an artist in his writing and who brings these people alive for you just as a novelist would bring his characters alive.

■ ■ ■ ■

Ned Sheldon, in early life, became a very well-known playwright, a very successful one. An extraordinary man. But what he did later in life was even more extraordinary than what he had achieved in the theater. Several books have been written about him. One of them is called *The Man Who Lived Twice*.[31] Early, when I came back from Germany in 1911, I found Ned already a famous man, all doors open to him everywhere, a rich man now, and very much in touch with all the people in the theatrical world, sending flowers to this actress and that actress; engaged to one of the most beautiful women of the period, Doris Keane, herself a talented actress, who would later star in Ned's play, *Romance,* which he was writing at the time. That play was the story of a young clergyman who falls in love with an opera singer. He's in love with her glamorous world, and she with his, to her, so much higher world. The play ends tragically. Actually, it tells Ned's own story, though Ned was a playwright, not a clergyman, and Doris Keane was an actress, not an opera singer. While Ned was engaged to marry Doris, this dreadful arthritis deformans began in his hip. I noticed it first one evening when we'd been out to dinner together at Sherry's. Ned took me to these expensive places and had tables reserved everywhere. He wouldn't walk home (I always liked to walk) because his hip hurt him so much.

The arthritis spread slowly through his body. He had every available medical help. Everything was tried, from Krishnamurti the Hindu sage to Christian Science, psychotherapy, all the medical treatments there are, sulphur baths. The disease crept remorselessly through his body, until very soon he was lying on a water bed, prostrate, slightly inclined, unable to move any part of his body except his lips. He couldn't move. All his joints were ankylosed. He had to choose the position in which he would remain for the rest of his life. Finally, his eyeballs were destroyed; he was left totally blind.

And there Ned lay, for some twenty-odd years—twenty-five or twenty-six years—in his apartment at 35 East Eighty-fourth Street, the penthouse of that building, just off Madison Avenue. That room became the place where many of the most interesting people went to visit him. Playwrights went there to read their plays and to get guidance from Ned, for he was an expert. Among his closest friends were the Barrymores and people quite different from that—another very good friend was John Buchan, the Governor General of Canada, who spent a great deal of time with Ned, whenever he came to this country. Krishnamurti, the modern Christ; and Paul Robeson, the singer; writers, painters, actors, and actresses, of course, galore. The women would come. They would always put on their most beautiful clothes before they visited Ned. Although he couldn't see them, he loved the rustle of a silk dress. They would bring flowers that he could smell, and they would go through their parts for him. Sometimes a whole troupe would go up there and give a play, around his bed, that he could listen to. Julia Marlowe went through all her old Shakespearean roles for Ned. Fritz Kreisler brought his violin and played solo for him.

Ned never liked to have more than one person at a time. He would give you dinner at his bedside. A little table was brought in, and cocktails. He had a cook and a butler, an orderly and a masseuse, a waitress and a secretary, a reader who read aloud to him several hours a day. Everything needed to take care of him, everything that money could buy, he had. He was massaged every day to prevent circulatory troubles, thromboses, and other things.

Ned was the hardest man in New York to see: everyone wanted to see him. I went to see him on an average, I should think, about once every two weeks. Ned would ask me to come, and we'd have a wonderful evening together. Very occasionally he would break his rule, and Van Wyck and Eleanor and Phyllis and I would be invited together, and he would have four people there. Then his face was more beautiful than ever, he was so happy. Listening, not saying much himself but listening to our talk, gave him great joy. He was a most extraordinary man.

He was one of my chief props. I used to read my poems, and he was often critical, but also he would praise. It could be very reassuring. It was sometimes difficult to leave him. I had to get up fairly early in the morning to go to the office, and when it got to be eleven o'clock, I'd want to go home, and Ned would say, "Oh, do you have to go now?" and I pictured him just lying there through the long night. But I would have to go.

It was such a privilege to see him, but his parting word would often be, "You'll come again soon, won't you?" And you knew that he really— that he depended upon people coming to see him. In this way he made a life for himself. He lived in others. He couldn't sign his name. He told me that with one elbow he could press down a little on a buzzer that would summon somebody when he wanted to have the bed cranked up or cranked down. He would be fed through a tube before you came to dine. I just can't describe the quality of that man, the effect he had on one. When you came into that room, you came into the presence of a disembodied spirit. The spirit was there, but there was no body it could use, except the lips—yet his gusty laughter and heartiness belied his crippled condition. I remember one time there was a quarrel going on in the kitchen between the cook and the butler, and it got rather noisy, and I said to Ned, "I'll just close that door." "No," cried Ned, "Leave it open. I want to hear who's winning."

He didn't have any false embarrassment about his condition. You could talk with him about blindness. I never saw him give way to depression, except once. One day when I was there he said, "Come nearer," and I did. He whispered, "Doris is dying." This was Doris Keane. Then, from under the black mask that covered his eyes, tears began oozing out. Doris died. She left her ashes to Ned. He kept them in his room. It was the great romance of his life. He never got over it.

He never married her. The engagement had to be broken. And it probably was a blessed thing because this way it remained a high and unsullied romance. Doris Keane, I think, had many doubts about marrying Ned. She was a woman who lived very freely, didn't conceal that she'd been completely promiscuous. She had had two husbands, and I doubt whether the marriage would have lasted. But as it was, the friendship lasted, and Ned took a great interest in Doris's daughter by her first marriage. After Doris's death, the daughter came to see Ned, over and over again. His love for Doris remained for him on the highest level of romance. In his play he tells the story of it. It's a very sad play. In the end, the young clergyman— the opera singer leaves him, because she knows that he won't be happy with her—goes back to her apartment not knowing that she had secretly left that day so as not to subject them both to a scene that she knew would be unbearable. And he stands in the empty apartment, and an organ-grinder in the street outside begins playing. It's one of the most desolate endings I've ever seen.

Ned went on writing plays, dictating them. He wrote several plays in collaboration with others, and some on his own. There was a play called *Lulu Belle,* which he wrote. But he didn't repeat the really big successes of his early youth, and he usually had to have a collaborator to work with him and to manage all the theater part of it.

Ned seemed to me the greatest human being I've known. He never wavered. His mother told me that when he was first told by the doctors that he was going to be totally blind, he went through a real dark night of the soul. After a week he came out of it and never referred to it again. He died at the age of about sixty or sixty-one, and as he was my age, that would be about twenty years ago. The telephone rang, right here in this apartment, in the bedroom, and I answered it, and it was Ned's mother. She said, "Come over immediately. Ned has died." She wanted me to write the obituary, get it to the papers. It wasn't necessary to write it. The papers all had obituary notices. Ned's death—that was another big loss. Oh, what a loss that was! I must show you his picture.

[13 March 1967]

AT EAST HAMPTON THERE HAD ORIGINALLY been a colony of painters. A great many painters went there, say, eighty years ago. Some very well-known ones were in the summer colony there. East Hampton itself is a very old town, founded by Connecticut people way back in the seventeenth century, the early part of the seventeenth century. There were two groups of people that later settled there, or three groups, you might say. One was actors and people connected with the theater, and then there were the painters. Childe Hassam was one of the painters whose work still commands attention. There was Thomas Moran, and another brother whose first name I forget—I think it was Edward Moran, a very good painter. The Morans were a family of painters. I remember seeing old Thomas Moran, who lived to be over ninety, pacing the beach—this tall, lean man with a hawk-like face, his eye on the water and the beach, and I suppose enjoying it and getting impressions for other paintings. He's a painter who has been somewhat overlooked now because he was purely representational and also made the mistake of going in for grandiloquent subjects. As we know, the things that are interesting in art are very often rather commonplace things, nothing extreme. No one ever painted a good painting of a thunderstorm or an earthquake. Thomas Moran would paint the Grand Canyon over and over again—the Grand Canyon by moonlight, the Grand Canyon at sunrise, and so on. They are very fine paintings of that school, but regarded—well, disregarded today.

I suppose of the painters there today, few of the old tradition remain. Jackson Pollock, in later days, lived at East Hampton. I knew him, but not well. He was an attractive man. He was a hard drinker, too, and my wife and I had some pretty unpleasant experiences when he brought us back

Edward Sheldon (courtesy of New York Public Library)

from his studio in his car, driving about eighty miles an hour. It was all right when we were going through sandy East Hampton roads out towards Springs, where he lived. But when he got on the main highway and in the village of East Hampton, where you're not supposed to go more than thirty-five miles an hour, it made one uncomfortable.

His method of painting—— He was just as much concerned (he was one of the early action painters) with what he did when he painted as he was with the work itself. He would put his canvas on the floor and then drip paint on it. But he was perhaps one of the most interesting of the abstract painters. I just mention Pollock because this tradition of a painting colony in East Hampton has persisted, and there is quite a colony there still. I don't know the names of these men as well as I should. I suppose there are some very distinguished painters there now. And sculptors, too. Willem de Kooning has been going to East Hampton in recent years, and the sculptor Jacques Lipchitz has also spent many summers there. I'm not sure whether he goes there now, or not.

But, to go back to the old times, the two names that come to my mind are the ones I mentioned, Childe Hassam and Thomas Moran. In the sun-bath of the bathing pavilion at East Hampton, when I was a boy, I used to be quite impressed by seeing, sitting naked in the enclosed sunbath there sunning themselves after a swim, Childe Hassam and John Drew—and sometimes John Drew's nephew, John Barrymore, would be there sitting on the bench, too—and sometimes a man who was my ideal in youth of absolute and fascinating evil. He was a Gallatin, Jack Gallatin. He was supposed to indulge constantly in sin and sinful practices, in all the known and even the unknown vices, and I used to admire him from afar as a boy. He looked very pale and exhausted and bored. He drank quite a good deal, too. He and John Drew used to have interesting conversations in the sun-bath, and I tried to sit as near as I could to overhear them. I never succeeded in this.

Another man who was often found in that group—it was like a little club—was Albert Gallatin, the distinguished brother of Jack Gallatin. Albert Gallatin was a broker and a very good one, but he also painted quite well and played the piano simply marvelously. His great love was Wagner, and when he played Wagner everyone was spellbound. He was an amateur, a broker who went in for the arts. Then there was another man who's been forgotten now, but who was a very good sculptor, John Roudebush; he used to join this group. I never knew Childe Hassam well or, for that matter, Thomas Moran, although I knew Moran a little better because the families were friends. My grandfather, William A. Wheelock, who had been one of the early New York crowd that first formed the summer colony at East Hampton, was a friend of Thomas Moran, and I think bought some of his paintings.

I was going to say that another member of the group—well, not really a member of the group but one of the summer colony there—was a woman, at that time Mrs. Leonard Thomas, wife of Leonard Thomas, the broker, a very attractive man. Mrs. Thomas had literary ambitions. She was born Blanche Oelrich, the daughter of an extremely well-to-do family, and a very beautiful woman. John Barrymore came down to East Hampton for weekends quite often and stayed with his uncle, John Drew. Apparently this beautiful Mrs. Leonard Thomas made a deep impression on Barrymore, and as the husband was away all week working in New York, and Mrs. Leonard Thomas was there all summer long, he didn't hesitate to take advantage of this. I don't remember whether the Leonard Thomases had any children or not; I was at an age when I wouldn't have noticed those things. Later on, as I got older, I did notice that Barrymore was paying a great deal of attention to Mrs. Leonard Thomas. Eventually there was a divorce, and Barrymore married Mrs. Thomas, who then burst out into a new personality under the name Michael Strange. She wrote poems under the pen name Michael Strange. She wrote a sort of second-hand, Whitmanesque, imitative kind of poetry celebrating every kind of freedom, especially the freedoms that she thought were desirable, and all seemed to go very well.

One summer the John Barrymores rented the house belonging to the parents of my beloved friend, Phyllis de Kay, and Michael Strange wrote one of her best poems about that house, which was a unique house, such as only the de Kays would have built. They were a most unusual family. After the house was built, the first summer the whole upper story caved in. It was one of those concrete buildings that was rather an experiment at that time. But instead of being dismayed by this, the whole family was so happy that no one had been injured that they went down into the big downstairs room and they danced. There were ten of them—father, mother, and the eight children, of which the young girl who is now my wife was the eldest.

I saw a good deal of Michael Strange later on in life, because she became a friend of my very old and dear friend Edward Sheldon. She used to be one of the guests at dinner at his bedside on some of those occasions when I was the other guest. Occasionally he stretched a point and had two guests, and Michael Strange and I sat on opposite sides of this little table at his bedside and talked to Ned or to each other. Ned of course would then get Michael Strange to recite her poems. And he would also ask me to recite mine, but I always refused out of vanity, because, to be quite frank, I didn't want to be included on the same program with Michael Strange's poems, which seemed to me so very amateurish, such bad and false and show-off poems. I recoiled from this and made excuses.

Michael Strange also came into the picture because she submitted a book to Scribners, which I turned down. It was an autobiographical book, the story of her life, which had been an interesting life. Michael Strange was the sort of person who had lived in a Bohemian way in her youth and was a rebel against the conventional. She had tramped all over Hungary or some other country with practically no money, living in this way because she wanted to. When she submitted this book I turned it down because I didn't think it awfully good. Max Perkins, however, who was remarkably perceptive as an editor, thought it would have a sale. I don't know whether he thought it was good or not, but anyway he took it on,[32] and this involved him in long sessions with Michael Strange in her apartment.

After the divorce from Barrymore—— That marriage ended unhappily; Barrymore became very difficult, and he got caught up in alcohol. He was a man of some genius, but he went down before old Brother Alcohol. He and Michael Strange were divorced. I don't know the ins and outs of it. They had as their confidante in this painful process Edward Sheldon, whom everyone confided in, and Ned did succeed in straightening Barrymore out—twice I think. Michael Strange and Barrymore would come to Ned's bedside, separately, and Ned would hear one side of the story and then the other side of the story, and he did straighten out John Barrymore, for whom he had a great affection. Barrymore worshiped Ned. He would do anything for Ned. He even was willing to give up alcohol for Ned, which was the supreme test. Ned straightened him out because he felt that Barrymore had a really great talent as an actor and that if he had only stuck with it, he could have been an even greater figure than he was. Ned was the one who advised Barrymore to take serious parts, to play Hamlet and so on. Well, eventually Barrymore and Michael Strange were divorced, and, if memory serves me right, Michael Strange, or Blanche Oelrich, as she had been, then married Harrison Tweed, who was an important New York lawyer. It was at this time, I think, that she was writing her autobiography, and she had a separate apartment so as to be able to get away from household duties, where she wrote.

It was there that Max had to go in the evenings to work with her on the autobiography.

Now, Max was not at all a philanderer and as you know had a very considerable contempt for women. He was married and had five daughters. He was not at all a man of the type who was going to be seduced by a beautiful woman. I think Michael Strange was very much fascinated by Max, who was an extremely good-looking man, an attractive man. They had long sessions toiling over Michael Strange's manuscript, which Max got her to cut and re-shape, with his extraordinary skill. He used to tell me amusing stories about it. At this time Michael Strange was a communist. You had to be a communist then. She would tell Max that there must be no classes in society; it must all be just one homogeneous, democratic group. Then every now and then she would interrupt her discourse to shout at the maids who were working in the kitchen, "Kate! Mary! for God's sake, stop rattling those dishes!" This amused Max very much. The book was quite a success sales-wise. I think Max was right, and I was wrong. I think perhaps I had a little feeling—— I tried not to let these personal feelings enter in, but she seemed such a terrible show-off, and that probably was just what sold the book. Because it was full of rather outrageous things, and she was a remarkably vivid human being.

Eventually Michael Strange was divorced by Harrison Tweed, and, I gathered from Ned, this was to her the most terrific blow of her life. She was a woman who was not accustomed to being rejected. She was accustomed to being the rejecter. The experience of finding a man who actually didn't want to live with her, who got fed up with her, came as a great shock. After that she went in deeply for religion, but the religion had to take on a show-off character also. It took the form of her getting engagements in certain churches to chant her religious poems before the congregation. She would have worked it around that way, you can be sure, and she was so attractive and magnetic that she held them spellbound with this not-very-good poetry. I won't even call it poetry—not-very-good verse, let us say.

■ ■ ■ ■

I knew Zoë Akins very well. I met her through my old friend Sara Teasdale. Both of them came from St. Louis, or from the environs of St. Louis. Zoë was the daughter of the postmaster of a town not far from St. Louis called Humansville. She came from a well-to-do family, I think without very much—what is the word we use today?—cultural background. But she had talent. I saw a good deal of Zoë, right up to the time when she went out to Hollywood. Zoë had been a poet, and her first book was published by Mitchell Kennerley, I think, the same publisher who published the first book of Edna Millay, the first book of Vachel Lindsay, the first book of Orrick Johns and of other interesting poets. Zoë was also published in England by Grant Richards. I can't remember the title of her first book, but that was the first and almost the only book of poems she did publish.[33] Later in life she had a very bitter experience—I think Zoë was a rather daring young woman for those days—that seemingly made a profound change in her. I think she lived quite freely. I think she had affairs with various interesting people. She was not a beautiful woman—quite the contrary—but she was an attractive woman and an interesting one.

During the First World War a young airman fell in love with Zoë or at least was infatuated with her, and they had a long affair. He was the son of wealthy people in St. Louis who, I think, had known Zoë's family so that they had certain bonds and backgrounds in common. The love affair was enhanced and intensified by the fact that he was soon to be called up for active duty as an airman. He was training over here. Then he was sent overseas. Zoë, I think, was as much in love with him as she could be with anyone. I think she was perhaps rather light in those ways, but this time she seemed to be involved quite deeply. He was a good deal younger. I think he was ten or twelve years younger than Zoë, and this was one of his attractions for her. He was sent overseas. I don't remember whether he came back at the end of the war, or whether he came back wounded and honorably discharged from the air force, but in any case his family got hold of him and began—— I think in the meantime, over there, he'd had various romances, as men at the front were apt to have. But his family got hold of him and said: "Look. . . ." He had promised to marry Zoë. He had proposed to her before he went overseas and had declared there was no other woman for him but Zoë. But they talked him out of it, saying, "Look, you're still very young. This woman is a great deal older than you are. It's an unsuitable marriage for you, and it will not be happy."

He had, I think, lost interest to some extent. I happened to be with Zoë at the little apartment she had downtown one afternoon at tea time—that means rather potent drinks—and the telephone rang. Zoë went to the telephone, and I pretended to be engaged in a book, but I couldn't avoid hearing the conversation, and I heard her say (whatever his name was, I've forgotten, I think it was Tom)—"You can't do this to me! Somebody's got hold of you! Oh, this is just dreadful—don't tell me. I don't want to hear about it——" and so on and so on. She burst into a flood of tears on the telephone. I can't remember just what was said, but it was quite brief, and she hung up and sobbed and was very shaken, and I tried to comfort her as much as I could, but she was incoherent. I said, "I think probably I'd better go. I'm only in the way."

"No, I want you to stay. I want to tell you what's happened." She pulled herself together, and she told me that he had—can a man jilt a woman? I suppose so—anyway, he had. The effect on her was remarkable. She pulled herself together with great success, her face hardened, and she said, "I am through with romance. Never again. I would never have believed this of Tom. He loved me deeply, and I loved him deeply, and we have exchanged vows, and this—— I'm finished. Power is what I'm going to get from now on. Money, money, money, money, and power. I am going to write plays." Zoë had written plays before. She had written a play that had had some success when played by amateurs, here in New York. I think it was played at the Comedy Club or some place of that sort. It was called *The Magical City*. It was all about New York. It was in verse.

"No more poetry! No more romance! I'm going to get ahead in this world, if I do nothing else." And she started in, and she did. She wrote a play called *Déclassée*. Ethel Barrymore—who, by the way, I omitted from the East Hampton roster. She used to be there for weekends. I used to see her in bathing, and there were various leading ladies of John Drew's to be seen on the beach during the off season. Well, to come back to Zoë. She wrote this play, *Déclassée*; Ethel Barrymore read it, took it, and starred in it. It opened on the road and came to New York, made a great success, a great deal of money. Zoë got the power she wanted. She came to New York and took a suite in a very swank hotel of those days—I don't know whether it still exists—called the Holland House. It was on Fifth Avenue, a little below Thirty-fourth Street, I think. There she spent one winter. She had a car and a footman and a chauffeur, and she lived in grandeur—was very much, you know, the idol of the theatrical world. She was a grande dame and delighted in it. All her dreams were fulfilled. Every time she went out of the door, she, as I noticed on several occasions when I was with her, would hand the doorman or the porter a dollar bill, and likewise on coming back.

I had in the old days met at her apartment T. S. Eliot quite often when he was still in this country. He and Zoë were friends from the old St. Louis days. Eliot in those days was a very different man from the man he became. He was as yet not widely known. He was very silent; I didn't know him well. I'd known him at college very slightly. He was two classes later than me. I think he was 1910 and I was 1908. I knew him partly through Conrad Aiken, 1910, whom I knew better. Eliot was very silent and reserved, didn't say very much. Actually he was a very mischievous man, had a wonderful sense of humor—the same thing that came out in the poems later, in satire and also in pure humor, as when he talks about Grishkin, the Russian woman with the marvelous full-blown figure which, as Eliot has it, "Gives promise of pneumatic bliss."[34] He had that kind of humor.

Very shortly after that, Eliot went to England, where he eventually became the absolute arbiter of culture on two continents. He changed the taste of two continents. Both here and in England the romantic school of poetry was thrown into the discard, and the Metaphysicals, John Donne and all the rest of them, became the right poets to admire. Eliot also became *the* representative poet of his generation, and eventually the Nobel Prize was awarded to him.

I never knew Conrad Aiken very well, either. I saw him occasionally at college when we were both publishing poems in the *Advocate* and when I was publishing so many poems in *The Harvard Monthly*, where Conrad often appeared with a short story. He is a fine short story writer, as well as a very fine poet. I've seen him on and off. Conrad lived part of the time in New York, but usually he would live out of town, in Brewster, Massachusetts, and sometimes in Savannah, his native city, in Georgia. So I can't say that I knew him very well, except as an editor. Scribners published his poems, and I've always been an admirer of his poems from early on. I was Conrad Aiken's editor at Scribners in the later years. His books had a good sale, that is, for poetry. Conrad is one of the best and had the distribution that a good poet would have who works at it long enough to build up a following.

He's a strange man. He had a very difficult history. As a child, I forget at what age but at a rather impressionable age, he heard his father kill his mother and then kill himself. This produced shock, as you may imagine, and I think is responsible for some of the macabre elements in Conrad Aiken's poetry. And also perhaps for his great interest in Freud and in Jung and in the whole modern school of psychoanalysis, because he had to get help, to straighten himself out, after this. I think it was a childhood experience at the most impressionable age when it would be very dangerous. Conrad is a man who has many warm friends. His work does have a certain ophidian quality, if I may use the word; there is a strain of morbidity in it. But it has great beauty. He's one of the few poets of our time capable of great aural beauty in poetry. Today, of course, the visual, the image, is the thing that interests most poets, but Conrad Aiken has persisted in writing poetry that has a beautiful aural texture. Magnificent, some of it is—and he's very modern, too, in his psychological and metaphysical interests. The worst thing that could be said about Conrad Aiken's work is that he's written a great deal of poetry that has perhaps somewhat the same general quality and tone, so that some people complain of a certain monotony in it. Like all important poets he has a great bulk of work to his credit. I think you can almost measure a poet's stature by his bulk. If he's a good poet, he will have, if he lives long enough, a great mass to his credit, and not just—— There are exceptions, of course. Eliot's one, for instance. Eliot published very little poetry—was extremely fastidious about what he published.

We saw a good deal of Zoë, my wife and I, later in life, even after she'd gone to Hollywood. Zoë went on with her work as a playwright, you know, and had other successful plays—I think *The Greeks Had a Word for It* was one of them. But on the whole, she failed after that. She wrote and had many plays produced, but they never went on to big successes, and eventually she capitulated to Hollywood and lived out there as a scriptwriter. She did publish one more book of poems, later in life, not as outstanding as her earlier works, and she never again was completely successful as a playwright. She came east from time to time, and my wife and I used to see her. We had gay parties for her. She would come and have dinner alone with us and talk, bringing her little dog "Zoë" that she'd taught to be almost human. She would tell the dog that she wasn't feeling very well, and the dog would begin to whimper and shake its head (it was a little Pekingese) and be very unhappy. Or she would say, "Somebody trying to steal Mama's purse, somebody trying to steal Mama's purse!" and hang onto it fiercely, and the dog would immediately rush forward and attack Phyllis and me in the most terrific rage. The dog had also been taught to say its prayers and she—it was a little bitch—would crouch and put her paws up in an attitude of prayer. Very sweet.

It was through Zoë, partly, that I met Mrs. Patrick Campbell,[*] who was staying in this country at the time, and Mrs. Campbell paid me a handsome compliment in her autobiography. She said, "Mr. Wheelock is the only man I have met in America who has the old-time courtesy, what I call

[*]Celebrated British actress (1865–1940).

deep courtesy." I was amazed to hear this, but it was very pleasing to hear it from a person as critical as Mrs. Patrick Campbell.

I was detailed to take Mrs. Campbell to a party at the University Club where the Abbey Theatre Players were speaking. They were not putting on a play there, but they were to speak, and we sat at a little round table with strangers, because they were serving drinks before the speeches. A kindly western woman of a very American type, who saw that Mrs. Campbell didn't know her or the other people at the table—and I didn't know them, so I couldn't have presented them to Mrs. Campbell—leaned over and said, "I am Mrs. So-and-so." Mrs. Campbell didn't deign any answer. Then this nice friendly western woman, with a very Chicago twang, said, "I spent the summer in London last year. Have you ever been in London, Mrs. Campbell?" I thought Mrs. Patrick Campbell would probably annihilate this lady, but it shows her greatness of spirit that she did no such thing. She said, "Oh, yes—you know, I am an Englishwoman; I have lived in London most of my life." She then did her best to put the poor woman at ease.

However, when the speakers began, it bored Mrs. Patrick Campbell. The speechmaking didn't interest her. She said to me, "Recite poetry to me." I didn't know what to do. I was quite young, and I was rather over-awed by Mrs. Patrick Campbell. So I began in a very low voice to recite Keats, and "Louder," said Mrs. Patrick Campbell. She was very imperious, you know. I recited a little bit louder. Immediately, all around there was this "Sh! Sh!" from the audience—"Shut up," they were almost saying. "Don't pay the slightest attention to them," said Mrs. Patrick Campbell. "Go right ahead. It's so much better than these speeches." I went on to Swinburne and other poets. An usher came and said, "You'll either have to stop or——" And I was in agony, because I hate doing things like that. "You'll either have to stop or leave." Mrs. Patrick Campbell said, "Pay not the slightest attention to him. Proceed." So we *were* asked to leave. That's the sort of person Mrs. Patrick Campbell was.

Her great sorrow at the time—or not sorrow so much as anxiety— was that she was very short of cash. She was thinking of going out to Hollywood, though she loathed the idea, to try to turn an honest penny. But in the meantime, she was hoping to sell the love letters Bernard Shaw had written her. Bernard Shaw had been madly in love with Mrs. Patrick Campbell—whether they had an affair or not, I don't know. I can hardly picture that cautious man, Shaw, indulging in this. But they were, I gather—she showed me some of them—very frank letters. Of course Shaw would not give permission to have them published until after his death and the death of his wife. He said, "I will give you permission to have them published but not now. I have to think of my wife," and so on. "It would be very painful to me to have them published now." They would have brought her in a goodly sum of money. So eventually she had to go to Hollywood, and there her feelings were deeply hurt. She told me later, when she came back from Hollywood, that sometimes she'd been asked to do things or some of these young upstart directors had told her to do things differently, to change her style of acting. But she knew they were wrong, and she would say, "But I am Mrs. Patrick Campbell!"—and they would ask "Who's she?" They had never heard of Mrs. Patrick Campbell. Actually never heard of her! She belonged to a previous era. And this was the last humiliation.

Well, Mrs. Campbell had her own affectations and cruelties. I know that when I took her out to dinner, she would bring along her dog, Moonbeam, and she would feed her at the table, which was against the rules of the restaurant, but she just talked the waiter and the headwaiter down. Also Mrs. Campbell had an affectation of not remembering names. I know it was an affectation because she remembered most names very well. We saw her on and off through the years after my marriage, and my wife and Mrs. Campbell got along very well together. Mrs. Campbell would never refer to my wife when they were on a first-name basis, as they soon were—would never refer to her as Phyllis. She would always call her Doris. This was to show that Mrs. Campbell was so important a person she couldn't be bothered remembering every name. Her own name was Stella, Stella Campbell.

We saw a great deal of Mrs. Campbell until the dear lady went back to England. I don't know what happened to her before her death, but I imagine she had rather a hard time. During the Second World War, Mrs. Campbell and I were driving in a cab, I think to the party at the University Club which I have already described, when she burst out—this was in the early stages of the war, or perhaps before the war had actually begun— "Oh, how I admire that man Hitler!" I said, "What?" "I think he's simply wonderful. Everyone else talks about things, but he just goes ahead and does them." I thought I'd have to express my opinion, and I said, "I have no use for him at all. I think he's a very evil and a very dangerous man. But I suppose every human being has some redeeming qualities." "Yes," said Mrs. Campbell, "everyone except my husband." This was her second husband. Her first husband, Patrick Campbell, a very gallant soldier, had been killed in the Boer War, and she married later in life a very sweet and pleasant older man who was rather dull, I gather, and whom she found very dull.

■ ■ ■ ■

Robinson might be interesting to talk about: Edwin Arlington Robinson, the shyest man that ever lived and the most aloof. I met him at a party given in his honor, I think by Louis Vernon Ledoux. Ledoux, himself a poet, was an old friend of Robinson's. Robinson, as you know, had no money, and he refused to do anything except to write very remarkable poetry, which didn't bring him in any money at that time. So most of his life he lived in the empty apartments of friends who were away or in rooms that they could spare for him. Louis Ledoux was one of the dearest and most generous friends.

I remember another party in honor of Robinson and of another poet, a woman who was well known at that time—she's forgotten now—Josephine Preston Peabody. She had achieved the distinction of taking with her second book of poems—she published many through Houghton Mifflin—taking a prize in England. Mrs. Peabody worshiped the poetry of Edwin Arlington Robinson, as indeed most poets then did. He was certainly the premier poet of the time. Scribners published his fourth book, *The Town Down the River,* in 1910, before my time. One reason that Scribners took it was that Theodore Roosevelt, while president, had discovered Edwin Arlington Robinson's poetry. Roosevelt was swept off his feet by it and recommended it to Scribners, and they published it. It didn't have much of a sale.

They did not continue to publish Robinson. The next book that Robinson came along with was *Captain Craig*, and Scribners felt they could not take it on. It was a single poem. As you know, Robinson's poetry was the poetry of the underdog, of the failure, of the unsuccessful man; he celebrated the man who had the courage to be what he wanted to be at all costs. And *Captain Craig* was the story of a down-and-out old sea captain who became a derelict. It was in blank verse throughout and quite long, and if there's one thing that's difficult to sell it's a book of poems, and the one thing that's even *more* difficult to sell is one long poem—much more difficult than a book of short, lyrical poems. Robinson took it everywhere, and it was turned down everywhere.* Eventually Macmillan published an

---

*Houghton Mifflin published the first edition of *Captain Craig* in 1902.

enlarged edition, and it was an absolute flop. Robinson's name was becoming widely known, and Macmillan became his permanent publisher. He also wrote plays—unsuccessful plays—in verse.

I seem to be drifting away. Back to the party. The only point of the party for me was that Robinson was to be at it. He had written me, and it's characteristic of him that he did this occasionally. I had sent him a copy of my first book, *The Human Fantasy*, and he wrote me a letter, which was affirmative—for him. He was very cagey about praising anything new, but he said he had liked the book and would I come and see him some evening? I did come to see Robinson. He was living at that time—this was after dinner, he'd asked me to come at half past eight—he was living in the empty apartment of Louis Ledoux, and it was one of the most awkward evenings I've ever spent. In the first place, I was rather overawed to be in the presence of Edwin Arlington Robinson, alone. He sat down at one end of the room—a room in which there was very little furniture that wasn't covered over with cloth, the way it is when an apartment is closed for the summer, and he pointed to a chair for me at the other end of the room, and his first remark was, "I hope you don't drink or smoke because I have nothing to offer you." I did both drink and smoke, then, but of course I said no, I was not interested, it was absolutely immaterial to me. There was nothing. He was poor. We talked about poetry. My instinct was to move my chair up and sit closer to him, but I was afraid to do it. So we spent the evening talking at long range.

We talked about other poets, particularly friends of his. One of the men who was a friend of Robinson was Ridgely Torrence, a very good poet who's since been forgotten. And Percy MacKaye, and William Vaughn Moody, and one or two others I can't recall at the moment. I don't think their names would mean very much today. Robinson brought my poetry up. He was a very kind man; it's just that he was mortally stricken with this kind of inability to—well, shyness, pathological shyness. This was what caused him to become an alcoholic. Like all very shy people, he discovered that the one thing that banishes shyness is alcohol. But he did get control of it later on in life. For a while it pretty much did him in.

Well, anyway, that evening there was nothing to drink. Robinson talked very kindly about my work. He did make some suggestions, very good ones, too. He said, "I'm glad you've written a whole book of poems about the city because we need to get that into poetry," and this is the same thing that had been told me by another writer. When my first book, *The Human Fantasy*, came out, I had a letter from William Archer, an English writer on the theater who translated Ibsen. I had sent him a copy. He liked the book for bringing the city into poetry.

At the party that I'm trying to get back to, Josephine Peabody was most anxious to talk to Robinson, whom she had never met but worshiped from afar. But there again, Robinson miffed it. He had the smallest, most pursed-up mouth I've ever seen; the mouth almost seemed to indicate that it was not to be used for anything but silence. When he found where Josephine Preston Peabody was sitting in a sort of a wall sofa, he went and sat at the opposite end of the room, and he never said one single word through the entire party.

They were serving drinks, but he was not offered any. I suppose they'd been told it was kinder not to. He was given soft drinks. Josephine Preston Peabody finally—she was shy, too, and rather in awe of Robinson— came over and tried to talk to Robinson, but all she could get from him were monosyllabic answers. "Don't you think that So-and-so"—some English poet, perhaps—"is a very fine poet?" "No," said Robinson. That was all. Then she'd have to start a new line: "I'm so devoted to the poetry of A. E. Housman, *A Shropshire Lad.* Don't you think some of those things are lovely?" No answer. "Which of his poems do you like, Mr. Robinson?" "None of them," said Robinson. And so on. That gives you a picture of what it was like.

I was satisfied just to be there. This was the first time I'd seen him in public. I'd met him before, at this meeting I talked of. He did occasionally do nice things in that sly, mischievous way of his. I remember going to a luncheon party given by a man who was the editor of the old *Outlook*— Harold Trowbridge Pulsifer, a poet who's been completely forgotten and was forgotten during his lifetime, and it broke his heart. I think he died earlier than he normally would have because he felt he was a complete failure. He edited the old *Outlook*, and he was a well-off man. The latter was held against him, of course. Poets should be poor, or they should be drunkards or maniacs or drug addicts if they want to get much attention. Harold was always giving parties for poets, and this one was given in honor of Robinson.

Harold Trowbridge Pulsifer was a friend of Theodore Roosevelt— Roosevelt was not yet president at this time—and Roosevelt often wrote for the old *Outlook*. There was that connection, and so Robinson came to the party, and I was sitting at a table a long distance from Robinson's table, where better-known people were seated. But about the middle of the meal the waiter handed me a little piece of paper, and on it was written,

"How's the Black Panther?" This was the title of a book I'd just published
—this must therefore have been 1922—"How's the Black Panther?"
signed "EA," Edwin Arlington Robinson—which thrilled me to the core,
you know, to think that Robinson should even know the title of my latest
book. I knew he didn't expect an answer, but I was so pleased.

Robinson did nothing else but write poetry. He did have a job at one
time, as you know, in the subway because President Theodore Roosevelt
got it for him. He reported for work two or three times, as a supervisor,
but was always told to go home; there was nothing for him to do today. He
finally took the hint and never went on the job but just received this modest emolument every month. It was a beautiful thing for the president to
have done and made it possible for Robinson to live quietly and do his
work. Eventually his books, each one getting finer than the other——
Man Against the Sky contains some of his great poetry. I think it contained
that beautiful, very strong poem on Lincoln,* the only really good poem
on Lincoln that's been written, although old Edwin Markham had done
quite a good one. Eventually his *Tristram*, which was a retelling of the old
Arthurian story, was taken, I believe, by the Literary Guild, so that people
in Fifth Avenue buses—you'd see them reading *Tristram* instead of the
newspapers. He made a little money and increased his audience enormously. It's held greatly against Robinson today that he did this, because
you shouldn't write about old Arthurian legends. You should write about
the Crisis of our Time or about the sordid or the violent.

Robinson became a great poet, and he is a great poet. His vogue is
gone at the moment. He's not mentioned by the elite any more. It's unfashionable to admire Robinson. But he will come back. He's a permanent
poet, I'm sure. No one could do work like that and not have it last. It has
real life in it.

What I'm going to say about Robinson now concerns him only tan-
gentially. There was another party, and a very fine one, given by Harold
Trowbridge Pulsifer at his apartment, a party consisting entirely of poets.
I remember, as I came in, I was met at the door by Pulsifer himself. Before
going on with the story, I must explain that T. S. Eliot's *The Waste Land* had
just been published. Pulsifer cautioned me as I came in, "Please do not
mention Eliot's *The Waste Land*." I said, "Why not?" "Well," he said, "Please

*"The Master" was the first poem in Robinson's *The Town Down the River* (New
York: Scribners, 1910).

don't, because Elinor Wylie is here, and she has said that this is the greatest poem of our era, that this poem will be remembered forever. It's the voice of a generation speaking in a new way for the first time. Robinson has said that if it is so much as mentioned or discussed, he will leave the party immediately. So please don't mention it!" Of course, no one did. Poor old Harold had to be at the door to warn each guest about this as he or she came.

Now, to go back to Robinson again for a moment. I didn't see much of him in those later years, and what I could say would be what everyone knows, so there's no use in saying it. He spent every summer at the Mac-Dowell Colony. A special allowance was made for him. You're not supposed to spend more than so many summers in succession there. There Robinson did all his magnificent work, under, for him, ideal circumstances, up in New Hampshire where he loved the country and where he was given solitude. Yet in the evenings, as you know, the people working there all get together at supper or dinner and have a social time. That was just enough society, and he was the lion, of course, of the colony.

Robinson died early, you know—I think he was only sixty-two—of cancer of the colon. People who saw him during his last illness were people much more intimate with him than I was, but I wrote him a letter and got an acknowledgment—I don't remember whether it was from Ridgely Torrence, or someone else equally close to him—saying that Robinson had been pleased to hear from me and wished me success in my work, which was a great deal for him to say.

Robinson was always aloof. He always looked ill. He was very pale and had this small mustache—not the Hitlerian kind, but still small—and a shrewd expression on his face, with the tiniest mouth, as I've said before, that I've ever seen: an ingrown type of person, who is not really meant to be a gregarious social being. It was a great effort for him to be with people. He was the most modest of men. He really had absolutely no vanity. It would have been good if he'd had a little more. In other words, I think he suffered from an extreme inferiority complex. Most shy people do, and I don't think all his fame—because he did have a great deal before his death—changed his opinion of his own work, which he probably knew, couldn't help knowing, was good, but perhaps felt wasn't *that* good. Very often a poet gets praise from the wrong quarters, and it all seems rather silly to him.

I don't know Marianne Moore well, but she certainly is the sweetest, kindest person who ever lived and also—although people laugh at me

Edward Arlington Robinson (courtesy of the Watkinson Library,
Trinity College, Hartford)

when I say this—a very modest person. She has said that she didn't know whether what she wrote was poetry. She didn't know what it was; it was something, but whatever it was, she said she didn't think that it was poetry. The great success that Marianne Moore has had is based upon many factors, one of them I think being her personality, that of a great person, a great human being. She answers every letter sent to her by the humblest person, saying something, very briefly, but she answers them all. Part of her appeal is the fact that this lonely little spinster woman—I say this without any derogation—is in a sense the Grandma Moses of modern poetry. Then, of course, she got her start with the intellectuals when T. S. Eliot said she was the only woman—and one of the few writers—in America doing something original in her form. Eliot wrote the introduction to her volume of *Selected Poems*. That's enough to put any poet on the map—just as in the old days, with musicians, if Wagner in his time said anything for you—— He didn't always. He and Liszt together listened to the work of a young composer, and when it was all over, Wagner turned to Liszt and said, "Nothing is lacking except talent."

I've known Marianne Moore only through meeting her at the National Institute and through telephone talks and meeting her at cocktail parties. She used to live in Brooklyn, and I've never been to her home in Brooklyn. She now lives in New York. She has said very nice things about my work. I don't think she cares particularly for it. How could she? It's so aural, compared to hers, the sort of thing she would rather avoid doing, I think. But she's very modest and very charitable toward all. I've had the pleasure of introducing her occasionally on the platform and writing a citation for her work, which I can genuinely admire for its qualities. She has been very pleased by this, very appreciative, which many people are not.

In connection with that, I think it's an amusing fact that I wrote the citation for Eliot when he got a Litt.D. at Princeton many years ago. Eliot had not suggested me; as I say, I knew him very slightly. Mr. Scribner, who of course was a great Princeton figure, said that they wanted the citation by someone who was a poet, and would I write the citation for Eliot on his getting this Doctor of Letters? And I did. Not in Latin, in English they wanted it. I think if Eliot had known that I'd written the citation, he mightn't have liked it. I don't think he had a very high opinion of my work, which has remained in the romantic tradition that he was so much against.

Edgar Lee Masters I knew very well. I didn't know him well until late in life—that is, late in his life. I did not know him during the early years when he was little known. He was a friend of Zoë Akins. Masters had enough feeling for poetry to discern the remarkable qualities in Sara Teasdale's work, and Masters and I met, I think, at first through an interchange of letters about some poem of Sara's. Masters had published, before I met him, his famous *Spoon River Anthology*. This again was a book that—— You might be riding in a Fifth Avenue bus and you'd see some man (you know, it's amazing for a man to be seen reading poetry) reading a book, and you'd look over his shoulder (you shouldn't do it, you know), and you'd find it was *Spoon River Anthology*.

I got to know Masters in his old age. He was a very unhappy man. He went on writing poetry, and some of it was quite interesting, rather influenced by Thomas Hardy; but he couldn't get anyone to publish most of it. He had published books of poems before *Spoon River*, which were, frankly, not very good. He had published the first one at his own expense, through the firm of Richard Badger and Co., a vanity publisher. But *Spoon River* was published by Macmillan and swept the country. It's a landmark in American poetry, not only because of its extraordinary humanity and its social significance, but also because Masters had a true dramatic sense; he could create character in very short poems.

I met Masters after this great success, when he was writing volume after volume of lyric poetry. He tried to recapture the success of *Spoon River* by issuing *Spoon River, Second Series*—which was a mistake. He should never have tried to do it again. It fell flat. He published another book called *Domesday Book*, which was somewhat along the same lines, the voices of the dead speaking from their graves, declaiming their own epitaphs as in the old Greek anthology. He was an unhappy man, very unhappy. He went to his grave without any of his later books being published, and they're not published today, and they never will be.

I think Masters must have left three or four complete, large manuscripts of books of poems, unpublished. However, I did succeed in getting Scribners to do three of his prose works.[35] He did a splendid biography of Vachel Lindsay, whom he greatly admired. It was a satirical book. It was called *A Poet in America*. It showed how Vachel was scorned and destroyed, allowed practically—he and his wife and children—to starve, and how he was forced into suicide by this, and then how later everyone rushed forward to peer and praise and to charge for going through the room where he'd worked and died. It was a very, very tragic and satiric book. It didn't have much success. Then Scribners went on and published a book of his on Walt Whitman, which was a good book but a failure, and still another book, I think on Mark Twain, which was not a good book. It was written when Masters was old and failing.

I used to go to see Lee, as he now had asked me to call him, at the old Chelsea Hotel where he was living. In his old age he was a combination of great sweetness and rather boorish manners. He'd been a lawyer. He'd never wanted to be anything but a poet, and he'd neglected his law practice much to the anguish of his wife—who, I think, had to put up with a great deal. Lee was a very vital man, and he married early in life a woman whom he outgrew. I'm sure she was a fine woman, but their marriage was not happy. He didn't make enough money. He was always writing poetry, which didn't pay, neglecting his law practice, and eventually he gave it up. I was glad that I did have a part in furthering his life and work on two occasions. One was when Lee was in hospital, desperately ill—I think it was lobar pneumonia—and penniless. I'd been to see him, and I knew what the situation was. I happened that year to be one of the judges of the Shelley Award, and I was able to get the award for him. There were two other judges, neither of whom wanted to give it to Edgar Lee Masters, and I got it for him by dint of making it clear what his plight was and what a fine poet he was. This prize is supposed to be given to people who are really in need, and it made all the difference. I think it was only $1,500, but that was a fortune to Lee at the time.

Then, again, I was able to help him get these prose works published by Scribners, and he received advances on them. We used to see each other a great deal, and I enjoyed our meetings. We talked mostly about poetry. I always met him at the Chelsea, because by then he had some difficulty in walking. I think he'd had a slight stroke. But he did come and have dinner with Phyllis and myself on several occasions, and also when we had other guests there, and his manners were very crude and sometimes even distressing. If he wanted to retire to the bathroom—the language he would use in asking permission to do so—he never hesitated in coming right out with it in a loud voice. I remember it was disturbing to Phyllis's mother, who was there on one occasion. I didn't mind it so much, except for the embarrassment of it.

Lee finally became quite old and had to undergo an operation. I don't remember whether it was the usual old man's operation, prostate, or what it was. I went to see him at the hospital, and I went especially to see him when he was afterwards relegated to a so-called nursing home outside New York, I think somewhere in the Bronx, where he was very unhappy and very lonely. It was a broken-down sort of place, the kind that a man

(Courtesy of Harry Ransom Humanities Research Center,
University of Texas, Austin)

would go to when he couldn't afford anything better—the dreariest place—and to see him really was tragic. I wasn't well enough off to arrange to have him properly taken care of, and none of his friends were.

However, he had got enormous comfort, the latter part of his life before his health had become so bad, from a young woman who appeared to have fallen in love with him. She was extremely attractive, unmarried, a young woman, I think who had lived quite freely but a fastidious person, too—no vulgarian. She just devoted herself to Lee. It was an extraordinary thing, a man so much older, and I would not have thought him a man that one could feel romantically about, but they had an affair, even though Masters was quite well on. Apparently he'd retained his virility remarkably into old age. And this was the one star in his heaven.

Lee had left his wife. This young woman also lived in the Hotel Chelsea, and she and Lee were together a great deal. She would be much of the time in his apartment, cook meals for him, take care of him, be mistress, mother, confidante: everything all in one. Lee was an amusing man— a bold, masculine type. She was brokenhearted when he died. She was the only one besides myself who went out and saw him at this nursing home, and she made gallant efforts to raise money to have him moved out of it.

Lee had left his wife and got a divorce a year before this, and he had remarried a schoolteacher, a typical schoolmarm—oh, my, a woman of the most terrific strong-minded, high-minded type. I think he must have been absolutely broke when he married her, absolutely desperate at entering old age with no prospects. She had enough money to take care of them both, and she was dazzled by Masters's great fame. And he had escaped from her. There was great bitterness of feelings. He had left her and gone to the Hotel Chelsea to live and made this very happy relationship with this young woman, who had a job and was self-supporting, but I don't think had any extra money. What Lee lived on while at the Chelsea, I do not know. Then he came out of this nursing home. He now really needed someone to take care of him all the time, every minute, and this young woman could not do it. And Lee had to go back to his wife—who had by then taken a great dislike to him and felt that he'd treated her abominably. She was that kind of a person, very vindictive. And there he was, bedridden and helpless, in her hands for the last years of his life.

Stark Young is a man whom I knew only late in life. In fact, my friendship with Stark Young was due almost entirely to my wife. Stark did not like women. He belonged to that division of mankind which might be called the third sex or, as my wife calls them, "the chosen sex." He took a strong dislike to most women. My wife was one of the few exceptions; he admired her erudition, her love of art, and, not least, her wit. I became Stark's editor at Scribners, and we got along famously.

Stark Young was certainly the top critic of the theater in his day, but he also had great talent for writing itself on any subject. While I was his editor he wrote a book called *The Pavilion*.[36] This was his autobiography— so amusing, written with such economy, never laboring anything. He didn't bother to follow any chronological sequence. Most amusing, delightful book, and a great deal more than that.

As his editor I used to come and see Stark at his apartment, which was right down this street, Fifty-seventh Street, a little nearer to Second Avenue, on the same side of the street, where he lived very happily for many years with a most delightful, lovable man, William McKnight Bowman— or Wales, as we all called him, because in youth he'd looked a good deal like the Prince of Wales. It was like a marriage. Stark was a heavy drinker. Bowman kept him from harming himself with drink. When Stark came here alone without Bowman on one occasion he did disgrace himself completely by drinking much too much. It was terribly embarrassing for Phyllis and me. I had to put Stark to bed here, and it was a dreadful occasion because he had lost control of all his bodily functions. It was most unpleasant. Phyllis made some coffee, and I got Stark to drink it. When he revived and could speak, he said, "I know you are going to tell Wales. You'll tell Wales about this." I said, "Of course I won't tell him about it." "Will you promise me that?" I said, "Yes." "Your promise will be just like everybody else's. So many people have promised me that, and they've always gone and told Wales." He said, "I couldn't bear to have Wales told." Stark was so devoted to this man, and this man had been so good to him and so concerned about him—the only person who really cared about him, keeping him away from this sort of thing—that it would be like offending God, almost, to offend Wales. I promised him that I would never mention it, and I never did, and my wife never did, although we used to see Wales quite often alone. And that won us Stark's friendship.

I did give Stark some ideas when he submitted, as he occasionally did, some of his poems to me. He'd always written poems. He never published any, because he had no particular—— He didn't think of himself as a professional poet, so I could be quite frank with him. He thought that some of my suggestions were good. But as for giving Stark suggestions on his own real work, he was not the kind of writer that one could give suggestions to or ideas, any more than you would have given them to Hemingway, or any more than you would, as an editor, have edited Stark or Ernest. Or Santayana, for that matter. Because when the material came in it had already been revised many times. It was in final form.

They were very professional writers and artists, all of them, with that terrific conscience a real artist has. I've often thought that a very good definition of an artist would be "Somebody who does things the way they should be done"—because most of the work of the world is done in a very slipshod manner. The work isn't interesting enough to demand more than that. I mean, clerks in a post office or businessmen usually do whatever they think it's necessary to do to get by. An artist does the thing the way it should be done—that's all. It must be done the way it should be done, in the absolute sense of the word. A writer like Stark would, I'm sure, although he never talked about this, take a sentence and rearrange it in all the different ways that it could be rearranged before deciding which one was the right one. He would go over it, revise a thing three or four times. He didn't quite go to the extreme that George Moore, the English writer, went to. After he had finished all his revisions, he would translate his book into French, as he said, "pass it through the filter of another language," then put it aside, come back to it, read it in French, and translate it back into a fresh English version. I suppose he felt it gained something from this. Well, these maniacs—of course, all artists are maniacs when it comes to trying to achieve perfection—sometimes get very fine results by their most peculiar methods.

Stark—I don't know whether this is peculiar to homosexuals—did have a certain malice in his nature. We had lunch together quite often, and sometimes we would be sitting—— We used to go to a place which is still running in New York called Maria's. Stark was something of a gourmet—always, you know, running down American food and American restaurants. As I was saying, we would sometimes find ourselves sitting next to a table where there was a couple having a romantic luncheon together, and on those occasions Stark would always manage, in the course of his conversation, to bring in four-letter words—all the four-letter words that there are—so that I was wincing and quivering in anguish. Imagine, these young people, so nearby, subjected to this! The first time he did it, I spoke to Stark about it.

"What's the difference?" he said. "I should worry. I'm going to say whatever I want to say." I pressed it still further, and he was offended. So on later occasions, it made it very trying for me. All I could do was to try my best to distract his attention. But he did it deliberately. It was a form of brutality. Malice. He did the same in talking about friends of mine. He seemed to want to convince me that everyone in the world was a homosexual. He had a great animus against Edward Sheldon because he claimed that Edward Sheldon, by getting engaged to Doris Keane at a time when he was already stricken with this terrible disease, interfered with her career. Then he went on to say, "Anyway, he should never have got engaged; he was a homosexual."

I'd say, "Ned homosexual? You're crazy. He was no more a homosexual than Stalin was, not that I'm comparing him——" "So was Stalin," said

Stark. "Didn't you know that?" I said, "Then I suppose the next thing you'll be telling me that Max Perkins is." "He is, he is," said Stark. "Why don't these people come out honestly with it? I believe in honesty," he said. "I hate these people that pretend———" And this was a form of brutality, too. He never dared to tell me that I was one. I think he thought that would be too absurd. But everyone that I knew apparently was. Edward Sheldon was, and Max Perkins was. So finally I asked him a very irreverent question. I said, "The next thing you'll be telling me that Jesus Christ was." "He was!" said Stark. "It's well known that he was. He never got married." And so on.

Well, that's just one side of him. He was a man of absolute courage, absolutely forthright about things. He was not a man who would say, out of politeness, what he didn't really mean, which is an unusual trait, sometimes very unpleasant, but it has its admirable side. He was pretty contemptuous of almost everyone, so that his friendship, when he really gave it, was quite an honor, and when he once gave you his friendship he was a very loyal friend. We became very fond of him. I think he was really more devoted to Phyllis than he was to me, and this is extraordinary, because he had no use for most women. But Phyllis was learned in things that Stark was learned in—old Italian theater and architecture—and this was amazing to Stark to think that any woman should know about these things. He was always making fun of women, and his favorite phrase, remember, was, "I had so-and-so here the other day" (some well-known actress)—"stupid goose!"—because she didn't know about certain things, because she got certain things wrong. Some famous actresses are not learned—why should they be? They don't have to be erudite. I remember Phyllis and I had drinks with Zoë Akins one day in the later years when Zoë was staying at the Ritz-Carlton that used to be on Madison Avenue, and while we were there, Helen Hayes, Tallulah Bankhead, and some other well-known actress who was playing in *The Glass Menagerie*—I can't remember her name*— came in for drinks, and Phyllis and I met them. They seemed the most elementary people as far as ideas are concerned. Their talk was mostly gossip about the theater. It doesn't follow that because you are a famous actress, you are an intellectual, but Stark was always making fun of them.

Then Stark had a stroke, and a pretty bad one. It was one of those cases where a certain part of the brain was destroyed, in Stark's case the part that is able to interpret type. He'd take up a book and look at it, and the printed words just didn't mean anything anymore. And then he would

---

*Julie Haydon.

cry. It frightened him. He could understand spoken words. That's a different brain center. But he couldn't remember names anymore. Wales would bring him over here. Sometimes Stark would say, "I want to—— I want to—— I want to see my neighbors." He couldn't remember the name Wheelock, but Wales knew what he meant, and Wales would bring him over here and prepare to come upstairs with him. "No, I want to go up alone," Stark would say. He would come over bringing a bouquet of flowers for Phyllis, and he couldn't remember her name, but when he came in the front door he would say, "For my neighbor," as he handed her the bouquet. He knew who she was, but he couldn't remember her name.

He lived on in this condition for about three years, and I have never seen anything more touching or more beautiful than the devotion of his friend William McKnight Bowman. Wales was an architect. He had to give up his business for the time being. Stark became so helpless that he had to be in a wheelchair. Wales would take him out in that wheelchair every morning and afternoon. He'd wait on Stark hand and foot, take care of him in every possible way, with infinite love and tenderness, and was with him when Stark died. He had finally had to be hospitalized. There never was devotion between man and woman more beautiful or touching or profound than the devotion of these two men to each other, and especially the fostering devotion of Wales, who was slightly younger than Stark.

Stark was not greatly given to appreciating the work of other people. He was rather egocentric. When he found anything that he could sincerely like, it would usually be some image or some—you know, one detail of the poem. He never expressed any particular admiration for my work, that I can remember.

The last memory I have of Stark is not an unpleasant one—very characteristic. It was on his eightieth birthday. Oh, I had met him often in the street in a wheelchair, but this is the last time we'd been to his home, at 320 East Fifty-seventh, and Wales had arranged with the greatest care this party, with all these friends, for Stark's eightieth birthday, and all these gifts had been brought. Stark sat in a wheelchair enjoying the whole thing hugely, although he couldn't remember the names of any of the people, and Wales would read his birthday messages to him, because now Stark couldn't read. I remember, when the other guests had gone, Stark had asked Phyllis and myself to stay. Wales was out of the room for a moment. Stark was able to move his arms. He reached down under the chair and fetched up a pint bottle of bourbon and drained practically half of it off and then quickly put it down again underneath his wrapper or wherever it was. Forbidden by Wales. Just, of course, the worst thing he could have done, for a man who's had a stroke is not, I believe, supposed to drink that much. But the mischievous look on his face as he did it! That was his *real* birthday gift, to himself.

Stark died some time after that, and just the other day Wales died. He came here to dinner with us last week. He seemed himself, perfectly normal, and there were other friends here, and Wales was charming. He went home that night and was found dead in his bed—died in his sleep that very night. He had a very bad cough. He was an incessant smoker of cigarettes, and I spoke to him about it. I said, "Wales, if you don't mind my saying so, you really have a bad cough there. I notice every time you light up a cigarette it makes it worse. Couldn't you cut down a little bit?" He changed the subject, didn't want to hear about it.

After Stark's death Wales moved heaven and earth to have a memorial service worthy of Stark Young. Stark, like many other writers, had gone out of fashion and was neglected in his old age. But there was a small cult that worshiped him as a writer on the theater. Wales got up this memorial service which took place in one of the theaters, I've forgotten which, downtown, and he was able to get all of Stark's old friends together for it. Martha Graham, for instance, came and Harold Clurman and Kim Novak and John Gielgud, a great friend and admirer of Stark's. And I was asked to read from one of Stark Young's books. I chose something from his novel, *So Red the Rose,* the one book of his which has had a really popular sale and gone into paperback, a beautiful, beautiful novel about the South.

At this memorial service, before we went on stage, before the curtain rose, I saw Martha Graham, whom I'd never met before, standing, looking perfectly unconcerned, leaning up against part of the scenery, and John Gielgud was near her. I went up to her and said, "I wish I felt as calm as you do. I'm out of my depth here with all these great stars of the theater." "Calm?" she said. "I'm just trembling from head to foot! I always am, before I go on." And Gielgud said he was in the same condition. He held out his hand. It was shaking like an aspen leaf. Then I knew that my nervousness was nothing unusual. I asked Sir John, "Have you felt like this every time you went on throughout your lifetime?" "Every single time," he said, "you go through this. And if you didn't, you'd be no good." I can see now how tremendous the temptation must have been for people like John Barrymore to fortify themselves beforehand, so as to avoid this. I asked Gielgud, "Don't you think it's bad for your heart action and circulation, to

Stark Young (courtesy of *Dictionary of Literary Biography*)

get into this condition so often?" "Not at all," he said, "Doesn't do you the slightest harm. It's purely functional, purely a reflex." It was a beautiful service, and all managed with such love by Wales. What a true friend. He spent the rest of his time trying to keep Stark's memory alive.

I met Charles Bedaux by virtue of being an editor at Scribners. Just to give a little of his background, Bedaux was a Frenchman who had begun as a poor boy and had worked on the subways in Paris. He had been what's known as a sandhog, working on the construction of new branches of the subway. Later, by reason of his invention of a system called the Bedaux

Efficiency System, which was bought by industrialists all over the world—a system and method of organizing work that produces a speedup without the workers' realizing what they are being maneuvered into—he made a fortune. He was a millionaire many times over.

Bedaux brought in the manuscript of a novel he had written, one of those baroque novels that he loved, an extraordinary thing, set back in the Middle Ages and full of barbarities, castles, dungeons, tortures, and so on. It was absolutely impossible from a publisher's point of view, and I turned it down. He wasn't satisfied. I didn't, frankly, know then who this Charles Bedaux was. He called me up and, in a most courteous manner, wondered whether it wouldn't be possible for me to talk to him and tell him why we'd turned his book down. He said, "I'm interested in going on with my writing." Well, I didn't want to. You know, it's very painful, trying to explain why you turned a book down, and the author always tries to persuade you that you made a mistake. However, he said, "Have lunch with me." I finally said yes. What else could I do? He was so friendly. I said, "Where shall I meet you?" "Where else," Bedaux said, "than at Jack and Charlie's?" I don't know whether it's still in existence—one of these very expensive places. We met there, and we talked about his writing.

I discovered in the course of our conversation that Bedaux was a tremendous admirer of Thomas Wolfe's work. He read him and read him and read him, and he said that about once a week he and his wife would take a real rest. They would stay in bed for a whole day, and he would read aloud to her from Thomas Wolfe, and she would read aloud to him from some French writer, and they would just enjoy being completely cut off from the world. He particularly loved Wolfe's *Of Time and the River*. He said, "I don't know how many times I've read that aloud to Fern."

Bedaux wanted to have other luncheons, and I enjoyed having lunch with him. He talked about himself, and we talked politics, and he said, "Of course, you know that there's a big change going on in the world. You've seen what Hitler is doing, and you see what Roosevelt is doing in this country. Franklin D. Roosevelt has become a dictator in this country, and all this idea about democracy is sheer nonsense. The whole world is going to go Fascist." And he added, "You will see that the Duke of Windsor, the erstwhile King of England, is going to return to the throne, be recalled to the throne by his people as dictator." I said, "Do you know him?" "Know him?" he said. "He's one of my closest friends." I said, "Do you know Hitler?" "Hitler's a dear friend of mine," he said. "I have a house in Berchtesgaden, right next to his. Yes, indeed, we're old friends." I said, "Is Hitler an attractive man?" "He's a *fascinating* man," he said. "Don't you know how children love him? He's got that magnetic charm that a man of genius has. The tenderest-hearted man in the world. But he's politically wise. He knows that brutality is necessary. The world——Democracy won't work." I said, "I can't agree with you on that. I'm a Jeffersonian Democrat." "All the worse for you," he said. "It's going to go very hard with people like you in the days that are coming. I'm sorry for you. I hope you will read and change your opinions. I'm sure you're an intelligent man, and that you won't stick to one idea."

Then I recalled that my Uncle Tom, Thomas Hall, who had been professor at Union Theological Seminary, in New York—my mother's favorite brother—had married a German woman, married the daughter of the professor of botany at the University of Göttingen and that he and his wife had returned every summer to the house which she inherited there. He had been Roosevelt Exchange Professor in Göttingen and had retired there after his wife's death until recently he had died. He had left a will in which he bequeathed a small legacy to a cousin of his wife's, a woman who had married a Russian, lived in Czarist Russia, lost everything in the Revolution there, and then had come back to Germany, after her husband's death and was now working in a department store in Hamburg to make a living. Uncle Tom had helped this cousin a good deal. She was a baroness, Baroness Cari von Englehart. He had left her this small legacy in his will. I was co-executor of his estate, together with the Bank of New York, and the Bank of New York had looked into the situation, and they had told me, "According to German law under Hitler, the estate of your uncle is taxed fully in Germany, not only that part of it which is in Germany—the house and land he owned there—but his entire estate, including his American stocks and bonds. This, in addition to the U.S. inheritance tax, will be so heavy that there will be no money left for the legacy. That will be the first thing that will have to go. This woman will get nothing." I said, "That's dreadful. Surely something can be done."

Now I thought of this problem, and I spoke to Bedaux about it. "Don't say another word," he said. "I'll take care of that for you. Now, I tell you what you do—you know German?" I said, "Yes." "You write German?" "Yes, I can write German." "Write me a letter in triplicate. Put the whole situation before me, the need of this woman, the way German estate law operates to wipe out her legacy, and send me those three typewritten copies. Sign them yourself before a witness. Then don't ask me any further questions. I assure you that the woman will get her legacy."

I did this. Nothing happened for about—oh, I think nearly a year. In the meantime, I'd written letters to the Baroness von Englehart and suggested that she leave Germany for Switzerland. I hoped I might be able to get the legacy to her there. She wrote me back a frightened letter, which she had mailed outside the German borders—I don't know whether she'd gone to Holland or what—"Never write to me again if you're going to touch on any of these subjects. It's extremely dangerous. One letter that you wrote me—if it had fallen into certain hands, and everything is censored, though not too efficiently—might have led to my arrest, trial, and possible execution. Evasion of taxes is now a capital offense in Germany." That ended any efforts on my part to get the legacy to her. I had suggested her coming to the United States. That was impossible, it seemed.

But before the year was up, while at work in my office at Scribners, I was told that there was a gentleman to see me. His card indicated that he was a representative of a bank in Den Hague, which is The Hague, and I went out to see him, and he asked me for identification. Fortunately I had on me my Blue Cross identification card or something of that sort. I was identified. And he said, "Can we go somewhere where we can talk quietly?" I took him into the library, and he said, "I have arranged matters so that the Baroness von Englehart will receive her legacy in full." He said, "The way we do it is this. This legacy will not be paid in ordinary German marks, because those marks would only just suffice to pay the full tax on your uncle's estate, but we are paying it in a thing called *Speermarken*—it's too involved to explain, but we get around the difficulty in this way; we are not breaking any German law. I have had the personal permission of Herr Hitler and of Hjalmar Schacht in this matter. And I can assure you that this will go through. But before it goes through, you will have to trust me. It is necessary that I have in advance your receipt as executor."

I said, "Well, my receipt alone won't be satisfactory. I shall have to get also the receipt of the co-executor of the Bank of New York." So I went and had a talk down there—its only four blocks down from Scribners—while this man waited for my return. The people at the bank were terribly impressed with my power as an executor. I didn't have time to explain it to them. I have since told them about it. But I persuaded them finally that there was nothing to lose. "If we don't do this, the baroness will get nothing. If we do do it, she may or she may not get the legacy." So they signed and I signed. About a month after that, I got a letter from the baroness, saying she was very happy, that she had received her legacy, and that all was well. She had bought an annuity. It wasn't a big legacy. She was quite old, perhaps seventy-five, and she had given up her job in the department store. She had enough money to live on from this annuity.

This was the beginning of the war, the Second World War. The Baroness Cari von Englehart had enough time left to enjoy her annuity for about two years; then when the American blockbusters bombed Hamburg, she, with several thousand other people, perhaps a hundred thousand, I don't know, took refuge in the Hamburg subways, and the blockbuster bombs landed right on the subways, and they were all destroyed. Legacy and all.

Bedaux submitted other books, but there was no agreement. There was no quid pro quo. I'd told him that, right off the reel. I said, "You know, Mr. Bedaux, we'd like to publish a book of yours and we very well might, but this kindness on your part is———" "Oh, no, no, don't," he said, "I'm not that kind of a person at all. I'd just like to help you out, and I'd like to show you what kind of a man Hitler is, that he has humane———"

Bedaux had an office in New York, and I had lunch with him there quite often. It was at the very top of the Chrysler Building, right up in the tower there, most romantic place, just as in his baroque novels. You would look out and see these gargoyles, these strange figures that are at the top of the Chrysler tower. He had this little hideaway up there, and he would bring out his books. He really had the feeling of a writer. But the next thing that happened was that Bedaux was to bring the Duke of Windsor to this country for a speaking tour, and it was all noised about in the newspapers. Then objections were raised by the labor unions here. They said that if Bedaux came over with the Duke of Windsor, his life would not be safe, and the Duke of Windsor's life would not be safe. The association was a very unfortunate one, from the point of view of labor. They hated this speedup system. The whole thing was called off.

Then I lost track of Bedaux until I took up *The New York Times* one day and read that Charles Bedaux, a United States citizen, had been arrested in France on the charge of trading with the enemy. A later issue of the *Times* said that this had obviously been a mistake; Bedaux was a good loyal citizen of the United States, and the whole thing was going to be dropped. Much as I hated to do it, I felt that it was my duty to write to Cordell Hull, then Secretary of State. I wrote and told him exactly what I knew about Charles Bedaux, and Hull wrote back saying, "This is most interesting information; we're very glad to have it." Later I was visited at Scribners by two agents from the United States Intelligence Department. They interviewed me for several hours and took notes. My action was one I have never been able to feel very happy about. Bedaux was arrested. He was brought back to this country for trial for treason, and on the way over he committed suicide. Every time I go by the Chrysler Building, I think of that office where Bedaux gave me such good lunches and was so kind to me. And yet he was a snake in the grass.

[20 March 1967]

I KNEW ALAN SEEGER WELL. He was a good deal younger than I was. I met him at college. Alan was the younger brother of one of my closest friends, Charles Seeger, the musician, who later became professor of music at the University of California and was at one time well known as a very modern composer in the twelve-tone scale. In any case, the thing that interests me in the case of Alan Seeger is something you find in a great many poets, a tremendous death wish. Now, why poets, who are so much aware of life and in love with life and intoxicated by life—why they should have so strong a death wish is hard to understand. Perhaps the two things are bound up with each other, death being an inevitable part of every life.

Alan Seeger is a good case in point. His desire to enter the Foreign Legion before we had gone into the war at all was, partly at least, the expression of a desire for death. Alan was living in France at the time the war broke out. He had gone there after very unsuccessful years in New York. He was not suited to holding a job or doing any routine thing, and in France, as soon as the war broke out, he enlisted in the Foreign Legion and was sent to the front. His one wish, expressed in all his letters and poems, was that he might have the privilege of dying for France. He exposed himself unnecessarily, took on all the most daring missions that other men rather sidestepped, and eventually, as you know, after having written his best-known poem, "I Have a Rendezvous with Death," was killed in a bayonet charge. I've forgotten the name of the place right now, but I think it was at Belloy-en-Santerre. Alan was found dead with his rifle stuck in the ground, the bayonet stuck in the ground, and a white cloth tied to the stock, in the hope that this would attract the attention of stretcher bearers, but he had died before they came.

Here is one case in point of a romantic and a poet, a most interesting character, who had the promise in him of very fine things to come, yet seemed to want to die. He had never been happy or at rest until those years when he was at the front. I couldn't say a great deal more about Alan Seeger. We all know that he was a poet, and we know that he wrote very much in the old tradition. He was a scholar, too, and much influenced by early French and English poets. Alan never married. In fact, I don't know how old he was when he died, but I shouldn't have thought it was much more than twenty-five or twenty-six, and he was penniless and not willing to hold a job of any kind whatsoever. Supported by his father and mother, who were very anxious for him to get on his own feet.

Then I think of other men, other poets. All of them for different reasons somehow or other found it necessary to end their lives prematurely. I think particularly, for instance, of Delmore Schwartz, a poet not only of great promise but of genuine achievement. Delmore's difficulty was one that many poets suffer from: he had a tremendous ego. He felt that he was not only a good poet but a very great and important poet. And when, after years of some success, instead of the success continuing, it fell off, and he lost his vogue—other poets came along who seemed to interest the public more—and he disappeared from the scene, that is, from any important position in the literary world, it was more than he could take. He was a morbidly sensitive man. Also, he suffered from not having any money and refusing to take a job, or when he did take one he wouldn't keep it. Delmore got more and more sorry for himself and more and more desperate and more and more depressed, until finally he destroyed himself.*

I knew Delmore Schwartz because he used to go regularly—that's when I met him—to a New Year's Eve party given by Margaret Marshall, who for many years was editor of the *Nation*, the old *Nation*, and is a writer herself. Many writers and especially poets used to gather there, and I saw something of Delmore then. He came to the Scribners offices sometimes to see me to ask advice about the practical side of things.

Then, a great friend of Sara Teasdale's, Marguerite Wilkinson, herself a poet—— Her reason for suicide was one which I'm told is quite common, although it seems very bizarre to me. Marguerite committed suicide because she was afraid of death. She couldn't bear living with the prospect of death inevitably looming on the horizon. The process of death frightened her. She used often to say, "How does one go about it?" And I used to tell her, "You don't have to go about it. It goes about you. You probably won't know when you're dying, any more than you knew when you were being born"—which, by the way, must be a much more drastic experience than dying. We all dread death, of course. We wouldn't go on living if we didn't. The very core of every living thing is the absolute determination to

---

*Schwartz died from a heart attack that may have been induced by a combination of drugs and alcohol.

go on living. It's useless to worry about death, but it was a neurosis with Marguerite Wilkinson. She just couldn't think of anything else. She couldn't sleep at night for the fear of it. Being a very courageous Spartan woman of New England heredity, she did what Goethe used to do. Goethe, you remember, used to go up to the top of the highest buildings and look down because he was afraid of heights, and he went mountaineering and so on. So Marguerite did all the most dangerous things. She would go down to Coney Island and swim and swim very far out, testing herself to see whether she could get back again. She did other daring things. She was happily married to a very fine man who taught at New York University. But one day she went down to Coney Island on this test of courage—she was particularly afraid of the water—and swam out too far. And we shall never know whether she did it on purpose or not, but she drowned.

Others come to mind who had this same—not really feeling so much as, apparently, an absolute necessity to commit suicide. Life seemed to narrow down for them, the way it does for cattle in the stockyard when they go to slaughter. The passage gets narrower and narrower and narrower until finally there is no escape, no way of turning aside, and there is nothing ahead but death.

John Gould Fletcher was another suicide. Fletcher was one of the best known of the Imagist poets. He and Amy Lowell and H. D. (Hilda Doolittle) and Richard Aldington and Ezra Pound and R. S. Flint made up the movement called Imagism. Fletcher was one of the most successful of the group, one of the best. He was a strange man, not as attractive as some other poets have been—frankly, something of a bore because of his complete unawareness of the state of mind of people around him. Van Wyck Brooks told me how Fletcher had come to call on him without an invitation one day when Fletcher was in Westport, where Van Wyck and his first wife were living at the time. He came, he said, just for a half hour's chat. He stayed for four or five days, without having been invited, because he wouldn't stop talking about the genealogy of his family, the Fletcher family, which had taken on enormous importance in his mind. Van Wyck Brooks and Eleanor Brooks found it a little bit hard to take.

Fletcher was born in Little Rock, Arkansas. He married twice, I think, the last time to a woman older than himself, an Englishwoman, a very fine woman, who stood in relation to him, I should say, more as a mother than as a wife. In any event, there was a pond on his place, and one day John Gould Fletcher, for no reason that anyone could assign at the time, no immediate reason—he had appeared perfectly cheerful—walked slowly out into that pond until the waters closed over his head. He didn't know how to swim, and he drowned.

Orrick Johns was one of the small St. Louis group of poets. He was talented and made some impression at the time. His poems were semi-humorous and were widely published. He did labor under the handicap of having lost a leg, I forget how. He had an artificial leg which he found very unromantic and which bothered him a good deal. Orrick was a young man when he killed himself. Just how he did it, I don't know, but I remember Sara Teasdale being very much upset about it. And I was, too. He was one of the first of that group who had written me such enthusiastic letters about my first book, *The Human Fantasy*, and I felt as if he were a man who really knew what I was trying to do.

Then, one of the most tragic cases of all was a young poet who, I still insist, although he's now completely forgotten, had great talent. His name was Walter Stone. In one of my annual volumes called *Poets of Today* I included Walter Stone's book.[37] Beautiful work, and quite his own, although in the tradition. There is just as good work done, and just as individual work done, within the tradition as among the experimental poets. Beethoven revolutionized the symphony, but Bach wrote great music in the forms that were to hand for him in his time. And William Butler Yeats, who wrote in the traditional forms, is certainly just as great a poet, I would say, as Walt Whitman, who wrote in revolutionary forms of his own. Tennyson had just as much talent, although he wrote in the traditional forms, indeed, a good deal more talent than so good a poet as e. e. cummings, who did things in an entirely new way.

Stone wrote within the tradition, but his work was highly individual, and I was very much impressed by it and published him in this volume. I think one of his difficulties may have been that he was terribly in love with his wife, Ruth Stone, who is also a poet and in some ways a more brilliant poet than Walter and more appreciated than Walter was because she was more experimental, more "in the movement," as they say. Also I think that she perhaps was the one who turned the other cheek. He was the one who was in love, and she was the one who accepted it all and wasn't particularly excited about it. At least, that's the impression I got when I met her and saw them together.

Walter had received a scholarship, I believe, or a foundation award, I forget which, that took them to England, and he was working very hard in London to get a Ph.D., which he badly needed to bolster his teaching career. While he was working on this night and day in London, his wife,

Ruth Stone, was off somewhere with the children. I think they had three daughters. And Walter was left rather alone. I don't know, perhaps his thesis wasn't going well, and he knew that his wife was having a book published by Harcourt, Brace, a book of her own,[38] while the best he could do was to be one of three poets in one of the volumes in my *Poets of Today* series. He got depressed. His poetry was full of the love of life, but he took his belt from his trousers, twisted it around a door knob, and managed to kneel down in such a position as to strangle himself to death. Horrible!

■ ■ ■ ■

I was Cardinal Spellman's editor, and it was an interesting experience. I think the first book of Spellman's that Scribners issued was a book of prayers. After that his real secret hope and almost passion was discovered: he wanted to be a poet. That was the one thing Cardinal Spellman wanted more than anything else. He'd written verse all his life. He showed me his poems. I have the greatest respect for Cardinal Spellman. I think he's an absolutely sincere man, an extremely able man, a very hard-working churchman, and a great asset to the church because of his enormous administrative and business ability. That may not be the thing that you think is particularly appropriate for a cardinal, but after all, a cardinal, the head of a diocese such as the archdiocese of New York, is running a big business, and he has, in addition to his other duties, to raise large sums of money every year for the running of the organization, the machine, of which he is the head. Spellman is a spiritual man in his own way in that he sacrifices the trappings of spirituality for really doing something for his church.

The first time I met Cardinal Spellman he amazed me. I was asked to have lunch at the residence, at the Cardinalcy there on Madison Avenue, and I came in and was met by several priests. There were one or two others coming to lunch that day, two bishops, I think. I was the only layman. The cardinal had not yet come in. Finally the small, round, chubby figure of Cardinal Spellman, considerably overweight and rather short, came in with his chin over the top of a pile of packages. I remember the top one was Fig Newtons. And his first remark as he entered the room carrying these packages—these were things he had bought for the household—his first remark as he entered the room was, "Well, how's the market doing today? What's U.S. Steel doing today?" I thought it a most extraordinary opening remark for a Prince of the Church.

However, I became very fond of him. Sometimes when I would go to see him and was waiting in his study, he would come in through a side door from the cathedral, just covered with perspiration and exhausted from the service that he'd been conducting. He really did the work—I think still does—of two or three men. He has the great faculty of getting other people to work for him. He called his priests "my boys with the round collars." He said, "I keep them right up to snuff. I don't stand for any nonsense from any of them."

Cardinal Spellman would show me these poems of his with an almost childlike reverence for me as a poet—me, a younger man who didn't have any of the abilities that he had or his exalted office. He seemed to feel that the most important thing of all was to be able to write good verse. I used to be perfectly straightforward with him. I would even have to correct his meter. His ear was so—when it came to verse—so elementary that he was capable of writing a line that was not metrical, in a form where such a line would stand out like a sore thumb because it didn't conform to the measure that he'd chosen for the poem.

However, His Eminence seemed to take some interest in me as a human being, too, because when I was in the hospital—with nothing serious; I think it was phlebitis—he sent me a most magnificent—— I believe they're called floral emblems, a whole little stand that a flowering vine was growing on, monstrously expensive things. On his card was written, "For John Hall Wheelock, prayerfully, solicitously." I think Cardinal Spellman had hope that he might influence me. He knew from my poems that I was not an orthodox believer, and yet he knew that I was not a negative person, and perhaps he thought that I was ripe for conversion.

We have remained friends. I used to work with him over these poems. I would take them home with me and sometimes do elementary work on them, simply correcting the meter and pointing out the false application of certain words he'd got wrong in his mind. He had, for instance, the idea that "fulsome" was a word of praise. He would write "the fulsome love of God"—but of course, "fulsome" means insincere and excessive. I'd have to point out things like that. Also his sense of the word "gracious" was very strange. But he was a humble man, truly humble, and I suppose humility is perhaps the greatest quality any human being can have, and one of the rarest—genuine humility, not the pride that apes humility, as the phrase goes. He did have genuine humility, and he had this burning desire to be a poet.

Sometimes I would be going home from work at the end of the day, and I would pass up Madison Avenue by the Cardinal's residence, and Cardinal Spellman would come running out into the street, come behind me and take me by the arm and turn me around—"Could you come back for just a little while? I wrote a new poem last night." He'd lie awake all night working on a poem—this busy man. I would always, if I could, if I didn't have other engagements, come back to his study. He'd hand me the new poem and then sit, absolutely motionless, with his eyes fastened on me, intent, waiting for the good word, you know. I'd try to say something nice about the poem.

Well, the books were published. Scribners didn't feel that they could say on the jacket of a book by Cardinal Spellman that this was the work of a poet, but we could say that here was very serious and sincere verse by a great churchman. What made them worth publishing was the fact that they had a big sale. He never kept a penny of any of the money earned by his books. It all went to the Foundling Hospital which he had started; he kept nothing for himself.

I remember sometimes, frankly, going home by some way other than Madison Avenue, for fear that Cardinal Spellman would come out and seize me when I was in rather a hurry. But he was a dear man—is a dear man and a brave man—and suffered the most cruel reviews of his work. I too was made fun of by certain poets and critics who wrote, "This is Wheelock's idea of poetry; he's fostering the work of Cardinal Spellman." But Cardinal Spellman took it all in his stride. His humility protected him. He knew that he was not really a poet. For a long time he made it a habit, on public occasions, to recite his poems instead of making a speech. I don't think he could even recite his poems; he had to read, and people found this very trying; they used to dread the occasions when the Cardinal did it. Somebody must have told him about this, and he never did it again. He stopped writing verse. He's given it up.

I see Cardinal Spellman occasionally, and he always sends me a Christmas card. He has said flattering things about me. He evidently thought I was kind, and he told Mr. Scribner. Mr. Scribner was very much amused—this was Charles Scribner III, and he'd seen another side of me, and we'd had drinks together—but Cardinal Spellman always insisted, "That noble creature, John Hall Wheelock." I suppose I appeared so to him because I never got impatient and because I like him. He's an honest man and a good man and a man who was cursed with this ambition to do something that he could never really do very well. What poet is there who doesn't wonder whether perhaps he's not in the same case? For we all think what we do is good, you know, while it remains to be seen whether it is or not.

Another churchman of a very different stamp was a man that I met because he, like myself, used to spend his summers in East Hampton, Paul Tillich, the great Protestant theologian. We had many things in common. In the first place, I was greatly drawn to his book called *The Shaking of the Foundations*,[39] the book in which he describes what has happened to the modern world. He compares religion—which he defines loosely as some sort of ultimate concern with what life is about and what the universe is about—to a cement that has held the bricks of society together. He was very broad. He felt that the honest doubters were nearer to God than the extremely straitlaced orthodox people who look down their noses at those who have doubts. In fact, he felt that to doubt and to wonder about things that no one can really know about definitely was a sign very often that you were more religious than the hard-boiled orthodox were.

In this book Tillich shows very dramatically how what is happening to the world is the shaking of the foundations, the foundations that were based upon certain ethical and moral principles which derived from divine sanctions. If you tell a man that he's got to do thus and so because the mayor said so or because you said so or because the president said so, he can always come back and say, "Well, what of it? I'm just as good as he is." But if he believes that God said so, then it's unanswerable. When this cement of faith which bound society together, a society in which people were willing to cooperate and some to play a less important role than others because they all were brothers and they all believed in the ultimate meaning of life, when that cement crumbled away, then you got the shaking of the foundations and the sort of thing we're going through.

We had another bond, Tillich and I, in that I speak German and have been a student in Germany, and of course he was a typical North German Protestant, a fine-looking man, very big and also very serious, painfully so at times, very sincere, with a most attractive wife, Hannah, who just lived for him and to help him in his work. Tillich was, like many Germans, a prodigious worker. During the last years of his life, I saw a great deal of him. It was a time when he was worried because he'd had a heart attack and had now been chosen to deliver a very important theological address in Geneva and another one at the University of Chicago. Also his major work was in process, a three-volume work which outlined his principles and his system of thought.[40] He felt that he had these tremendous opportunities before him and that his strength was failing. Tillich was then approaching eighty, but he got all those things done. He went out to—I don't remember whether it was Geneva, now, but anyway it was a very great opportunity. It was the city in which the great Kant had once delivered the same lecture and other famous men, after him. Tillich completed his great work, his three-volume work, his magnum opus, and he delivered both the lectures, the one in Chicago and the one in this European center, and then he died. It was wonderful that he was able to do it all.

I must tell one story about Tillich that shows his other side. He was a man who would take a drink with the best of them, and he could enjoy humor too, although he was pretty serious for the most part. He used to sit on the beach at East Hampton under a beach umbrella in the blazing sun. I would sit and talk to him, and all sorts of young men would come up, disciples of his. Sometimes they were houseguests, young budding theologians, and they would argue with Tillich all day—metaphysics, theology, and so on.

I got talking to Tillich about his method of composition. Did he find in working that it was the same as when you are writing a poem? He told me that his most fruitful hours were in the evening, when he had a bottle of Rhine wine before him, and he would work slowly into the small hours of the morning until the contents of the bottle was consumed. He said that seemed to start his thoughts up better than anything else. One day, I went to the beach and saw Tillich at his usual post under the umbrella, but one leg was extended and resting on a small chair, and the great toe had a huge bandage around it. I asked him, "For Heaven's sake, Dr. Tillich, what's happened?" "Gout," he said. I said, "And what is that due to?" "Overwork," he replied.

Somerset Maugham is a man whom I met once in my life, possibly twice. I met him at a dinner party given by Padraic Colum's wife, Molly. Padraic and Molly Colum were both very old and dear friends of my wife and myself. Padraic Colum's a most distinguished poet and writer, and Molly Colum wrote books, too. She wrote two books, both of them excellent. The first was called *From These Roots*[41] and was a study of the forces that have made modern literature—that have made, for instance, the work of James Joyce and T. S. Eliot and others. The other was her autobiography *Life and the Dream*.[42] Padraic, of course, is one of the best-known poets of Ireland. He was with Yeats in the Abbey Theatre. Yeats said of him that he was the most talented younger member of the Abbey Theatre group.

At this dinner given by Molly at a little restaurant called the Hapsburg House, just around the corner on Fifty-sixth Street, Somerset Maugham was one of the guests, and my wife and I had also been invited. Maugham was a great friend and admirer of Padraic and of Molly. But to come to my story—there was a lady in New York, and I think she's still living, though she's now very frail, Mrs. Murray Crane, the widow of a former governor of Massachusetts. Mrs. Crane used to have what she thought of as a salon. On certain days, perhaps once a month, a distinguished group of writers would be invited to gather at Mrs. Crane's house for informal discussion and to stay for dinner. And the reason she could get them was because Padraic—who was always financially on the rocks; both he and Molly had a hard time making both ends meet—Padraic would act as Mrs. Crane's impresario, shall we say? Padraic knew all the important writers, and he could get them when no one else would have been able to get them to come to such a gathering.

On the occasion I'm thinking of, this lady, Mrs. Murray Crane, had asked a question to start conversation. She asked Francis Hackett, the critic, who was there—a very distinguished man, no longer young—if there was any poem that he would like to recite, any poem from the period that was under discussion, the rather decadent *Yellow Book* period of Aubrey Beardsley. Hackett immediately launched out into that most beautiful poem by Ernest Dowson, of which the refrain is, "I have been faithful to thee, Cynara, in my fashion."[43] It's a poem about a man's hunger for a lost love, persisting throughout a series of dissolute, promiscuous affairs, undertaken in an effort to forget her. These end in feelings of desolation and disgust, voiced in the cry, the assertion, "I have been faithful to thee, Cynara" (she is the lost love) "in my fashion."

Hackett read it extremely well, and after he had finished, Mrs. Murray Crane turned to Marianne Moore, who always came to these salons, and said, "Miss Moore, what is your feeling about this poem?" Marianne Moore spoke up and said, "Who is Ernest Dowson? Never heard of him." You know, he was one of the most exquisite poets of the period. "Never heard of him," Miss Moore said. "But I know he's not a good poet, because his use of the word 'fashion' is forced by the rhyme." She didn't seem to realize that in England even today that's a very common phrase, meaning "in my way" or "in my own way."

After Miss Moore got through, Somerset Maugham raised his hand to show that he wanted to speak, and Mrs. Murray Crane told him to go ahead, and he said, "Miss Moore, have you ever had a hangover?" "Certainly not," said Miss Moore. "Well, then, how could you be expected to understand this poem? This is a poem expressing a state of emotional hangover on the part of a man who's in love and has not kept faith with his love, outwardly at least. The feelings involved resemble those of a hangover, and unless you had some knowledge of that, you wouldn't be able to understand such a poem." That ended it. I thought it was a good answer.

Somerset Maugham, as I think we all know, was a homosexual. He was not purely a homosexual. He was what they call "double-gaited," ambivalent, or however you want to put it. I'd known this in the old days. Ned Sheldon had told me about him. Ned would tell me about other people who came to his bedside, and one evening he said, "Somerset was here the other day, and I'm ashamed of him." Ned had very strong moral feelings. He had very definite standards about things. What had disgusted him was that Somerset, as he called him, who was spending the summer in East Hampton, had got a young society girl into trouble by a promise of marriage and then welshed on it, said he couldn't go through with it, and offered to make some sort of a financial settlement. Ned was disgusted and said that he told Somerset, "I don't ever want to see you again if this is what your standard of conduct is going to be." Under the persuasion of Ned, Maugham married the girl, and she had her child legitimately. He did the right thing—that is, from that point of view—but the marriage ended in divorce.* His greatest novel, *Of Human Bondage*, is his own story—the story of a young man who falls in love with a woman not of his class and of being rejected and humiliated by that woman, as so often happens.

I would like to talk about Oscar Williams, probably the best contemporary anthologist. He seemed like the last man in the world that you would imagine had a passion for poetry. Yet he had, and he was a poet himself. He was one of the winners in the Yale Series of Younger Poets. They publish each year a young poet who is selected out of all the manuscripts that are submitted. As the man who was editing the series at that time was, I believe, Wystan Auden, it was a great distinction to be chosen, and Oscar Williams's book was chosen. I do not remember the title of it,† but I do remember one line from it, which I think only a man of imagination could have written. Oscar was married, and very happily married, to a woman

---

*In 1917 Maugham married Syrie Barnardo Wellcome, who was English; they had one child and were divorced in 1929.

†*The Golden Darkness* (New Haven: Yale University Press, 1921).

who was a painter, Gene Derwood. She painted under her maiden name. Oscar, in writing of the first years of marriage, speaks of all the happiness, but somewhere in the poem: "And I am lonely for my loneliness." I think that says a great deal in one line.

Oscar's great talent was as an anthologist. I secured him for Scribners, and he did a series of anthologies that have sold in the millions: *A Little Treasury of Modern Poetry, A Little Treasury of British Poetry, A Little Treasury of American Poetry, A Little Treasury of Great Poetry, A Little Treasury of Love Poems, A Little Treasury of World Poetry in Translation*, and so on. Not only Scribners but many other publishers have issued anthologies of his. The Scribners contract didn't bind him to give everything to them. And all his anthologies had a tremendous sale. Oscar was a great impresario. He did all the work himself. He wrote to all the poets, typed the letters himself, selected and collected the poems, got all the permissions from the publishers involved, handled all that correspondence, made all the payments when Scribners turned the checks over to him, made the bargain with the publisher that controlled rights—the shrewdest bargain that any anthologizer has ever driven—he wore the publisher out by his persistence. For instance, in the *Modern*, he insisted that he must have Eliot's *The Waste Land,* which had never been given in its entirety to an anthology before. He must have Wallace Stevens's "The Man with the Blue Guitar." He must have Hart Crane's *The Bridge*. He must have these long big poems, the most famous poems of these poets, in their entirety, notes and all. And finally, overwhelmed by Oscar's sheer persistence, the publisher would say, "All right, all right, as long as you don't come round again. Take it, yes, you can have it—yes."

We split in the end because his demands were so great and also because Mr. Scribner got very angry with him, as you may recall from that previous episode. So the relationship had to be terminated.

Oscar was a perfectionist. He made up his own dummies; he pasted the whole thing together, measuring every line, so that the poem would fall in a certain way on the page. He tried to place every two-page poem on facing pages, so that you wouldn't have to turn over. He'd work it out to the millionth of an inch, paste up the whole dummy exactly the way the book would be, just taking these long galley proofs and cutting and pasting them up. Then he followed the book through in every single detail. One Sunday his wife called up and said, "Jack, I don't know what to do with Oscar, but he's just getting impossible because he says the dust jacket for the new anthology has not got quite the same area of cellophane on one side as it has on the other, and he doesn't think it looks very nice. Also he doesn't like the color of the ribbon"—the little bookmarker ribbon. I said, "We can't do anything about that."

"No, but I can't stand it. You've really got to talk to him about it." So they came up here, and Oscar talked about it all day long. He was almost having a nervous breakdown over it. He was a perfectionist. He carried that through all the way. He was also a man of mystery. I didn't discover until Gene Derwood's death, when I went to the service—the service for Oscar's wife—that the tall young man sitting in the pew with Oscar, who later introduced him to me as Strephon, was their son. Neither Gene or Oscar had ever referred to him, and I'd never seen him before. They'd kept it a secret from everyone that they had a son.

Another mysterious thing: when Oscar's estate came to be settled, I was called in by a lawyer who happens to be a friend of ours (I don't know how he got involved in it) and whom Oscar had appointed as the lawyer for his estate. It seems Oscar's estate ran into a very large figure—this man who didn't have a nickel, and lived down off Wall Street in an empty loft somewhere, he and his wife, that they paid practically nothing for, and that had only cold water, and no elevator before 8:00 A.M. and after 6:00 P.M. and was up about eight floors. And you know what made his estate so valuable? The letters he had received over the years from all these poets. From T. S. Eliot and from Yeats and from Wallace Stevens and others equally well known. He had kept them in great boxes—he'd never thrown anything away—and they had a tremendous value. That was his whole estate. I was called in to try to help this man to an appraisal of the actual value, for inheritance tax purposes, of these things, because the tax authorities were claiming they had an even greater value than they probably had. Also this lawyer had never before dealt with a literary estate. I don't know why Oscar appointed him. Perhaps this man had been kind to him.

Oscar disappeared very suddenly. I couldn't go on with him at Scribners. It was too difficult. I was caught between the upper and the lower millstone. Also we'd quarreled about various matters. Then, not having seen him for several years, I would occasionally run into him. The last time I saw him was at the annual ceremony of the National Book Awards. Oscar came up to me with someone—he always had some beautiful girl in tow after the death of his wife— and he said, "Miss So-and-so, I want you to meet Mr. Wheelock. Mr. Wheelock is my editor—or used to be my editor." This always irritated me, being introduced as Oscar's editor.

Well, anyway, one day at a cocktail party I was told by the editor of the *Hudson Review*, Joe Bennett, that—— I happened to mention Oscar, and he said, "Yes, poor devil. He's dying you know. He's dying of cancer of the throat." Oscar had a difficult death. I wrote him a letter, telling him that I was sorry that we'd differed about things but that I hoped he could still feel— in spite of our differences, I held him in great affection—and that I hoped he could still feel the same way about me. I never got any answer to this, but I suppose he wasn't in condition to write letters.

At this party given by our friends Mr. and Mrs. Donald Adams— J. Donald Adams was one of the editors of *The New York Times Book Review;* he wrote a column for them every week called "Speaking of Books"—they had invited as guests of honor Marilyn Monroe and Dame Edith Sitwell, the English poet, who was over here at that time and is a very formidable lady, as everyone knows. My wife and I went to the party, and when we arrived I found a circle of people, like a horseshoe, at the center of which sat Dame Edith. The seats on either side of her were vacant. Everyone was afraid to sit next to Dame Edith because no one felt that he or she would be able to keep up his end with so learned and witty and devastating a person as Edith Sitwell. I certainly had no such ambitions, but I was shoved into a seat next to her, by Donald, who said, "Here's just the man we want—just the man you want to talk to, Edith." So I found myself next to this great lady. We got along very well, simply because Dame Edith, like myself, was a great admirer of that much-underestimated poet Swinburne, and we talked about him endlessly.

The other guest of honor had not showed up, and that was Marilyn Monroe. Then I was told by Jackie—that is, Donald's wife, Mrs. Donald Adams—that Marilyn was always late to everything—that this was one of her great difficulties—but that she would come. Dame Edith waited as long as she could, and we'd just about exhausted the subject of Swinburne, on which she contradicted me several times with the manner of a superior to an inferior. I didn't challenge her because I thought, "That's just her way."

Then, suddenly, after Dame Edith had gone, this couple appeared, Arthur Miller, the playwright, and Marilyn Monroe. As they came in, everyone in the room rose, as if for royalty —everyone, that is, except my wife and a friend of hers who were talking together. They remained seated, not out of disrespect but simply because women do not rise except for royalty, and they did not regard this couple as royalty.

Arthur Miller and Marilyn Monroe stood before the assembly, facing us, holding hands together, behind their backs. This was a little embarrassing, a public display of affection that went on steadily throughout the evening. I was presented to Marilyn Monroe. She certainly was most attractive. I did my best—I'm not very good at making conversation with someone I meet for the first time—and Miss Monroe gave me just one look and said, "You need another drink." This, I felt, was not very high tribute to my conversational talent. However, I took another drink, but I didn't go back to talk to Miss Monroe. Later a strange thing happened. It shows how easily one misjudges people. At the annual ceremony of the National Institute of Arts and Letters I had come down from the platform and was waiting for my wife, who was in the audience, when suddenly I saw coming toward me Marilyn Monroe. Her husband, Arthur Miller, had been taken into the Institute that day. As she approached she seemed to be looking at me, to smile and wave her hand. I thought, oh, she never would remember me; she must be waving to someone behind me. I remained perfectly impassive. I heard afterwards from Donald that her feelings had been hurt—she had this idea that people looked down upon her as a rather second-rate movie star, and she thought I had high-hatted her, as they say. I felt miserable about it. It shows how poorly we judge people. I'd thought of her as being rather snooty and upstage because of her fame. But no, not at all. She suffered from a terrible inferiority complex.

Richard Watson Gilder was a very powerful figure in New York as head of *The Century* and also a very public-spirited man who did more to clean up the slums and other evil conditions in New York than probably anyone else. He died early from spending himself to the point of exhaustion. He has been made a great deal of fun of by people who think of him as one of the old conservative crowd. Actually, he was a friend of Walt Whitman, one of the first appreciators of Walt Whitman, at a time when people were very squeamish about Walt Whitman's poetry. He was also a friend of Albert Pinkham Ryder, the American painter, whom some people disapproved of so much, yet Gilder's reputation persists as a "nimble poet," a man who was purely genteel.

It is true that Gilder was included, during his lifetime, in the "Household" series of the standard American poets: Longfellow, Whittier, Holmes, Lowell were all enshrined in these red rough-cloth volumes. And on my class day at Harvard, in 1908, to which I'd invited Phyllis de Kay, her uncle Richard Watson Gilder came to Cambridge. His son George was graduating also. Richard Watson Gilder rather attached himself to Phyllis and me, and in the afternoon when there was going to be dancing and gaiety in the Yard, he spirited us away to Mount Auburn Cemetery, where many of these American poets are buried, and we spent the afternoon standing with bowed heads at the graves of Longfellow, Holmes, Lowell, and whatnot, Gilder feeling all the time that he was now one of this great company. It was a rather dull afternoon for two young people who wanted—— But we were over-awed by Gilder, and I was being very polite because I knew that he was an influential man. Also because he was the uncle of my beloved Phyllis, I couldn't do anything about it, and the whole afternoon was spent standing at these graves.

There was another man that I eventually found it very hard to take— he did me a great deal of harm with his praise, his acclaim of me—Alfred Noyes, the famous English poet. My father was amazed. My father, who didn't care too much about my poetry and rather teased me about it and made fun of it all, was for the first time shocked into feeling that I might amount to something when he took up *The New York Times* and read there that a famous English poet, Alfred Noyes, arriving at the Port of New York, had said to the reporters crowding about him that America had today one magnificent poet, John Hall Wheelock. Noyes said, "Not only is he a great poet who uses the traditional forms in a new way, I predict that in twenty years from now he will be known on both sides of the water as the best poet of this era."

At this time Noyes was quite an influential man. Swinburne had let his mantle fall upon him, as it were, and had seen a lot of him. Noyes's encomium was therefore emblazoned on the jacket of my next book. But eventually Noyes became the laughingstock of the modern crowd, and he deteriorated so as he went on. He wrote jingly verse. One of his best-known poems was "The Barrel-Organ," the one with the refrain, "Go down to Kew in lilac-time, in lilac-time, in lilac-time; / Go down to Kew in lilac-time (it isn't far from London!)" He got to doing that sort of thing. Then he wrote a long, very rhetorical and overblown poem about the lives of the great astronomers, in which he dwells with awe on the great distances between the stars. In other words, Noyes came to represent everything that modern poetry hates. I was connected with him to this extent so that the dear man's praising me to the skies really did me a great deal of harm.

He wanted to meet me, and he and his wife came and had dinner with us, and I remember calling up Padraic Colum and asking whether he and Molly would also come and that Padraic said in a hushed voice, "No, I could never be in the same room with Alfred Noyes." The reason for this was that Noyes had apparently been on the committee that had something to do with the execution of Erskine Childers, the Irish patriot, at the time of the Troubles. Noyes had made himself very unpopular by being a pacifist during the First World War and coming to the United States and teaching at Princeton instead of enlisting in England.

But he had been a great poet in the beginning. His long epic poem *The Armada,* a very fine thing, too, ran in *Blackwood's Magazine* as a serial for, I think, two years and was greatly admired by Swinburne, the greatest living poet of the age. Noyes was just the opposite of what had usually been thought of in England as a poet. He was a robust man who had been stroke on the Oxford crew, and he was greatly interested in science. He was in his day considered very modern, but very often if you start out very modern, you end up as an old fogy as the newer crowd comes along, and Noyes became the most reviled figure of all. Praise from Alfred Noyes came to be the kiss of death.

Noyes belonged, in a way, to an older generation that had a different point of view. I remember at Scribners, for instance, the feeling was very different from what you would get today. When I would spend a weekend with Mr. and Mrs. Arthur Scribner at their beautiful country place in Mount Kisco, I was treated royally. They would have a house party, perhaps with ten people there, and we'd go boating on the lake and fishing and have a wonderful time. Mr. Arthur Scribner would be friendly, and he and I would travel back to New York in the club car on Monday morning like two boon companions. Then I remember the first time I committed a serious social error. Coming back from lunch on that Monday, I stepped into the elevator in the Scribner Building to go back to work and found that Mr. Arthur Scribner was in the elevator. I spoke to him, and he cut me dead—because now I was an employee and not supposed to speak to him. Not during business hours, except on business matters. If Mr. Scribner wanted to speak to me, he would, but for me to make social conversation with the august head of the firm—— It was one thing on a weekend when I was at a party as a guest, but now I was just an employee. That would never happen today, you know. That was the reason that both those men, Mr. Charles Scribner II and Mr. Arthur Scribner, were known by their employees throughout the firm as "Chilly Charles and Arctic Arthur."

■ ■ ■ ■

I'd like to talk about Alan Paton, whose editor I was. Scribners brought out his *Cry, the Beloved Country* in 1948 and, later, a book that I worked with

him on, trying to get him to compress it and above all to change the title
he had given it, *Too Late the Phalarope*. I said, "Alan, nobody—— People
are going to be—— You're going to lose sales because when they go into
a store, they are going to be shy about asking, 'Do you have *Too Late the
Phalarope?*' They won't know just how to pronounce *Phalarope,* and therefore many will be put off from asking for the book. Do change the title."
No, Alan wouldn't hear of it, and it did affect the sale, I'm sure. He is a
most attractive man, more like a Scotsman than anything else I can think
of, and he speaks like a Scotsman, although of course he is from South
Africa and lives near Natal and is the great champion of the blacks and the
great enemy of apartheid. His books are indirect protests against racial dis-
crimination. *Cry, the Beloved Country* is a marvelous book. Paton has been
the head of a reformatory for boys in the outskirts of Natal, and he knows
the blacks well. He has written this one magnificent book. *Too Late the
Phalarope* is a very moving book, too.

Paton was terribly cocksure about a lot of things. I think he was
extremely vain, really. Many great people are. I remember one incident
that made a deep impression on my wife as well as on myself. We were in
this very room when Alan was having dinner with us one night, and he said
to me in his Scots voice—he pronounced my name "Jeck"—he said, "Jeck,
they tell me I'm the most modest man in the world, despite all me great
achievements. Is that the truth?" I didn't know what to say. I couldn't think
of anything to say that wouldn't be wounding. Finally I came up with—
"Well, Alan, all I can say is that I'm absolutely the vainest man in the
world." He hesitated for a moment and then said, "Well, now, maybe I
shouldn't have said that." But I thought the naivete of that question has
been really delightful.

Too Late the Phalarope had a very fine theme. It was based upon the
theme of miscegenation in South Africa. This story is the story of a young
police officer in Natal, devoted to his father and mother, who is attracted
to a black girl. He loses his self-control, and they have this love affair. It's
most dramatically told. The big moment, from the point of view of the
reader, is reached when the young man comes home one night and finds a
note fastened to his door, which simply reads, "We saw you." He goes into
an agony of fear. The next day he goes on a picnic with his family, and he
keeps thinking that he is their destroyer, that they're doomed now. But it
turns out that this note fastened to his door was just a joke by another
police officer who'd seen him coming out of a bar somewhere, and it had
no relation whatever to his affair with the black girl.

Alan Paton, poor man, I believe is under house arrest in his home in South Africa. He came to this country several times and lectured and was made much of everywhere, and he saw a great deal of my old friend Van Wyck Brooks, who was also very much interested in anti-segregation. My wife and I saw a lot of Alan. Now he's not allowed a passport. He can't leave his country. I think he's more or less confined to a certain area. He has given hostages to fortune: He has children, a son who's in business in South Africa, and other children who are involved in one way or another. If he isn't going to destroy them, he has to keep his mouth shut. It's a major tragedy. If he's written more, they haven't allowed it to be published. I don't think they'd allow any manuscript of Paton's out of the country unless they censored it first.

Well, to go back to my oldest and perhaps closest friend, Van Wyck Brooks, there's one little anecdote that I have always thought amusing. After Van Wyck's first wife, Eleanor, died, he was desolate and very lonely. He did have a rather childlike, helpless, dependent side. He came to New York and took an apartment across the hall from where my wife and I were living, and we tried to do what we could for him. My wife, that spring, went back to England on a trip. I couldn't go, because of my job at Scribners, and an old friend of my wife's and mine, a childhood friend, Gladys Rice, at that time Gladys Billings, who had had two divorces and was now living in an apartment here in New York, invited me to come to a dinner party she was giving. Gladys knew that my wife was abroad, but she was giving this small dinner party and asked me to come alone. And so, knowing how lonely Van Wyck was—I was worried about him because he'd been brooding so much—I said, "Could I bring Van Wyck Brooks?" Gladys was very much excited and said, "Why, of course bring him, and tell him that Allen Tate is coming, too."

I spoke to Van Wyck, and he said, "Yes, I'd like to go very much." "You've never met Gladys Billings?" "No, I never have." I said, "Allen Tate is going to be there, too." "Oh, then I can't go," said Van Wyck. "Why not?" "Allen Tate is my literary enemy." I said, "Oh, don't be ridiculous. I don't believe he's anyone's enemy." "Anyone who doesn't like my work is my enemy," said Van Wyck, "and I will not be in the same room with him. He's my enemy, and I will not go." I said, "If you don't go, you will miss a very enjoyable time. It's good for you, you know, to see people. You admitted that yourself the other day, that you can't go on grieving forever. Allen Tate is an attractive man and you're an attractive man, you'll like each other enormously. Why not take a chance on it?"

I finally persuaded Van Wyck, and he went. It was at this party that he fell in love with Gladys, his hostess. He fell in love just as a boy might fall in love, really head over heels. Van Wyck was not a great man for walking—in New York he usually traveled by taxi or bus—and when we left the dinner party I said to him, "Let's get a cab." "No, I want to walk back," he replied. "I'd like to talk to you." And he pumped me with questions about Gladys, all the way home. The next day he called Gladys up and asked if he might come to tea. They had tea together. But she kept him— she could see that he was quite smitten, and in fact he told her so—she kept him dangling for quite a while. In the meantime, a very nice older woman, a widow who had been a friend of Van Wyck's first wife and Van Wyck for many years and was not too well off, had come as a paid companion to run his household for him, in the apartment across the hall. And she told me she got pretty fed up hearing about Gladys—Gladys this and Gladys that and why doesn't Gladys call up, and so on. Poor lady, she had rather hoped perhaps that she might be the next wife of Van Wyck Brooks, although she was a bit older. There was no reason why she shouldn't be. She was a very charming lady. Well, eventually Van Wyck and Gladys were married, and it was an extremely happy marriage. It lasted for sixteen years, until Van Wyck's death. Gladys has just published a book about it, *If Strangers Meet.*[44] It's getting wonderful reviews.

I never said anything about my old friend John Reed, who's buried beside the Kremlin wall. When I was at Harvard, John Reed was one of my contributors on *The Harvard Monthly.* He began as a poet, you know, and he used to send me his poems, and then later, when I became an editor of *The Harvard Monthly,* he submitted his poems to *The Harvard Monthly,* and I published a good many of them. We got to know each other very well, and it's always been a mystery to me why John Reed—how John Reed—came to be the fiery revolutionary that he later was. When I knew him at college, he was a slightly overweight, extremely quiet, pleasant man who suffered terribly from adenoids, which gave his voice a curious muffled quality, and who wrote verse that was in no way to the left or liberal. In fact, I regarded Reed as rather old-fashioned. His poems were anything but radical. There was a poem about New York City, in which the one phrase that I still remember, "moon of the tides of men," was used as metaphor. This quiet creature apparently developed into a rabid revolutionary, and wrote the book—what was it called?—*Ten Days that Shook the World.* In Russia Reed was turned into a hero of the time—old John Reed, who used to send in those very mild poems. I don't remember just why Reed went to Russia. I think he originally went as a reporter for some newspaper, doing some articles on Russia. This was before the upheaval. Then he was caught up in the Revolution.

John Hayward is a very touching character. He was another one of those heroes in a sense, like Edward Sheldon. Hayward was considered in London to be the finest, the greatest authority on French literature in perhaps the world, certainly in England, and a regular contributor to the old *Times Literary Supplement.* From childhood, he'd been a cripple. I never knew just what it was he suffered from. It seemed to be the combination of a spastic condition superimposed upon polio. He lived in a wheelchair. Hayward was a heroic man; his spastic gestures were hideous, the flailing of his arms; and he had the greatest difficulty in writing. Yet his profession was that of a writer, a scholarly writer, and he became a great influence in the literary world of London. When you saw him, you wondered how he endured it. He had a spastic condition of the face so that his tongue hung out, and he grimaced. He went through life in this condition, yet he had beautiful women in love with him, and he was a brilliant, most amusing man. Hayward became the companion of T. S. Eliot. They lived together in Cheyne Walk, there in the Carlyle Mansions, where Rossetti had lived. After the breakup of Eliot's first marriage, he and John Hayward formed this menage and lived very happily together. A tragic thing happened when Eliot fell in love with his secretary, Valerie, and had the only really happy seven years of his life after his marriage to her. He had to tell John Hayward that he was leaving, and it was like a man who's leaving his mistress or his wife. He just couldn't face up to, you know, telling him. So he left a little note, in the classic fashion on the hall table, and disappeared forever.

Whenever we were in England we used to see Hayward, but this was after the break with Eliot. We hadn't gone to England often while I was with Scribners. It wasn't till after my retirement that we were able to go so often, and then we saw a lot of Hayward, and he very much enjoyed talking to my wife, who is more learned than I am, as well as more amusing. Hayward took a great liking to Phyllis, and he tolerated me as the husband. I enjoyed him. He used to write me affectionate letters. I think he felt that if I'd married anyone as amusing as Phyllis, there must be some virtue in me.

There is another Englishman who interested me, C. Day Lewis. There are four English poets that are always linked together—W. H. Auden, C. Day Lewis, Stephen Spender, and Louis MacNeice. I've only met C. Day Lewis a few times. But the most amusing occasion was one I'm going to tell you about. I've written one prose book, which has done very well; I wish my books of poems would sell equally well. I'd tried my very best to get this book published in England but with notable lack of success. Finally I was told by the agent, "I know what I'll do, and I think this will solve our problem. C. Day Lewis is now a reader for Chatto and Windus; I will send it direct to him, and they will certainly—— Day Lewis will take it."

Then I met Day Lewis. My wife and I went to dinner with a friend of ours, Janet Adams Smith, and Day Lewis happened to be one of the other dinner guests, and we got talking, and I told him my difficulties in getting the book published in England. In fact, he rather brought it up himself. I was cagey about talking about it, but he looked me right in the eye—I'd just learned, I think the day before, from the agent, that it had been turned down by Chatto and Windus also—but C. Day Lewis looked me right in the eye and said, "Well, I can tell you one thing that I feel absolutely certain of—you never had it rejected by Chatto and Windus." I have never known whether that was malicious, or whether the book made so little impression on Day Lewis that he didn't remember it or perhaps that he didn't even read it. But there was nothing I could do except to smile.

I'd like to talk about Percy MacKaye a little bit. There was an interesting man. He was a man who'd had a great vogue in his day. His big five-act plays in blank verse, *Sappho and Phaon* and *Jeanne D'Arc,* were playing in Boston when I was at Harvard. They were successes, which is unusual for a poetic drama. Then later MacKaye wrote huge pageants that had some success, and he wrote the comedy that some people at the time thought was *the* great American comedy, called *The Scarecrow,* which ran on Broadway for a while in 1908. But in his old age, as he grew less and less remembered and less and less thought of, certainly by other poets, and forgotten by the general public, MacKaye became more and more pompous and was the perfect image of the poet, the conventional image of the poet, with his eye in a fine frenzy rolling, you know, and disheveled hair and hollow cheeks. The makeup was absolutely perfect, but the work, as he got older, deteriorated a good deal. However, during the last years of his life, Mac-Kaye devoted himself to a very ambitious scheme. He thought that Shakespeare hadn't done a very thorough job with *Hamlet* and decided to add another act to it of his own, and he worked on it, and he got it published during his lifetime.[45]

One of the interesting things about Percy MacKaye, or Percy, as everyone called him, was his absolute confidence in himself, which never failed, and his extraordinary sentimentality, really. He had been tremendously in love with his wife, and she must have been a long-suffering woman because they were poor most of their lives, in spite of his successes, and had a good many children, and Percy was always the center—this great poet!—and she was always just the self-effacing wife. But after her death, MacKaye lived at The Players club in Gramercy Park, and on the anniversary day of their marriage, he would give a dinner for, say, thirty or forty people at The Players, and he would have an empty chair where his wife was supposed to be sitting, and all his remarks were addressed to her in this empty chair. In fact, I was told by someone that he had had a doll put there to take her place. I've since heard that that was not so. But it was an empty chair he talked to. Where he got the money for these big parties, heaven only knows.

MacKaye had other rather headlong qualities. When you went to see him, you couldn't get away in less than two or three hours because you never got to a point in his talk where there was a break, so you could leave without being rude—and his talk was always about himself. Occasionally he did tell me (it never thrilled me very much), he said, "I voted for you at the National Institute last week"—then I would learn that I had failed to get in. He was always voting for me, and I never got in. I thought it would have been much better if he hadn't told me that he'd voted for me. I'm not only in now, but I've also been elected to The American Academy of Arts and Letters, which number only fifty out of the Institute's two hundred fifty members.

I don't think I really have anything to say about Edmund Wilson, except that he was the most difficult author I ever had to deal with. For instance, he was doing an editing job on the prose of John Peale Bishop, who had been an old friend of Edmund's. Allen Tate was doing the poems, and Edmund was doing the prose.[46] Edmund kept putting in more and more and more, and I kept saying, "You know, we have to hold the price of this book down to"—whatever it was, perhaps $4.50. Edmund wrote me back insulting letters, saying, "Don't give me any of that publisher's———" and then a four-letter word. "That book will be sold at the price that was decided on, even if I make it double the size," and so on. I just couldn't do anything with him. He was insolent and rude and unreasonable and irrational, and yet he's done such fine things. I admire Edmund for the steady way in which he has turned out work without any deadlines. All on his own initiative, he's gone on and on and done so many interesting and good things.

Wilson had a propensity for rewriting, which went right on into page proof. As you know, an author is allowed to make changes free of cost up to a certain percentage of the total cost of composition. After that, it's charged against the author. But Edmund would go right on making changes even in page proof, where changes are very costly indeed, because it very often means re-paging. And yet he always stated that he wouldn't stand for one nickel of any of this, that that was just a lot of publisher's rot and hogwash. In the end, of course, the publisher usually had to make a compromise of some sort. I became very fond of Edmund, though. I never called him "Bunny," as all his friends seemed to. He's a much younger man than I am, but he called me Jack, and I called him Edmund. In spite of all our differences, we remained good friends, but he didn't remain with Scribners after the publication of some two or three of his books, and he's had several publishers since.

The other author of mine who was perhaps the next most difficult, in my editorial days, was Taylor Caldwell. Her books have had a tremendous sale. There were two stories I had in mind. One of them was this. Janet* and her husband went to—— I can't remember the place, but it was a seashore resort that rather distinguished people went to in the summertime, and many of them were writers, and even what might be called "intellectuals." Janet began throwing her weight around and telling them all that her books sold seven hundred thousand or a million copies, and when she got through talking and boasting about it they would just look at her and say, "Well, your books can't be any good if they sell that many." This was an eye-opener to Janet. "They must be utterly lacking in distinction," one man said to her.

Taylor Caldwell was a very difficult author to deal with on proof-reading. When I read her proof, I would make corrections, and I had to make a great many. At that time there were some authors whom we didn't correct in manuscript. We waited for the galleys. Eventually we had to put Janet on the manuscript basis because there was so much to be corrected in the galleys. She was so annoyed by my many rewritings and changes that she wrote on the proof-sheet, "Who the hell is writing this book, anyway, you or me?" On another occasion she commented, "Why don't you put your name on the title page with mine?"

Janet couldn't understand, for instance, that—— She had a priest, a Catholic priest in one of her books, who was always quoting from the Bible, a thing that Catholic priests don't often do. But worse, he was quoting from

*Taylor Caldwell, whose full name was Janet Miriam Taylor Holland Caldwell Reback, published fourteen novels with Scribners between 1938 and 1951. After she left Scribners, she published more than a dozen novels with other houses.

Taylor Caldwell (photo from dust jacket of *On Growing Up Tough* [1971])

the Protestant Bible, and the Catholics use what's known as the Douay Bible, which is a totally different text from the King James Version. I spoke to Janet about this—or wrote her about it—and she wrote back, "There is one Bible and only one Bible, and that is the King James Version, period." And I never got her to change it.

She thinks of herself, always has, as a great writer, a modern Dumas. She was quite a simple English woman, who came to this country in quest of a better chance to make a living. She'd made an unhappy marriage to a man who drank too much, and it ended in divorce, and she came over here with a trunkful of manuscripts—books of poems, essays, novels, short stories. She knew a great deal about English literature; she could, for instance, recite the metaphysical poets by the yard. She was intellectually, in those ways, very alert but a person of the simplest status socially and in cultural background. She came here and got a job with the Immigration Department as a typist, and while working there met a man named Marcus Reback, who was her immediate boss, and whom she married. She sent us a novel that had been turned down by a number of publishers. It was called *Dynasty of Death.* She'd never had anything published, although she'd been trying for years: books of poems, essays, novels, etcetera. We took *Dynasty of Death,* and it was a great success.

We went on publishing Taylor Caldwell's books for many years, and I was in charge of her books and of her when she came to town. That would be a whole volume in itself. My wife and I used to have them here, get up little dinner parties for them. They wanted very much to meet all the critics and writers. We had, frankly, to explain to our friends beforehand that Mr. and Mrs. Reback were nice people and that we were fond of them, and not to be surprised if they were a little on the crude side. Very often after dinner, we'd come back to the family room with Marcus shouting at the top of his lungs. "Now, Jack," he'd shout, "get after that book. Put a little pep in that campaign. Don't let the grass grow under your feet." And so on, all this business talk, you know, before our guests.

Eventually, of course, Marcus betrayed us. I don't think Janet would have. He wasn't satisfied. He had learned somewhere that Hemingway got fifteen percent royalty, and his wife was getting only ten percent. He said, "You mean to tell me you think Hemingway is as good as Janet?" What could I say? I said, "Your wife is a wonderful story-teller." "Story-teller, nuts," he said. "Is she a greater writer than Hemingway or isn't she?" I said, "Well, Tolstoy was a great story-teller." "I'm not talking about Tolstoy. Is she better than Hemingway? I know damn well she is. Now, what is your answer?" I said, "That is something I couldn't answer. I'm not a literary critic. I know her books do very well, and we're very happy to publish her."

Then they began to fool around with other publishers. This was after we'd published about ten books of hers, very successfully, made a lot of money for the house and for her. I was away on vacation, and when I came back Mr. Scribner said that various publishers had written in and said, "Taylor Caldwell has submitted her new book to us, and we would like to know——" They all played it perfectly straight and said, "Are you parting with Taylor Caldwell? Because we certainly won't take her on if you want to keep her." Mr. Scribner said, "We do want to keep her." So then they declined the book.

When I came back, I confronted Marcus with this, and he looked me right in the eye and said, "Whoever said that is telling you an absolute lie. That book was never shown to any other house. Never! It's a dishonorable thing to do and we would never do it." Then Mr. Scribner wrote them a letter about this and got the same assurance from Taylor Caldwell that they had never shown it elsewhere. Yet he had, in his files, letters to the opposite effect from five different publishing houses. Finally he wrote one more letter—a masterpiece, it was. He said, "We know very well that you wouldn't say what's untrue, and therefore we shall have to ascribe it to something in the nature of a miracle or a hallucination that five publishers think they received from you the manuscript of your new book. We are willing to write it off as a hallucination." But, of course, we didn't publish for her anymore. She's gone right on. I think her later books have had even bigger successes. They sell a million copies. She turns one out almost every other year.

Another person who annoyed me considerably during my life was Ted Weeks, the editor of the *Atlantic Monthly*. I met Ted Weeks—I forget where, at some cocktail party—and he was so nice and so terribly affectionate, much too—— I think it's always a little disturbing when you meet a person for the first time, and he immediately calls you by your first name, especially when you're a bit older. Also Ted would sign all his letters to me, "Affectionately yours, Ted." I'd been sending poems out to magazines for over fifty years at that time, and I'd appeared in all the magazines—everything from the little quarterlies to the big magazines like *Harper's* and the *Yale Review* and what have you. But I never got into the *Atlantic Monthly*. I never could understand it. So when I was on a more intimate footing with Ted Weeks, I talked to him about this, and I said, "Why is it that I can't seem to get my poems published in the *Atlantic?* I've been sending them in to you now for half a century, and you've never accepted one, yet during that time all the other magazines have published many of my poems. What's worse, when the other magazines decline a poem, I usually get a polite note from the editor, but from the *Atlantic* I get nothing but printed rejection slips." "Oh," he said, "that's terrible! Why don't you try us again? There must be a mistake somewhere." So I sent him, I thought, one of my best poems, and in about three weeks I got back a printed rejection slip. However, I eventually made the grade, and I have never understood why, because the poem they took was one of my poorer poems. Perhaps Ted was just embarrassed about the situation. Through it all, he continued with this terrific affection and first-name business.

I've always had a great admiration for Robinson Jeffers's poetry. I think he's one of the most underrated poets of our time, and I believe that some day he'll be recognized as the great poet he is. It's true that Jeffers is rhetorical, but, after all, great rhetoric can be great poetry, and he is one of the most prophetic poets we have had. You feel in those early poems of violence of his that they are the poems of a man living in the pre-nuclear age and foreseeing a great deal that came later. I don't see how anyone can deny the great beauty of his rhetoric and the absolute integrity of the man as poet. I think the dignity with which he bore the neglect, throughout most of his life, on the part of the elite, the literati, was an example that one could hardly surpass. He never complained. He kept on doing his work. I think some day he will really come into his own.

I went out to see Jeffers in his home in Carmel, California. He and his wife, Una, lived in a house he'd built with his own hands of stonework there. I was a little disappointed when we arrived, my wife and I, by the slightly overprepared event. When we reached the house, somebody was playing Bach on the organ. They knew we were arriving at this time. When we came in, there Una was, all by herself, playing the organ. And this strange man, Jeffers—this hawk-like, maniacal man, poet of violence and of nihilism—was not to be seen. But after some time, some conversation, Una said to us brightly, "Would you like to see Robin?" I said, "Yes, we would like to see him, very much." "I'll go get him."

Una went out, and she came back leading this lean, hungry, desperate-looking man. He evidently had been disturbed at his work. I knew just exactly the state of mind he was in, and I felt very—— I wished to God we weren't there. I knew I must say something. I knew how interested Jeffers was in birds and how large a part they play, especially hawks, in his poetry. I said to him, "Mr. Jeffers, your California birds differ somewhat from our eastern birds. I'm very much interested to know what birds you have here." Jeffers reached out with one arm to the bookcase behind him, a listless gesture, took a book and put it into my hand—*Birds of California.*

Our meeting was not a success. Later, when Jeffers came to New York, my wife and I went to hear him read at Columbia, and he read about as badly as anyone could. He destroyed those marvelous cadences of his by reading them flatly, out of some sort of self-deprecation, not wanting to appear to think they were good. My wife amused Jeffers greatly, when we had dinner with them afterwards, by telling him that I used to recite his poems to her at night when we couldn't sleep and that she much preferred my reading of them to his. He was delighted by this. He said he was delighted that anyone knew his poems by heart, and I did know a great many of them by heart. I had some correspondence with Jeffers after that, and he became very much more open with me.

Another interesting person—but she's been written up so thoroughly that I don't think I could add much of importance—was Amy Lowell. She weighed, you know, about two hundred eighty pounds; she was one of the Imagist poets. One of my friends said that she was "the only one hundred percent male" he'd ever met. She smoked enormous black cigars and affected to be very masculine indeed. I saw a great deal of Amy Lowell at one time because she was beginning as a poet then and was very anxious to be in touch with New York poets. She lived up in Boston, of course. She was a grande dame there. She was a sister of the president of Harvard, yet very much, frankly, on the make as a poet. This immensely wealthy woman was desperately eager to establish herself as a poet, and she did at the time succeed in doing so. Except for her life of Keats,[47] she is largely forgotten now.

I've had some strange experiences as editor. There was a writer whose work I admired greatly, a German, a refugee from Hitler's Germany, René Fueloep-Miller. I saw him suffer a humiliation. He was a most distinguished writer, highly regarded in Austria and Germany. Forced to leave Germany and come to this country, he was supporting himself and wife and little daughter—or trying to support them—by teaching and doing hack work. Mr. Scribner—this was Charles Scribner IV—was still a young man and had just taken over control of the business, with which he has done so marvelously well. But he was a little cruel at times. Fueloep-Miller had written a good popular book in the field of science. It really was a good book. It didn't pretend to be anything more than a popularization. Fueloep-Miller had been trained as a physiologist. After I had taken the book on, Mr. Scribner consulted some of the people at the Rockefeller

Institute, got them to read the manuscript, and they decided that it was not absolutely sound scientifically. Mr. Scribner laid great stress on this. He said, "You will have to tell Fueloep-Miller that we can't publish the book." I said, "I cannot do that, Charlie. I have given him my word, and the contract is signed. I'm afraid you'll have to do it." Charlie said, "I'll talk to him in your office, and you'll have to go along with it."

One afternoon we all sat down together in my office. Mr. Scribner, with great kindness, being as kind as he could, explained to Fueloep-Miller that he could retain the advance that he'd been paid on the book. "You can retain the advance, and you can go to another publisher with the book and get another advance on it," he said, "but we do not feel that we can publish it." "Why not?" said René Fueloep-Miller, and he insisted on Mr. Scribner giving him the facts. He said, "I never intended it, you know, to be a work of pure science. I intended it to be a popularization of what's going on in science now, and I think it is well suited to that." Mr. Scribner said, "We do not feel so here, and we are not willing to publish the book. I know that we've signed the contract, but we're asking you to break the contract and keep the money." Fueloep-Miller, who was a poor man, said, "I will not keep the money under these circumstances. I'm not accustomed to taking money for work that is not satisfactory." There was a long silence, and Mr. Scribner looked very uncomfortable. Then Fueloep-Miller added, "I always try to learn something from every experience, no matter how disagreeable." I've always remembered that. That sank in, I think.

[27 March 1967]

SOME OF THE WELL-KNOWN WRITERS for whom I was editor became my friends and some not. All of them were writers for whom I had respect. I think it's rather amusing, the divergence of experiences one has as an editor working with such a great variety of temperaments.

A man that I think of who was fascinating to work with in a way and yet extremely difficult was Colonel Charles Lindbergh, now General Lindbergh. He was touchy, and of course he was famed for his obstinacy and determination. He wouldn't have made that first solo flight across the Atlantic if he hadn't had those qualities. Coupled with them was an over-politeness and agreeableness that made them particularly distressing. You would say, "Colonel Lindbergh," as he was then, "I would suggest that this be reserved for the footnotes because it really disturbs the flow of your narrative." We were working on his *Spirit of St. Louis*.[48] He would immediately say, "Now, I think that's a good idea. You've thought it out carefully, and I can see that you've got a very good idea there. I'm very much pleased with it. On the other hand, I think I'll leave it just as it is." This proved to be the case with almost every suggestion that was made. As was afterwards proven, by reviewers' statements and other comments, Scribners, through their editor, was sometimes right about these changes. But Colonel Lindbergh was always delighted with them in the extreme—and then turned them down. In a way, that's more insulting than when a man speaks right up and says, "I don't care for that idea. I'd rather do it my way." Being so terrifically polite and agreeable is almost being patronizing, isn't it?

Anne Morrow Lindbergh, who was a poet and wrote extremely well, had more literary finesse and more quality in her writing than Lindbergh himself had, and she did go over the manuscript and helped him in various ways. Lindbergh was perfectly frank to admit this. But he was very often writing about things that Anne Morrow Lindbergh couldn't possibly have written about. Actually Lindbergh writes quite well, but his wife could improve almost anything that he did, in just little things, you know, and that was what she did do.

I got to know Lindbergh quite well. He lost interest in me, lost interest in my wife and myself, later on. We used to see the Lindberghs occasionally. We had dinner several times with them, and they came and had dinner with us. He lost interest in us because of two unfortunate occurrences. On one, he invited us to go to Darien, Connecticut, where he and his wife had their home, and he suggested that we take a train to—I've forgotten just where it was, some distance away—and that then he would transport us one by one to their place in Darien in his little two-seater plane. Well, my wife and I, although we know that Lindbergh is supposed to be the safest flier in the world and has never had an accident and services his own planes himself, in spite of all that we had a sort of superstitious desire not to go separately. If we could have gone together, survived or died together, that would have been one thing. I turned the invitation down. Lindbergh never quite forgave me for that, because it seemed to reflect on his airmanship.

Then another unfortunate thing happened. One very hot Sunday in August—this was when I was still an editor and had only a very short summer vacation—they invited us out to dinner at Darien. On the day that had been selected we got on a train which seemed to take a long time to reach Darien, we got out at the station, and there was no one there. I looked everywhere around the station. I looked in the parking lot outside the station, and I even looked into the men's room to see if he'd slipped in there for a minute. No trace of anyone. I then had a brilliant idea. I went

down to a little store very near the station and telephoned, asked the operator for Colonel Lindbergh's number, because it wasn't in the book. She
said, "It's a private number. There's no way of reaching him."

It seemed to us that they'd forgotten. We didn't want to embarrass
them by arriving at the house and perhaps finding some other guests there
or some other party going on. I quickly consulted the stationmaster and
found that there was only one train more back to New York that night. It
was due shortly. We crossed to the other side, jumped on the train, and
went home. My wife was a little unhappy about it all. It was an extremely
sticky, hot night, and we had had nothing to eat and didn't get back to New
York until after nine o'clock that evening.

As soon as we got back to our apartment, the telephone began to ring,
and it was Colonel Lindbergh. "Why in God's name? Where were you? We
had such a beautiful dinner waiting for you, and I was at the station looking for you high and low." I said, "Well, that's very strange, because we *were*
at the station." "*What* station? Now, describe the station." I said, "It was
Darien, Connecticut," and I described the station. I described going down,
and the name of the store where I'd made the telephone call, and Lindbergh said, "It just remains one of the great mysteries because I was there."

Since then we have learned, or we did learn some time after that, that
because of his extreme fear of publicity, Lindbergh would very often
remain in his car until his guests had started looking for him on the platform and that sometimes he overshot the mark a little and stayed too long,
waiting for the crowd to disperse. We may have acted a little hastily in
order not to miss that last train back to New York. But Lindbergh went on
about it, and he was terribly upset, and we got so tired explaining it all to
him. Evidently he seemed to believe that we were either fibbing or that we
had got out at the wrong station. They invited us out again, and we went
and had a very pleasant dinner, but after that, I think, these two events
rather cooled off the friendship.

The only other episode I remember shows how publicity-shy Lindbergh was. The head of our advertising department, with whom Lindbergh did business for a long time, almost every day, this man while out
for lunch saw Colonel Lindbergh standing in front of a drugstore; he had
come out of the door and was standing there for a moment. Being a
friendly man and a public relations man who believes in being friendly,
he went up to Lindbergh and greeted him, "Hello, Colonel Lindbergh."
Colonel Lindbergh stared at him with a stony eye and said, "I don't know
you. I don't know you. I'm not Lindbergh." "Well, I certainly thought you

were." "I don't know you. I don't know you. I have no business with you," Lindbergh replied, and he went off. It *was* Lindbergh, but he didn't want people around to know this. It shows how oversensitive he is, and that same trait was probably responsible for what happened at the railroad station. My wife remained a little upset by it because she thought frankly they'd just forgotten and had made up all these excuses.

Anne Morrow Lindbergh is a most attractive person, and she had become a great friend of Edward Sheldon and used to go and sit at the little table and have dinner with him in his apartment where he lay in bed, blind and paralyzed. She wrote a most impressive article about him in the *Reader's Digest,* in that series, "My Most Unforgettable Character"—the most beautiful thing that has ever been written about Ned, although two books were written about him, none of them nearly as good as what she said there.

We've remained friendly. There was however, one other unfortunate incident. The night they came to dinner with us we had also invited Van Wyck Brooks and his wife. That was Van Wyck's first wife, Eleanor Stimson, the niece of the then secretary of state, Henry L. Stimson. It was foolish on my part to have risked that combination. My wife didn't really know about it. Van Wyck Brooks was very liberal, in fact very much to the left, vice-president of the League of American Writers and other leftish organizations, and Lindbergh of course was extremely to the right, not to say fascist. And after dinner they quarreled. Van Wyck was not a quarrelsome man, but he got irritated because of Lindbergh's rather up-and-down manner. It was a very painful experience for us all. That, too, I think, put Lindbergh off.

I was editor for Nancy Hale for many years and grew very fond of her, and I think she liked me. We became friends. When she came to town, as she did infrequently, we would have lunch together and talk about her writing plans. Nancy was very tactful and treated an editor like a human being. In fact, she professed to liking my poems, and she's continued to like them. We correspond still.

Nancy had said that when I left—she knew I was going to retire; I waited until I was nearly seventy-two before I retired—she would leave. I had persuaded her not to do that. I said, "That would be very foolish because the other editors here, I honestly think, are abler editors than I am and very forward-looking, and you're much appreciated here. It's one of the best publishing houses in the world, after all. It would be very unwise to do that." Nancy promised me that she wouldn't. But one day, after I had retired, she came in unexpectedly. She was rather arrogant, you know. After all, she was a descendant of Julia Ward Howe and of Edward Everett Hale and heaven knows who else. She was told to take a seat and that Mr. Burroughs Mitchell, the editor who had inherited her as author after I left, was busy. Nancy, being a rather hardy soul, demanded to know who was with him. "Oh, another writer," said the receptionist. "Yes, but what writer?" "James Jones."

So Nancy waited very respectfully for another half hour, and then, when at the end of the half hour she was still kept waiting, she rose majestically and left. Later, a letter followed saying that she was severing relations with the house. This was a tactical blunder on the part of somebody, possibly even of Burroughs Mitchell, who is so very courteous and sensitive to these situations. If he'd only come out and shaken Nancy's hand and sat down for a moment and said, "Now, I'll have to go back again just for a minute, till I can get rid of this man," it might have been all right. But this way did not work. She just took the bit between her teeth and left Scribners. I know that Nancy Hale had had any number of publishers trying to get her, and perhaps this just provided an incident—you know, a good excuse.

Another writer who was not actually an author of ours, although I did try to get him for Scribners at one time, was William Carlos Williams, who has achieved such a big reputation, especially among the young people of today, and whose poetry, the best of it, is certainly very fine, indeed. Well, you would think poets would know something about one another. It seems to me I know the names of almost all the American poets who have published more than two or three books. But when part of *What Is Poetry?* came out in—I think it was the *Partisan Review,* I really can't remember, or *The New York Times Book Review,* one of those places—I had a very excited letter addressed, with characteristic casualness, to "Mr. John Paul Wheeler."

The letter began with that wonderful dash and brio that William Carlos Williams always had: "Dear Mr. Wheeler: Who in the hell are you, anyway? For you have certainly written the best essay on poetry I ever read in my life." Then he quoted phrase after phrase: how we pass through life in a state of anesthesia and that the arts, and especially poetry, wrench us out of this state to a fresh perception of reality and so on. All this enormous enthusiasm on the part of Carlos Williams—and I thought, well, this is rather amazing because here the arch free-verse leader—who says, "Damn the iambic measure" and "Smash the iamb" and so on—has written to *me,* admiring what I say about poetry more than anything he's read before! Very hopefully, I wrote back—I didn't even refer to his getting my name wrong—but I never heard another word from William Carlos Williams. As soon as he saw that it was John Hall Wheelock, an older man—well, about his age—he had no more use for me. That was rather disillusioning, I think.

Then there were other authors who presented problems. Marjorie Kinnan Rawlings, whom I knew very well, was one of the authors I'm proud to have counted as a friend. I was her editor for some years, after Max Perkins's death. She could write such beautiful things, but, like many good writers, she was capable of very bad work, too. Marjorie Rawlings, if she just wrote naturally about the things she was familiar with (as for instance in *The Yearling,* a touching, beautiful book, a profound book in a way), the results would be superb. She always had a slight sense of inferiority, a feeling that she was a popular writer and that she must be more literary, more "highbrow," and tackle some great theme. Whenever she did this the books she turned out were incredibly bad. I can't remember the name of the last one she wrote,* just before her death, which she felt was the greatest, most profound book she'd ever written—and I got worried right away. When I read it, it was about a farmer out west whom she hadn't really made real or three-dimensional and about his idealism in the cause of the farmers out there and of the laborers on farms and how he dies heroically in an airplane on a flight to a farmers' convention. The whole thing was this preposterous tripe because she had this lofty theme in mind. If she'd just sat down and written another book about the people in the part of the country that she knew so well, down there in Florida, she could have written almost a great book. I think *The Yearling* is perhaps a great book because it appeals to writers and people who are highly critical, and it appeals to the mass reader also. I tried very hard to get rid of this fixation of hers. Max Perkins had labored over it when he was her editor. But we never could accomplish anything.

Then there's another writer who is, I think, among the best poets of our time, Peter Viereck. I was the first to publish him. Viereck's first poetry book was called *Terror and Decorum.* I'd never seen anything of his before that. He didn't publish much in the magazines until after he turned in this book. It was first-rate work, and we took it on, and it won the Pulitzer Prize. We became friends. But Peter had an unfortunate trait that has alienated almost everyone. I think he suffered very much from the trauma induced by his father's disgrace. Peter's father, George Sylvester Viereck,

---

The Sojourner (New York: Scribners, 1953).

was a natural son of the German kaiser, by an actress, Edwina Viereck.* He was a journalist and a poet, and a very interesting poet, too. He wrote erotic poetry. When I say that, I mean that he broke the Victorian tradition at a time when the Victorian tradition was very strong. His poems don't wear well now because he was always writing about Sin, and Sin doesn't mean very much to people today. He tried to be very wicked in his poems, and of course things have gone so much further now that his efforts in that respect seem very puerile. But at his best he was a good poet. He had a wonderful ear. And he was bilingual. He wrote and published books of poems both in German and in English. Eventually, George Sylvester Viereck was caught giving aid to the enemy during the First World War, or perhaps even spying, and I think he spent fifteen years in a federal prison.†

By the way, I knew George Sylvester Viereck very well in his early years, when his first books were coming out. Even the great Richard Watson Gilder, the head of the Century Company and one of the most influential men in New York and a terrifically traditional poet, was so impressed by George Sylvester Viereck's talent that he published him in *The Century* —of course, avoiding the poems that might give offense.

I think Peter, his son, felt terribly the onus on him to prove that he was a good, loyal American citizen. He enlisted immediately when war broke out and served through the war—that's the Second World War; he was too young for the First. But he developed in his personality as a defense, I suppose against the onus that he'd felt—he'd been taunted about his father at school—an extreme aggressiveness, so that wherever he went he had his pockets full of circulars and other promotional material about his poems. If Peter met anyone, he'd bombard them with circulars and letters about his own work. He alienated people like Allen Tate and people like Van Wyck Brooks, people like Robert Lowell, people like Frost, Sandburg, and you could go on indefinitely. Eventually, his interminable aggressive flow of cerebration and extreme super-egotism wore out even his wife. She went out of her head and then accused Peter of railroading her into an asylum—which he had not done at all; her schizophrenia required hospitalization. His whole life became a great tragedy. On her recovery the

*George Sylvester Viereck's father, Louis Viereck, was born out of wedlock to Edwina Viereck and was believed to be the son of Kaiser Wilhelm I.
†George Sylvester Viereck was pro-German during World War I and was accused of being a paid propagandist for Germany. He was ostracized but did not go to prison.

breach with his wife was healed, but for a while, Peter's job at Mt. Holyoke College, where he is Professor of History, might very well have been lost because there were two sides to this. Some people believed the wife, some people believed Peter. Eventually he was cleared.

Now Peter has learned to keep quiet. He's bringing out a new book, and his conduct with regard to that shows what he has learned from his suffering. He never wrote me about the new book, although he is one of my poets. He hasn't bothered me with so much as a letter all these years. But his publisher approached me, and asked if I would be willing to read Peter's new book.[49] And if I was perhaps I'd be willing to say something about it.

I said I'd like very much to read it, and they sent me the proof sheets, and it's magnificent. I wrote the best recommendation I could, which they will use on the jacket of the book. Even then, not a word from Peter. You see, he's learned his lesson almost too well: to keep quiet. He learned by suffering, by finding that he had nearly become an outcast. None of the periodicals wanted his poems. Sometimes if a fellow lecturer would learn that Peter was to be on the lecture platform with him, that person would say that he'd been taken ill and wouldn't be able to come to lecture. Peter has learned through the agony he must have gone through with his wife, whom he'd met while he was overseas during the war—she's a Russian, most attractive person, too, very intelligent. They had children, and one of his sons, I think, is going to be a remarkable poet himself. Peter has learned from suffering something that had almost to be burned into him for him to take it in.

I had known George Sylvester Viereck in the old days—in fact, before he was married, before Peter was even thought of. George Sylvester Viereck, Padraic Colum and Molly Colum, old friends of ours, were important people in the Poetry Society of America, and they ran it. Another who also was very influential there was Edwin Markham. The society was run on a very high level because fine and interesting poets were the leaders. It has fallen off in recent years and has become—this is certainly a perfectly valid thing to become—a club for rather lonely poets who are not very successful and who like to talk about and criticize one another's work. But George Sylvester Viereck was the young rising star of poetry in those earlier days. His 1907 book *Nineveh and Other Poems*—always talking about Sin—was undeniably able verse, full of such lines as "The stain of one delirious night, / Not all the tides shall wash away." In a marvelous sonnet to the English language Viereck wrote: "What time my boy's heart heard as in a dream, / The choral walls of rhythmic beauty rise."

George Sylvester Viereck was a man of great ability, but so disgraced that the only way he could make a living—no one would have anything to do with him—was by writing pornographic books under a pen name, and he made a good income from it. He could turn his hand to almost anything, and he wrote pornographic books that apparently had a large sale in the underground market.

This was the father of Peter Viereck, who, I think, is one of the most interesting and original poets of our time, moving completely against the stream, the current fashionable stream in the poetry of our time. We published five of Peter's books—*Terror and Decorum, Strike Through the Mask, The First Morning, The Persimmon Tree,* and another, a play in verse, *The Tree Witch.* He got the Pulitzer Prize for his first book. Excellent poet. Not that getting the Pulitzer Prize necessarily means that you are.

Another very different author that I had charge of for two or three years was the great Italian art authority who had fled here from Italy because of fascism, Leonello Venturi. Venturi was a most delightful man. He stammered very badly. Before he began a sentence, he would always repeat one Italian word "*Gli*"—"*Gli, Gli, Gli*"—and then he'd get started. He secured the worst translators for these marvelous books of his on painting, written, of course, in Italian. He got Russians to translate them, and I worked myself almost sick rewriting some of these translations. The book, for instance, would describe a painting in which, according to the translation, "Two Clownesses appear" and things like that. You know: lion, lioness—clown, clowness. I got Venturi an extremely fine translator who also knows a great deal about painting, which is essential to the translation of a book on that art, namely, Francis Steegmuller, whose name you've probably heard.

Venturi and his wife used to have dinner with us from time to time. Both of them were very fond of my wife. Phyllis knows a great deal about painting and has lived in Italy. My wife also speaks Italian. One day, in this very room, the first time that Leonello came—he was alone in this country at the time after his flight from Italy—when he found that he was looking at the painting that hangs over our heads here, a production of the Munich School of painters—Meilsner is the name of the painter—he said, "Do you mind if I change my place and sit on the sofa over there, so I don't have to look at that Meilsner!" Venturi was very modernist; his great loves were Chagall and Picasso, but Chagall especially. He was an attractive man. He's dead now. We both became very fond of him, my wife and I.

Now, on this list of writers, there remains one more who is, I think, extremely interesting. He was a difficult man in his way, too, Willard Huntington Wright, and he was quite a wild boy. In fact, he was known, among some members of my class, 1908, as the "college ass." At that time he thought of himself as being a very great poet indeed. Certainly the makeup was perfect: the hooded eyes, the tormented face, the long hair. Willard was not really a cultivated man. He had a tremendous smattering of knowledge about certain decadent, minor poets—Ernest Dowson, Arthur Symons, et al. He did have a great admiration for George Sterling, a very rhetorical but, I always have thought, a very fine American poet. Sterling committed suicide years ago.

At college Willard got as far as the beginning of his sophomore year. I may have this wrong; it may have been the end of his freshman year. But anyway, a musical comedy came to Boston (I don't remember the name of it) that contained many attractive chorus girls, and Willard fell in love with and married one of them. I think they had been seeing a great deal of each other, and I think there was a baby on the way, and Willard—well, there was nothing to do but get married. I think he did this with great enthusiasm. She was a very attractive girl.

Willard had to leave college, then, and he was very hard put to it to make a living. He was a man without means, from a family of modest means and certainly not in a position to support a couple and a child. How he managed, I don't know. I didn't see him during those years. When I next met him, it was after I had come back from Germany in 1911, and we hadn't seen each other perhaps since 1905 or '06. There was Willard, after many experiences and vicissitudes, editing *The Smart Set*. You can read all about him in the recently published *Smart Set* anthology,[50] which is prefaced by an introduction giving the history of the magazine and a great deal about the various editors. Willard was the editor just before H. L. Mencken took over, Henry Mencken and George Nathan.

I remember how terrifically Willard impressed me. Here I was, holding a twelve-dollar-a-week job with an advertising concern, hard pressed to find time in which to do my writing, and really very immature, as I'm afraid I have always been—and am perhaps even now. I don't know, I seem to get old very slowly. And here was Willard, already a man of the world. He'd been my classmate, was my age, but he'd experienced everything. He took me out to lunch at some expensive, posh restaurant, and we had drinks. He used to keep a bottle of brandy in his office and drink from it, from time to time—while he was working. He had a very pretty secretary who he gave me to understand was his mistress. He took the brandy in order to maintain his virility during his various sexual orgies with other women, as well as with this woman, his secretary. I was lost in admiration of such an accomplished man of the world! Then, too, he published my poems in *The Smart Set,* many of them.

Willard went on to have a very strange career. In 1916 he published a novel called *The Man of Promise,* a really good novel which had no sale but did have great quality. He wrote what I'm told is one of the best books on French Impressionist painting. I think that was its title—*French Impressionist Painting.*[51] After that he did a book on Nietzsche called *What Nietzsche Taught,* published by Benjamin Huebsch, the publisher whose firm later merged with the Viking Press. That book did quite well. Then he did another book in still another field—I've forgotten what.[52] So here was a book of fiction, a book of art criticism, a book of biographical-literary study, and whatnot. Besides all this, it was Willard who brought into *The Smart Set* that daring freedom in the use of language and of subject matter later exploited by Mencken and Nathan. In other words, in his editing he exemplified what he gave me to understand his own life was like. I was green with envy and lost in admiration of this so worldly man. I seemed to myself, in comparison, abysmally pedestrian.

Willard carried everything perhaps just a little too far. I think probably it was the brandy that did him in more than anything else. Eventually he had a terrific crack-up, a nervous breakdown of the worst kind. He told me afterwards, when he had got over it, just what had happened. His illness had cost him his job. He was worn out, and he was penniless, and he was taken in by a kind French doctor here in New York, who recognized Willard as a man of talent, saw the straits he was in, took him into his home, quieted him down, and saw him through his nervous breakdown. Incidentally, as a therapeutic measure, he gave Willard the run of his library. Well, it all happened in this library; the doctor told Willard, "The thing for you to do"—Willard had great difficulty in sleeping—"is to read these mysteries and detective novels here. I'll guarantee they'll put you to sleep if you read long enough."

Willard browsed in this library, which was well-stocked, particularly in this field—books on poisoning, on murder, everything of that sort. In the course of doing this, he made himself a master of the mystery form

From left: Willard Huntington Wright (S. S. Van Dine), Ernest Hemingway, Charles Scribner III, and Maxwell Perkins (courtesy of Charles Scribner's Sons, Princeton University Libraries)

and technique. As you know, those books have to be written backward. He made himself such a master that while I was an editor—no, before I was an editor at Scribners, while I was still working in the bookstore—he came in and left with Scribners the typescript of his first mystery, *The Benson Murder Case,* written under the pen name S. S. Van Dine. Scribners published it, and he went on and did a dozen of them. Philo Vance was the detective, the "Sherlock Holmes" of the series. There was the *Canary Murder Case.* All had similar titles, and each had the distinguishing feature that it wasn't merely a mystery. In the course of the narrative he would develop some special subject; perhaps in one mystery it might be perfumes and their use by famous women throughout world history. Anyone reading these books would feel not only that he was reading a very exciting mystery but that he was broadening his knowledge at the same time. A cultural thing.

Willard went right on drinking brandy. He couldn't do his work except with large potations of this. His marriage had been a failure, and he had a great deal of difficulty getting rid of his wife. He had to support her and their daughter, both of whom lived in California, while he worked here in New York. Eventually he managed to get a divorce. Willard then married again, a very happy marriage, to a woman a year or two older than he was. Now he did his most successful work. For the rest of his life he did nothing except to turn out these mysteries. He was always dressed as if he'd just stepped out of a bandbox, dressed to the nines. He didn't wear spats, but his moustaches were carefully waxed like those of a Frenchman, and he carried grey gloves. Everything, you know, harmonized as to color—all that sort of thing.

Willard used to come in—Max was his editor, not I—but he would always drop into my office for old sake's sake. We'd been classmates for a short time, and both of us were poets. He'd read me I don't know how many of his poems that freshman year, and we'd been friends. Willard came in to see me in the later years, on a day when he looked very different. He'd wasted away. He looked like a very sick man, and he told me he had only a few months to live. He had cirrhosis of the liver. There was this interesting thing about it. Willard said, "I'm not going to complain. And I don't feel depressed. I've had a good time. I've had a wonderful life. I've enjoyed myself, and I've enjoyed my brandy. It's made my life exciting, and I'm enough of a sport to be willing to pay the price, and I have to pay it now. I always knew that I would have to pay it some day. But I don't care. I've had enough." And he died a few months after that. Willard was a most attractive man.

Then, another interesting character—I think he's one of the best translators today from the Latin—well, there are Richmond Lattimore and Robert Lowell and Robert Fitzgerald. This man, Rolfe Humphries, translated Virgil, translated Ovid, and is a poet himself. I was his editor at Scribners. We published, I think, four or five books of his, and then his *Collected Poems*—just as Scribners has done with Louise Bogan and Conrad Aiken and other poets. I was the editor that had charge of the work of these talented people.

Rolfe and I became friends. Louise Bogan and I have been friends for years, and she's a great friend of my wife's and myself now. But Rolfe was a very—not exactly psychotic, but very nearly so, and partly I think because he had not been overly successful. He was married to a woman much more successful than he was—a psychiatrist, with a big practice, whereas Rolfe taught at a girls' day school out in Jackson Heights somewhere for a pittance and then wrote his poems. His wife was almost too busy to see him. She was much the more important person. I think all this, added to a morbid sensitivity on his part, almost upset him mentally.

Then later in life when Rolfe published his superb translation of Virgil, he was called to Amherst and made a professor there. Every now and then, he'd lecture at Yale and other universities. He became *the* important person in the family, and his wife had to take a back seat. She had to move to Amherst. She lost most of her practice that she had had in Jackson Heights. I never met her.

Now the story I'm leading up to is—as you know, I was editor for Oscar Williams and got him to do those seven or eight anthologies for Scribners, the *Little Treasuries,* which were so enormously successful. When it came to doing the *Little Treasury of American Poetry* (I think that was the one) I was delighted that Oscar Williams had made so generous a selection of Rolfe Humphries's poems. Each anthology had toward the end of the book a picture gallery, the portraits of all the poets included, always in oval frames. I thought I had spoken to Rolfe about the inclusion of his poems, but I must have slipped up somewhere, because one day he came in and—he could be very violent and disagreeable in certain of his moods—and he wanted to know, in no uncertain terms, how the hell did he come to be in an Oscar Williams anthology? I said, "You've got a very good representation there." "Take them out!" I said, "You want them taken out? The *Modern Treasury* has sold several hundred thousand, you know." "Take them out!" said Rolfe. I tried desperately to get him to leave the poems in. He said he wouldn't appear in any anthology by Oscar Williams. He thought

Williams was a vulgarian, that he sucked up to more important writers. He added that Williams had included himself in his *Little Treasury of Great Poetry*. He gave himself more space there than he gave to Thomas Hardy. Rolfe said, "Any man who has the courage to put more of his own poems into an anthology than he's put in of Thomas Hardy's is a man I don't want to know. He's got too much courage."

I looked into the matter. Here we were in page proof. If you know anything about bookmaking, you will know what that means—to take out material when the book is in page proof means re-setting everything after that point. I went to Oscar Williams, whose business it was, I had always thought, to get the permissions. I supposed that he had got Rolfe's permission, but he hadn't. Oscar was one of those people that you could not persuade to anything. He insisted that this had been my job: "You are the publisher of Rolfe Humphries, and it was up to you to get his permission. If you didn't do it, why, you'll have to pay. Scribners will have to pay the cost of this thing." Well, the cost was going to run into a couple of thousand dollars. I didn't know what to do. I couldn't afford to pay it myself. Oscar wouldn't pay it. Perhaps technically it was my mistake. So I went to Mr. Scribner, and he, against his will and with some annoyance but very graciously, said the house would pay for it. I think I told you, I won't repeat it here, how annoyed Mr. Scribner was when Oscar forced me to put this in writing. It was a most difficult situation, and the house had to pay several thousand dollars to have not only all these poems taken out but everything after that re-set and all the pictures rearranged when Rolfe's was removed. The extreme feeling of Rolfe—that's just like him—was so strong that he would not be included in any anthology, however wide its distribution, edited by a man whom he regarded as having such a———

While I'm talking about these authors for whom I was editor—I think I've now finished that—there's one writer more I should like to say a word or two about. I was not his editor. He was published, I think, by Doubleday. His name is very well known today. By the time this interview is released, it probably will not be so well known—Morton Dauwen Zabel, a most sensitive man with a great zest for life. Morton was a most cultivated man, familiar with German and French and Italian as well as with the classical literatures, and a recognized authority on painting with an absolute passion for going to Europe and visiting all the art galleries. Morton enjoyed life so tremendously when he had the chance. Most of the time, he was teaching, and he was so able that in short order he became head of the Department of English at the University of Chicago. He rather attached himself to my wife and myself. He never married, and our apartment became his second home. Whenever he was in New York, he would come here and stay with us, and we enjoyed his conversation enormously. Morton would get so interested in what he was saying that he was the despair of the maid who was waiting on the table because it took him forever to finish his meal. He held up everybody and everything. But also he had this curious fear—we never knew the basis of it—concerning his health. Some horror hung over him. He looked like a perfectly healthy man, yet he never would take a drink. He never would eat anything that had much sugar in it, yet he was not a diabetic.

His one spree, abandoning the puritanical drive of hard work that he lived by, was to go abroad. Morton would have a sabbatical or a leave of absence for a certain length of time, and he would go over and just— I think he was of Austrian origin—glut himself on going to the Austrian Tyrol or to Rome or on visiting all the important libraries in London, let us say. And he would remember every single thing that he saw or heard on those expeditions. I remember going through London with him, my wife and I, when we were over there, through a street—it really became burdensome because he'd say, "You know that house? The architect of that was so and so; it was built in such and such a year. This club is the St. Botolf's Club. You know they have a very small membership; only one hundred two, I think, are allowed into the club. The architect was so and so———" Everything was like that, you know. It rather got to be too much.

But still this horror was always hanging over Morton. His sister died, his only relative, and some mysterious horror hung over that. I remember his last visit here. He had published only two or three books of his own,[53] but he had edited and written introductions for the works of many well-known writers. He was an authority on Henry James and on Joseph Conrad, and he had edited, with introductions, many of the works of these writers. His was work of extreme distinction. He always had a ready market for work of that kind—very much sought after by publishers.

But the last time we saw Morton, he seemed depressed. We didn't know the cause. He didn't talk as much as usual. Then he disappeared into Chicago, and we never thought anything more about it, until finally, just by chance, we read or heard somewhere that Morton had died in Chicago—that he'd been alone in the hospital. He had no family; he had hardly any friends in Chicago; he was respected but not particularly liked in the university there. And he had died. This horror, whatever it was, had caught up with him, the thing that he was always escaping from. He was such a talented man, and one of the ablest interpreters of Conrad and Henry James that there has ever been—certainly one of the most cultivated men I've known. Now Morton Zabel is going to be completely forgotten because he didn't leave enough enduring work of his own.

■ ■ ■ ■

I began writing verse as a child. When I say "as a child," I don't know just what age is covered by that word, but I remember my mother encouraging me about some verse I'd written when I was nine years old. I went on with this endless versifying of mine; it has been my great passion always. It recompensed me for many things. For instance, I wanted to excel in many lines, but I was ruled out in the field of athletics because I had a leaking heart valve that didn't work too well. I still have it, of course, but the heart compensates for it in time by getting bigger. I was not allowed to play football, and that was the great game at Morristown. I was allowed to play baseball, but I played it very badly. Eventually I became manager of the baseball team, and I was very proud of that, especially when we went to play a game out of town, and we came back, and the bus going up to the school dropped me off at our house as we passed it on the way, and the boys all gave a cheer for me. This was the sort of thing that I needed very badly. The one place where it seemed to me that I could excel was in my verse, and I did, and it recompensed me for many things. I was a shy boy, not at all sociable, and I'm still not very sociable. Some people have that temperament. I like to be alone.

When I went to college, I went on more intensively with writing verse, and of course I discovered—as all young people do, especially if they are poets—I gradually discovered all the great poets of the past. I remember reading Chaucer and Shakespeare and the older poets and the metaphysical poets and the Cavalier poets, all the great English and also all the great German poets, for my brother and I had had German nurses and governess, who taught us more than you would learn at any school. We spoke German exclusively with them. My father was interested in German, and my mother loved German poetry, so that I had the advantage of having two literatures. You discover Goethe, and then later on Heine, and then of course as you grow up, newer poets come into the picture. You discover the many minor poets, some of whom have written the loveliest things, Nikolaus Lenau, Eduard Mörike, Joseph Eichendorff, and then the more modern ones, Rainer Maria Rilke and Detlev von Liliencron, Franz Werfel and Richard Dehmel, and so on.

In English, the same way. It seemed to me that in school we had gone back and read the classic great English poets, and then as you went on you read the more modern poets yourself. You would go on from, for instance, Pope and Dryden and the poets of that period and of course Gray's "Elegy." One always gets bogged down in that wonderful piece of rhetoric. Then you come on later to poets like Keats and Shelley and then, still later, Tennyson, Browning, and Arnold and all that period, then the Rossettis and Swinburne and Yeats and the lesser poets like William Ernest Henley and Coventry Patmore and Francis Thompson.

I had an ecstatic youth because I was living in these marvelous things, and that made it unnecessary for me during those years to live in any other world. I could go down to the beach at East Hampton in the morning and watch the boys and girls, the more popular boys and the more popular girls having a wonderful time, and I would remain aloof, yet contented, for I was a poet and I had this other world that they didn't have. That was really the way it worked a great part of the time. I lived in a dream of self-sufficiency—which didn't mean that I didn't want the other things, but meant that I wanted them too much. I wanted them so much that I didn't dare enter into these fields at all for fear of being repulsed or finding out that someone else was better at it than I was.

However, at school I did go out for track, and I made gigantic efforts to do the thing that I admired most of all, namely, the high jump: that wonderful way that some of the boys had of jumping up in the air and then lying on one side and rolling over the bar, which I never was able to do. I remember the master who had charge of the field athletics saying, as I approached the bar "like some great beast" and by sheer brute strength forced myself over, "What a lot of spring there is in that boy if only he knew how to do it right!" Finally I tore the tendon in my left thigh in making a superhuman effort to clear the bar a little bit higher than I'd ever cleared it before, and I was laid up for quite a while. Apparently to tear a tendon is almost worse than breaking a bone. I only mention this in order to show what an enormous desire I had to succeed and to excel in some way.

When I got to college, I had a great deal more satisfaction there. There were these three magazines, *The Harvard Advocate, The Harvard Monthly,* and *The Harvard Illustrated Magazine,* all of which I flooded with verse. I eventually became president of *The Harvard Monthly* and my roommate, Edward Sheldon, president of the *Advocate,* and between us we practically controlled—— I mean, if a student wanted to be published in these magazines, he had to send his manuscript in to us. This gave us a sense of power. Ned didn't need it because he was always a very assured, self-confident personality. I never was.

Well, I went on with this, and then, as I think I've explained before, I was elected Class Poet, and I spent my summers at East Hampton in perfect orgies of verse writing. I did nothing else. I used to lie awake at night. I worked so late I couldn't sleep. Of course, I thought everything I did was marvelous. I remember sometimes having such a sense of elation from what I'd written—three or four strong cocktails would have been absolutely nothing compared to it. I didn't care what happened after that. I felt I'd done this impossible thing. I was treading on clouds. Then I would have the inevitable reaction, the feeling that everything I'd done was absolutely worthless. It was either one or the other.

Goethe says it all in his poem "Egmont," where he describes it: "Himmelhock jauchzend und zu Tode betrübt": "Shouting in ecstasy to high heaven, or dejected almost to death." I lived through all those. Then, in the winters at college, more orgies of verse writing. And I graduated as Class Poet, and my Class Poem was communist, practically, as I think I've told you before. My parents suffered very much from this dereliction of mine.

Then came the German period, in which I sacrificed my Ph.D. in order to write a great deal of verse and when I discovered many of the contemporary German poets; also Liliencron was very much in the air then, and Richard Dehmel. I went back and read many of the older German poets, even some of the poetic dramatists, such as Grillparzer, and I got drunk on Heine, and later when I came back to America I published a book of short poems, *Love and Liberation,* which was full of short lyrics, very much influenced by Heine.

The two-and-a-half years in Germany were extremely happy years in many ways, intoxicated years, intoxicated with the reading of poetry and the writing of poetry. Swinburne was a very heavy influence on me, and it's a bad influence at any time because his style is so overpowering. However, I did work out of it, and before I came back, I had written the poems that made up my first book, which I've spoken about earlier in these recordings, poems about New York City. That book was called *The Human Fantasy.* Those were not my earlier, pre-German period poems, which were published later in a second book called *The Belovèd Adventure.* It had seemed to me, or to some of my advisors, that the poems about New York were the most likely to find a publisher. Many of them were written when I was homesick in Göttingen, that small university town in the north of

Germany. It was the first time in my life that I'd been so far away from my family, and I knew that I was to be away for three years.

When I came back to America, toward the end of June 1910, I had a mass of manuscripts that I think, without exaggerating, was perhaps three or three-and-a-half feet high. I was absolutely stumped about what to do. I felt they'd all have to be published. I was not sufficiently critical, self-critical. Whenever anyone suggested he'd like to go through this mass of poems—there was an older man there in East Hampton that summer who had written and published verse: "Why don't you let me look through them?" he said—I wouldn't allow it. The poems were sacrosanct. I felt so intensely about them.

That autumn in New York, I turned in *The Human Fantasy* manuscript in terribly sloppy youthful handwriting to Henry Holt and Company, to whom I 'd been recommended by Mrs. Charles de Kay, the mother of the lady who is now my wife, and who was the wife of Charles de Kay, the art critic on the *Times* and himself a poet. Roland Holt, president of the firm, was a friend of theirs. He read the manuscript and declined it. Then I took it elsewhere and ended up by sending it to Mitchell Kennerley, who was publishing much verse. Kennerley wrote me a letter, the first serious letter about my work I'd ever had, saying, "I see in you a remarkable talent for fiction. You are not a poet. You have not got the qualities of a poet. You should write novels, and I shall be extremely interested to see your first novel." Part of his reaction was due to the fact that there was a prefatory bit of prose at the beginning of *The Human Fantasy*. I had made up a paragraph or two to serve as an epigraph, and at the bottom of it is said, "From an unfinished novel by F. F." I brought in those initials because they were the initials of a girl that I knew very well in Germany, and I did this for good luck, as it were. Kennerley thought, I suppose, that this was an excerpt from an actual unfinished novel of mine.

This rejection was a grievous disappointment. After the Kennerley rejection, my mother was very unhappy about my state of mind. She was a very kind person, quite phenomenal. I've never known anyone like her. In a sense, she died when she did because she thought it would be better so for her children. She had a very bad heart condition, and she wouldn't do anything about it. She was the most unselfish person I've ever known, the gentlest and the strongest; underneath that gentleness there was steel. She said, "Why don't you go ahead and get your book printed? I'll pay for it."

I sent the book out to various key people, and I had some really remarkable letters. They were not the sort of people who would say nice things about a book unless they meant it. If they didn't think very much of it, they would say something polite, but they would not go out of their way to be enthusiastic, as these people were. I did not know any of them personally. I had sent copies of the book to Edwin Arlington Robinson, to Richard Le Gallienne, to Percy MacKaye, and to the great doctor and writer S. Weir Mitchell, who ran a sanitarium for people suffering from nervous breakdowns. My mother had been a patient there, just before her marriage, when she couldn't make up her mind whether she wanted to marry my father or not. She wore herself out trying to make up her mind and took what was known as a "rest cure" at Dr. Mitchell's place. They'd live on a milk diet there and lie in bed all day. They don't use that method of cure anymore. Also, I'd sent a copy to John Masefield, who was not yet poet laureate, and to Walter De la Mare.

All these people wrote me—and also I sent one to Professor Barrett Wendell. I'd gone to his lectures at Harvard. I got really enthusiastic letters from them all, especially from Barrett Wendell, who wrote me a four- or five-page letter. Masefield wrote me a long one, too, as did Richard Le Gallienne. In that exquisite handwriting of his, he praised my book for its "impassioned, unsullied ardor of youth," and said how he wished he could have this ardor now. Weir Mitchell complimented me on the poems in the highest—and De la Mare— anyway, with enthusiasm, real response, which just kindled my heart and raised my hopes.

With my other books I didn't bother so much to send out complimentary copies. The next book that came out was *The Belovèd Adventure,* and that also was published by Sherman, French and Company, and again my dear mother enthusiastically paid for it and had me solemnly autograph her copy—just so sweet. The third book was *Love and Liberation,* which also was published by Sherman, French. Those books, by dint of hard work on my part—because one of the disadvantages of not having a real publisher is that you have to do all the promotion and all the distribution yourself. I would spend my weekends—I had a circular made—sending this circular out to everyone I could think of, writing to reviewers, writing to review media, sending out review copies, going to bookstores. I remember arriving—I had to go early, because I had to be at my job at 8:30—I remember arriving at Macy's very early in the morning much to the astonishment of the buyer there, holding my book in my hand. I went through all that sort of thing.

The result was that by dint of backbreaking work, the books had quite a sale. You know, usually, a poet's first book, if he sells five hundred copies he's doing well. I managed to work them to over a thousand.

My position then came gradually to be something like the position of the more favored poets today, where Robert Lowell will get the front page, perhaps, of most of the review media. So I got the front page of *The New York Times Book Review* and of *The Boston Transcript Book Review* for *Dust and Light*. Many anthologies now included poems of mine, and particularly one poem that found great favor. The poem was called "Earth"; it appears in *Dust and Light* and it's a longish poem. It was the leading poem in two anthologies. In other words, I had arrived, in a small way. The atmosphere was much less critical than it is now.

> Earth
> Grasshopper, your fairy song
> And my poem alike belong
> To the dark and silent earth
> From which all poetry has birth;
> All we say and all we sing
> Is but as the murmuring
> Of that drowsy heart of hers
> When from her deep dream she stirs:
> If we sorrow, or rejoice,
> You and I are but her voice.
> Deftly does the dust express
> In mind her hidden loveliness,
> And from her cool silence stream
> The cricket's cry and Dante's dream;
> For the earth that breeds the trees
> Breeds cities too, and symphonies.
> Equally her beauty flows
> Into a savior, or a rose—
> Looks down in dream, and from above
> Smiles at herself in Jesus' love.
> Christ's love and Homer's art
> Are but the workings of her heart;
> Through Leonardo's hand she seeks
> Herself, and through Beethoven speaks

In holy thunderings around
The awful message of the ground.
The serene and humble mold
Does in herself all selves enfold—
Kingdoms, destinies, and creeds,
Great dreams, and dauntless deeds,
Science that metes the firmament,
The high, inflexible intent
Of one for many sacrificed—
Plato's brain, the heart of Christ;
All love, all legend, and all lore
Are in the dust forevermore.
Even as the growing grass
Up from the soil religions pass,
And the field that bears the rye
Bears parables and prophecy.
Out of the earth the poem grows
Like the lily, or the rose;
And all man is, or yet may be,
Is but herself in agony
Toiling up the steep ascent
Toward the complete accomplishment
When all dust shall be, the whole
Universe, one conscious soul.
Yea, the quiet and cool sod
Bears in her breast the dream of God.
If you would know what earth is, scan
The intricate, proud heart of man,
Which is the earth articulate,
And learn how holy and how great,
How limitless and how profound
Is the nature of the ground—
How without terror or demur
We may entrust ourselves to her
When we are wearied out, and lay
Our faces in the common clay.
For she is pity, she is love,

All wisdom, she, all thoughts that move
About her everlasting breast
Till she gathers them to rest:
All tenderness of all the ages,
Seraphic secrets of the sages,
Vision and hope of all the seers,
All prayer, all anguish, and all tears
Are but the dust, that from her dream
Awakes, and knows herself supreme—
Are but earth, when she reveals
All that her secret heart conceals
Down in the dark and silent loam,
Which is ourselves, asleep, at home.
Yea, and this, my poem, too,
Is part of her as dust and dew,
Wherein herself she doth declare
Through my lips, and say her prayer.

Poets today are very highly trained in the field of literature, in the techniques of literature. They are highly critical, highly sophisticated. The way I really feel is that you can't know too much about anything. The more you know, the better. But I think the poet is born. That's an old adage, but it's true. I think that there are a great many working in the field of poetry today who are really scholars rather than poets, and whose chief interest is in scholarly allusion and technical brilliance of one kind or another. Yet among them there have certainly been true poets who have done some of the best work that's been done in this country. It has come about partly through the fact that so many more people are professionally involved in knowing about literature and therefore in command of the medium they're working in. That never does any harm, does it? Harm is done only when people who are attracted purely to the scholarly side go in and write poetry whose sole interest for them, and supposedly for other equally scholarly people, is the hidden allusions to be found there.

There was always a space of three years or more between my books, except for those first three, when I was unloading this enormous mass of manuscript. *Dust and Light* was published in 1919, and *The Black Panther* in 1922, and the next one, *The Bright Doom,* was in 1927. *The Black Panther* was the most successful book of verse that year. I had one great disappointment, however, which didn't really mean too much to me. It would mean more to me now than it did then because then I was rather arrogant, but I was told—— The three judges of the Pulitzer Prize that year were Wilbur Cross, who was governor of Connecticut and editor of the *Yale Review;* Louis Untermeyer, who was an admirer of my poetry and had written a chapter about my work in his volume *Modern American Poetry;* and another person whose name I cannot now remember. The first two, Louis Untermeyer and Wilbur Cross, told me that my book, *The Black Panther,* was the best book of verse published that year. So, as those prizes go by majority, I thought it was coming to me. But I didn't get it. It went to Robert Frost, who continued to get the Pulitzer every year for four years, I think it was.* He himself used to joke about it whenever he was lauded for this. He'd shake his head and say, "Yes, and it's a bloody shame. A bloody shame."

Well, I continued working just as hard, and I spent all my summer free time, which was very brief, mostly weekends, at East Hampton. I was getting at that time two weeks' vacation. At the end of the two weeks, I would usually telephone in to the manager of the bookstore and say, "Couldn't I take one week more?" As the manager of the bookstore knew that my great passion was writing verse and that it meant a great deal to me— I would say I was right in the middle of a poem—he would usually let me have it. Here's how I learned my writing habits. I loved to be outdoors, walking on the beach. Yet if you were writing a poem in the ordinary way, as I used to write them, you'd be indoors, with pencil and paper. So I learned to make them up in my head as I walked, and by the end of my vacation during those years, I'd bring back to New York in my head, without having had to waste any time putting them down on paper, all the poems I'd made during those three weeks. I'd remember it all, and I remember it all still. I remember all the different versions through which the poems passed. I revised and revised and revised, and I remember them all—and I was treading on clouds.

Then in the winter I went on writing verse in such spare time as I had, and I was able to keep it up until I was made senior editor at Scribners after the death of Max Perkins and moved into his office. There followed a period of fifteen years when I wrote extremely little. For now I was confronted not with a situation where work was given me to do and where

---

*The Pulitzer Prize for a volume of poetry published in 1922 went to Edna St. Vincent Millay, not to Robert Frost. Frost won four Pulitzer Prizes for poetry, but not in consecutive years. His awards came in 1924, 1931, 1937, and 1943.

Max as my chief would assign work to me, but I had now to use my own imagination in producing a list, and not only a list but a list that would bring in a great deal of money each year to the house. This got on my nerves. I had to devote all my time to seeing people who might possibly lead to this or to that or writers whom we might get for the house, entertaining them at our home or at lunch or going out to dinners, going to this and that. I had to spend my nights reading manuscripts and meeting people. For fifteen years, while I was forced to do so—by this time I'd married, and I had a wife to support—I gave up my poetry entirely. I think that there was much value in this because the impulse got dammed up in me and I was unhappy and things got so intense, that when I came to do my next book——

I omitted one step there. I had, during the time after my breakdown and hospitalization, the time when I was getting well, been encouraged by my psychiatrist to work on a volume of selections from my six books. This was published in 1936 under the title, *Poems, 1911–1936.* From then on, no book of mine came out, until shortly before I retired as senior editor for Scribners and published *Poems Old and New,* which contained a more drastic selection from the *Poems 1911–1936,* plus the forty-odd new poems I had written during those barren fifteen years. Certainly those new poems were better than anything I'd done before and revealed a much livelier self-criticism. But the main thing was the dammed-up force of an impulse that had been frustrated for fifteen years. This gave my later work much more intensity—channeled it, as it were.

The book after that was probably my best, *The Gardener and Other Poems.* It has some innovations, some poems that, to my generation of poets, would have seemed rather daring, such as the "Anima" poem and others. Then, in my old age, I have gone on writing. I regard eighty as old, and I'm not at all ashamed to be old. I'm going to wear a hearing aid soon. In fact, I've had it fitted already.

The thing that is interesting to me, when I look back, is the fact that my poetry has always been metaphysical in character. I remember as a boy one of the things I used to puzzle about in myself was that I never believed anything. That may seem a strange statement for a man to make who's a poet. As I grew older, I thought a great deal about the way things really are and tried to make out some scheme that would satisfy me. And I hit upon one. It is an over-simplification, but I still feel has in it a kernel of truth. I think that the great difficulty of human beings has been that they always tend to see things in human terms. Now, human life begins and ends, and human beings, in order to function, have to have a purpose. This is not true of the universe. The universe has never begun and will never end because the totality of things does not begin or end. Also the totality of things is not conscious. God, if there be a God, is certainly not conscious. He's totally unconscious, and the universe has no purpose, nor does it need one, any more than it needs to be conscious. The brain is a tool developed by an organism in the interests of survival, just like the hand. The parts of the universe that have to struggle with each other for survival must have, if they're going to be successful, the advantage of every tool, and the brain is one of the most effective of all the tools developed by certain organisms for their survival. But the totality of things has no consciousness. And if you try to apply the brain, with its human premises and motives, to the universe, you never get anywhere. That's the reason why the whole thing must forever remain a gigantic mystery. As you cannot grasp the moon with your hands, so you cannot grasp the universe with your brain. The universe is unconscious, but it has this tendency, which is built in, whereby wounds heal; worlds grow old and are broken up and new worlds form out of them; life arises wherever there's a possibility for life; illness, if there is a possibility for survival in the cells, is overcome. There is this tendency, and this tendency has borne us all along. You and I were there in the primeval slime. In fact we were there when the earth came out of the sun. We were in the fire. We were born of the fire, just as later we were born of the water; all of us have been sea animals. And we've had absolutely nothing to do with all this ourselves. It all happened to us, through this tendency of the universe to move in a certain way. Every day, each of us, every human being and every animal does a million things through his unconscious that he couldn't consciously do—indeed, he hadn't the faintest notion how they are accomplished.

I don't know how to make enamel. I make enamel every day for my teeth. I don't know anything about chemistry. I go through the most elaborate chemistry in digesting my food. The gradual construction of a human being in the uterus is achieved without the mother's help. The whole universe is an unconscious process, moving always in a positive direction, with great throes and upheavals in between—self-nourishing, self-surviving, self-surpassing, with no purpose whatsoever, for it needs none. Purpose is a human concept. Beginning and end are merely human terms. Consciousness is useful where a part of the universe needs consciousness in order to survive. But consciousness bears no relation to absolutes.

This has been my philosophy for a long time. I've never found it in any book. It is not Buddhism; certainly it is not any of the doctrines of the West. But as I have gone through life, I have realized more and more—although I've had an extremely happy life—that life is a tragedy. From the human point of view, life is tragic. Every life ends in tragedy. Yet I feel—and this is where I differ with the other poets of the age—I feel that it is a worthwhile tragedy. I'm glad I've lived. I don't expect ever to live again. I expect when I die that not only will my life cease, but the fact that I have lived at all will be wiped out also. Everything will be taken. I believe that life is tragic, and I think it's very worthwhile. I'm glad I've lived. I said that, too, in a poem, when I wrote about old friends who have died.

Dear Men and Women
(In Memory of Van Wyck Brooks)
In the quiet before cockcrow when the cricket's
Mandolin falters, when the light of the past
Falling from the high stars yet haunts the earth
And the east quickens, I think of those I love—
Dear men and women no longer with us.
And not in grief or regret merely but rather
With a love that is almost joy I think of them,
Of whom I am part, as they of me, and through whom
I am made more wholly one with the pain and the glory,
The heartbreak at the heart of things.
I have learned it from them at last, who am now grown old
A happy man, that the nature of things is tragic
And meaningful beyond words, that to have lived
Even if once only, once and no more,
Will have been—oh, how truly—worth it.
The years go by: March flows into April,
The sycamore's delicate tracery puts on
Its tender green; April is August soon;
Autumn, and the raving of insect choirs,
The thud of apples in moonlit orchards;
Till winter brings the slant, windy light again
On shining Manhattan, her towering stone and glass;
And age deepens—oh, much is taken, but one
Dearer than all remains, and life is sweet

Still, to the now enlightened spirit.
Doors are opened that never before were opened,
New ways stand open, but quietly one door
Closes, the door to the future; there it is written,
"Thus far and no farther"—there, as at Eden's gate,
The angel with the fiery sword.
The Eden we dream of, the Eden that lies before us,
The unattainable dream, soon lies behind.
Eden is always yesterday or tomorrow,
There is no way now but back, back to the past—
The past has become paradise.
And there they dwell, those ineffable presences,
Safe beyond time, rescued from death and change.
Though all be taken, they only shall not be taken—
Immortal, unaging, unaltered, faithful yet
To that lost dream world they inhabit.
Truly, to me they now may come no more,
But I to them in reverie and remembrance
Still may return, in me they still live on;
In me they shall have their being, till we together
Darken in the great memory.
Dear eyes of delight, dear youthful tresses, foreheads
Furrowed with age, dear hands of love and care—
Lying awake at dawn, I remember them,
With a love that is almost joy I remember them:
Lost, and all mine, all mine, forever.

Appendix 1

John Hall Wheelock: Bibliography

Books

Wheelock and Van Wyck Brooks. *Verses by Two Undergraduates.* Cambridge, Mass.: Privately printed, 1905.

The Human Fantasy. Boston: Sherman, French, 1911.

The Belovèd Adventure. Boston: Sherman, French, 1912.

Love and Liberation: The Songs of Adsched to Meru, and Other Poems. Boston: Sherman, French, 1913.

Dust and Light. New York: Scribners, 1919.

A Bibliography of Theodore Roosevelt. New York: Scribners, 1920.

The Black Panther: A Book of Poems. New York: Scribners, 1922.

The Bright Doom: A Book of Poems. New York and London: Scribners, 1927.

Poems, 1911–1936. New York and London: Scribners, 1936.

Poems Old and New. New York: Scribners, 1956.

The Gardener, and Other Poems. New York: Scribners, 1961.

What Is Poetry? New York: Scribners, 1963.

Dear Men and Women. New York: Scribners, 1966.

By Daylight and in Dream: New and Collected Poems, 1904–1970. New York: Scribners, 1970.

In Love and Song: Poems. New York: Scribners, 1971.

This Blessed Earth: New and Selected Poems, 1927–1977. New York: Scribners, 1978.

Afternoon: Amagansett Beach. New York: Dandelion Press, 1978.

Other

Wheelock, trans. in part. *Happily Ever After: Fairy Tales Selected by Alice Dalgliesh.* New York and London: Scribners, 1939.

Wheelock, ed. *The Face of a Nation: Poetical Passages from the Writings of Thomas Wolfe.* New York: Scribners, 1939.

Wheelock, ed. *Editor to Author: The Letters of Maxwell E. Perkins.* New York: Scribners, 1950.

Wheelock, ed. *Poets of Today,* vols 1–8. New York: Scribners, 1954–1961.

REFERENCES

Berg, A. Scott. *Max Perkins: Editor of Genius.* New York: Dutton, 1978.

Bruccoli, Matthew J., and Park Bucker, eds. *To Loot My Life Clean: The Thomas Wolfe-Maxwell Perkins Correspondence.* Columbia: University of South Carolina Press, 2000. Includes letters to and from JHW.

Clemente, Vince. "James Dickey Remembering John Hall Wheelock." *South Carolina Review* 32 (Spring 2000): 13–18.

Clemente and Graham Everett, eds. "Remembering John Hall Wheelock." *North Atlantic Review* 3 (Summer 1991): 6–97.

Delaney, John, ed. *Dictionary of Literary Biography Documentary Series,* Vol. 13, *The House of Scribner 1846–1904*; Vol. 16, *The House of Scribner, 1905–1930*; Vol. 17, *The House of Scribner, 1931–1984.* Detroit: Bruccoli Clark Layman / Gale Research, 1995, 1997, 1998.

Hubbell, Jay B. "A Major American Poet: John Hall Wheelock." *South Atlantic Quarterly* 72 (Spring 1973): 295–310.

Kennedy, Richard S. "What the Galley Proofs of Wolfe's *Of Time and the River* Tell Us." *Thomas Wolfe Review* 9 (Fall 1985): 1–8.

O'Connor, Robert H. "John Hall Wheelock." In *Dictionary of Literary Biography,* vol. 45: *American Poets, 1880–1945, First Series,* edited by Peter Quartermain, 429–434. Detroit: Bruccoli Clark / Gale Research, 1986.

Slavitt, David R. "Elegy for Walter Stone." In *The Carnivore,* pp. 55–58. Chapel Hill: University of North Carolina Press, 1965.

Taylor, Henry. "Letting the Darkness In: The Poetic Achievement of John Hall Wheelock." *The Hollins Critic* 7 (Dec. 1970): 1–15. Collected in *Compulsory Figures: Essays on Recent American Poets* by Taylor (Baton Rouge: Louisiana State University Press, 1992).

Untermeyer, Louis. "John Hall Wheelock." In *The New Era in American Poetry,* by Untermeyer, 215–230. New York: Holt, 1919.

Appendix 2

A Selection of John Hall Wheelock/Thomas Wolfe Letters

FROM: John Hall Wheelock   CCS, 5 pp., Princeton

July 17, 1929

Dear Wolfe:

I hope you don't mind my omitting the "Mr.", and that you will do the same in writing me. I was very glad to get your note of the 16th this morning, giving your complete address. Thanks so much for the cartoon from the Boston Herald, which was undoubtedly inspired by Scribner's Magazine, as you surmise—and which I have passed on to Mr. Dashiell. I am surprised that the Boston authorities haven't looked into the moral situations which seem to be prevailing in the Arnold Arboretum, according to your ornithological report.

I have good news and bad news for you. The good news being that your story is out in the August number of Scribner's,* and that I will ask the Magazine to send you your copies to the new address. In the back of the Magazine you will find a brief write-up about your work, and also what seems to me an excellent picture of yourself. The bad news is that some seventy-five pages of your manuscript have been mislaid in some way, so that I am obliged to send you proof of galleys 79 to 100, inclusive, without the original copy.†

From *To Loot My Life Clean: The Thomas Wolfe-Maxwell Perkins Correspondence,* edited by Matthew J. Bruccoli and Park Bucker (Columbia: University of South Carolina Press, 2000)

*"An Angel on the Porch," an episode from *Look Homeward, Angel,* was published in *Scribner's Magazine* to generate interest in the forthcoming novel.

†None of the galley proofs for *Look Homeward, Angel* survives.

These galleys go forward to your new address to-day by first-class post. I have read them most carefully and I think you will understand my various corrections and suggestions. They will require of course a most careful reading by yourself.

Please note that I have deleted, on galley 80, several sections which it seems best to omit. You and Mr. Perkins had agreed to omit these sections, when you went over the manuscript, but in some way the printer set them up. I think nothing is lost by their omission. In the same way I have deleted one or two phrases in other places.

Is there any danger of confusion through the use of the names "Sheba", "Horty" and "Miss Amy"?*

I have looked up and verified all your quotations, so you need not worry about these.

I wish I had time and space to tell you how my enthusiasm grows with the proofreading. I must content myself with the less gracious act of pointing out what seems to me a defect. If you do not agree with me, kindly disregard my criticism. It seems to me that the section beginning in the middle of galley 87 and running to Chapter 25, is too long. This is the section dealing with the conversation between George Graves and Eugene, and is full of literary allusions, very skilfully interwoven with the story. It is one of the best parts of the book but it loses by being too much prolonged. You don't want the reader to get, for a moment, the impression that the author is conscious of his own skill and virtuosity; and I am afraid this will be the feeling aroused if this section runs on as long as it now does. Won't you consider this, and if you agree indicate such parts as you wish omitted?

You have not yet returned to me revised galleys 71 and 72, together with their foul galleys; nor have you returned galleys 72 to 78, inclusive, together with copy thereto. I have received here page proof covering the first 70 galleys, which is to say about 250 pages, but as this page proof covers only revised galleys, which had very very few changes and as I am following page proof most carefully myself, I felt it was not necessary to trouble you with them.

The printer was a little bit upset by the very lengthy insertion which you made on one of our revised galleys. I don't suppose it is likely that you'll be making another of this kind. It is of course desirable to do as little of this as possible, on account of the expense and delay involved.

---

*Sheba in *Look Homeward, Angel* was Hortense (Horty) in "O Lost"; Amy in *Look Homeward, Angel* was Emma in "O Lost."

This is a tiresome letter, but I do hope with all my heart that you're going to have a fine rest and a happy time, too, up in Maine.

As ever, dear Wolfe,

Yours sincerely,

J. H. W.

To
Mr. Thomas Wolfe
c/o Mrs. Jessie Benge
Boothbay Harbor, Maine.
Snow Cottage, Ocean Point.

■ ■ ■ ■

TO: John Hall Wheelock   ALS, 16 pp., Princeton

Ocean Point, Maine July 19, 1929

Dear Mr Wheelock: Don't mind if I call you "mister" at present, but you must please not do it to me. I no longer have the slightest feeling of stiffness or diffidence toward you, I have on the contrary the warmest and gratefullest feeling toward you and Mr Perkins, but I could no more call you Wheelock than I could call him Perkins. Alone in my mind I know that I am now a man in years, and as I face my work alone I come pretty close at times to naked terror, naked nothing, I know that no one can help me or guide me or put me right—that's my job. Perhaps that is why in my personal relations with people I cling to the old child's belief—that there are older people who are wiser and stronger, and who can help me.—I am far from being melancholy—I am more full of strength and power and hope than I have been in years—I have in me at the present time several books, all of which are full of life and variety, and rich detail. If I can only put down finally the great disease and distress of my spirit—which is to take in more of life than one man can hold—I can go on to do good work—because all men are certainly bound by this limit and I believe my chance to learn and experience, and my power of absorption are as good as those of most men. I feel packed to the lips with rich ore, in this wild, and lovely place, all America stretches below me like a vast plain, the million forms that repeat themselves in the city, and that torture us so by their confusion and number, have been fused into a calmer temper—I am filled with a kind of tragic joy; I want to tear myself open and show my friends all that I think I have. I am so anxious to lay all my wares out on the table—when one thing that I have done is praised, to say: You have not seen 1/10 or 1/20 of what is in me. Just wait" Then I am tortured when I have talked to people that I have seemed too exuberant, too full of wild energy—I go away thinking they have this simple picture in two or three colors of me, when there are a thousand sombre and obscure shadings that have not been shown. I am full of affection and hope for this first book, but when you and Mr Perkins have praised it I have been stirred with the desire to do something far better—I will, I must show these men what is in me! Hence, again, we come to those reasons that make me say "mister" to some people—the spirit of the young man is thirsty for real praise, for admiration of his works: the creative impulse, which has such complex associations, may have roots as simple and powerful as this one.

It would be inexact to say that I feel that whatever I do is by its doing right—in my own life I am trying for greater balance sanity, kindness to other people—but when I write at present I want to wrench the most remote and terrible things in myself and others—whatever scruples and restraints from the traditional morality I have—and I have many—vanish under the one surpassing urge to make everything blaze with light, to get intensity and denseness into everything!—Thus when I write, my own lusts, fears, hatreds, jealousies—all that is base or mean—I drag up with strong joy, as well perhaps as better qualities, feeling not how bad these things may be, but what magnificent life this is, how little all else is by comparison. This is of course the most colossal egotism—but how else do people create? not surely, by telling themselves they are dull, and their affairs petty or mean? what profit is in that, or where's the improvement? In short there are moments when I work when I feel that no one else is a quarter my power and richness—my baseness is better than their nobility, my sores more interesting than their health—etc, that, one way or another, I am a fine young fellow and a great man. I know you will not despise me for this confession—there are people all around, especially the critics, who would rail and sneer at this, but under their silly little pretenses of modesty and cynical urbanity they are nasty little mountains of egotism—I merely work in this way, by feeling when things are going well that I am something tremendous like a God, but as a person I am no longer insolent or proud at heart, I feel on the contrary a constant sense of inferiority, often to people I am in no wise inferior to. Professor Babbitt* at Harvard could figure all this out in 40 seconds by his patented quack's system, and have all my various romantic diseases healed with a half dozen [tickets] of his own manufacture—but his brand of "classicism" is so much more romantic than my wildest romanticism that by comparison Plato might have begot me out of Lesbia.

I cannot tell you how moved I was by your letter—by its length, its patience and care; it is a symbol of my entire relation with you and Mr Perkins—I could not a year ago have thought it possible that such good luck was in store for me—

*Irving Babbitt (1865-1933), Harvard professor of French, denounced both romanticism and naturalism.

a connection with such men, and such a house, and editing and criticism as painstaking and intelligent as I have had.

I should have once said that it was like a child's fantasy come true, but I know this is not exact—a child's dream is swollen with so much false magnificence that much in life seems stale and disappointing to the young man. But a slow and powerful joy is awaking in me as I come to see that life has real wonder that is more strange and marrowy than our fictions. Consider this: I was a little boy born among great mountains from obscure people, I saw strange and beautiful things when I was a child, I dreamed constantly of wonderful far off things and cities— and when I grew up I went away and saw them I was a poor boy who grew up in anarchy—I said that one day I should go to Harvard, and I went. People who make jokes about Harvard would make a joke about this, but it was not a joke to that boy—it was magic—and the journey must first be viewed from its beginning. I read and dreamed about strange foreign cities—I grew up and went to see them, I met people in them, I wandered from place to place by myself, I had wonderful adventures in them. When I was 16 or 18 I hoped,—I dreamed, I did not dare to speak the hope, that someday I would write a book that men would read—now I have written a book, and a great publishing house is printing it, and men who have seen it have been moved by it and praised it. Seven months ago I came to Vienna from Budapest after months of wandering about in Europe: I had a scar on my head and a broken nose, I found there a letter from Scribners. Now I am writing this from a little cottage on the wild coast of Maine—the sky is grey and full of creaking gulls, the Atlantic sweeps in in a long grey surge. I have eaten delicious foods and drunk glorious wines in many countries; I have read thousands of noble books in several languages; I have known and enjoyed beautiful women, have loved and been loved by one or two.

Fools will sneer "How romantic!"—I tell you merely what you will easily agree to—this is not romantic, this is only a bald statement of a few facts in a single ordinary life. No man can say that there is a single garnishment or distortion of fact here—whoever chooses to believe there is no wonder and no richness here is only stupidly and stubbornly hugging fantoms of sterility. No— what one comes to realize is that there is a reasonable hope that one may cherish in life that makes it well worth living—and that the childish pessimist who denies this is as lying and dishonest a rogue as the cheap ready-made optimist— and that, indeed, of the two brands of rascals, the merchant who deals in Pollyanna optimism is a better man than he whose stock-in-trade is snivelling drivelly Pollyanna pessimism. The spirit that feels from its mothers womb the tragic [underweft] of life, and never sees the End as different from what it is, is all the more certain that sunlight is not made of fog, wine of vinegar, good meat of sawdust, and a womans lovely body of nitrogen, decaying excrement, and muddy water. To hell with such lying drivel—why do we put up with it?

I know that it is good to eat, to drink, to sleep, to fish, to swim, to run, to travel to strange cities, to ride on land, sea, and in the air upon great machines, to love a woman, to try to make a beautiful thing—all such as consider such occupations "futile", let them go bury themselves in the earth and get eaten by worms to see if that is less futile However, these despisers of life who are so indifferent to living, are the first ones to cry out and hunt the doctor when they have bellyaches

There is an island in this lovely little harbor—I can look out on it from the porch of my cottage. It is covered by a magnificent forest of spruce trees, and a little cottage is tucked away in a clearing under three mighty trees at one end. One end of the island (where this house is) looks in on the bay and on the little cottages along the shore, the other end fronts the open Atlantic. Now I fantasy about buying this island (which has 15 or 20 acres), and so strange is possibility that one day perhaps I shall. Several weeks ago when I knew I was coming to Maine I began to think about islands. Presently I saw myself owning one, living on one, putting off from the mainland (a decrepit old wharf) with my servant, in a little motor boat stocked with provisions—to the minutest detail I saw this place, even to the spring house where butter and milk and rounds of beef should be stored. This scene became a part of my dream—however blurred the actual details have become, I cannot say, the picture remains vivid, only the island I dreamed about has become this one here—I am unable to distinguish one from the other, so imperceptibly have the two fused (even to the rotten old wharf from which I fish)

In a child's dreams the essential thing happens—it is this that makes wonder —the long vacancies between the flare of reality are left out; he is, for example, on a great ship going to a strange country, the voyage ends, and the very next moment the ship is sailing into a harbor, he sets foot not on land, but on Paris, London, Venice. I am living in such a [place]—there is the harbor, with wooded islands in it, a little shore road that winds around by the waters edge, and all the little cottages, with tidy yards, bright flowers. Then immediately there is the ocean. I had ceased until recent years to believe there could be such scenes; and even now it does not seem real. I thought there would be preludes to the sea. But there are not. The other night I walked along the road. The little farmhouses slept below the moon, the gnarled apple trees full of apples getting ripe leaned over the hedges, and on the walls the wild wood lilies grew. You would not say along that road the sea was there, behind the houses, behind the fir trees, and the hedges, and the apples getting ripe, and yet you round a bend, and the sea is there. I thought there would be vast lengthenings into the sea, slow stoppages of land and rock, drear marshy vacancies, slow lapse and waste relinquishment of earth, but when you round the bend of the road the sea is there—he has entered at one stride into the land—this union of the vast and lonely with the little houses, the land, the little harbor, made a great music in me. I could not tell you all it meant, but it was like Milton standing by a little door. And I thought that if one came into this place on a ship from open sea it would be with the suddenness of a dream.

To unspin all the meanings in these things would take too long—and my letter is much too long already

I got the proof sent with your letter—through galley 100. I am sending off to you this afternoon the few galleys I had before—through 78 (including foul galleys for 71, 72) I am sorry the printer was upset by my one long insertion— I do not think it will happen again: I did it here to round out one detail in Leonard's life—much that showed the man in a favorable light had previously been cut, and I though it proper to add a little here. But I shall not do this again. I note carefully all you say—I shall study the boys-going-away-from-school scene, and cut where I can. I am sorry to know it is still too long—Mr Perkins suggested a very large cut out of it, which was made—I have a much fresher mind for it now, and will perhaps find more. I shall certainly send all the proofs I now have (through 100) back to you by Tuesday of next week—they should reach you Thursday. I still have ten or eleven days in this lovely place—that is, until a good week from next Tuesday—you would therefore have time to send me more. I propose to go to Canada when I leave here, for a week, and return to New York before August 10. It would be good if I had proof to take with me.

You gave me a great start when you said 75 pages of ms. had been lost, but on re-reading, as I understand your letter, it seems that we already have galley proofs for these pages—even if we haven't there is at Scribners a complete copy of the original mss. besides the one Mr Perkins and I cut. Of course what revisions were made in these 75 p. I don't know. It is a thrilling shock to know that you have already page proof for 70 galleys—of course I am excited and anxious to see them. I await eagerly the copies of the magazine with my story and the piece about my work—What's the use of acting coy and modestly restrained when you don't feel that way!

This is another day—a glorious blue-white cold sparkling day. Forgive the long letter, the personal rhapsodies—I have victimized you by making you the target. My next letter will come with the proof and be strictly concerned with business. I fish, read, and write here.

Faithfully Yours, Tom Wolfe

■ ■ ■ ■

FROM: John Hall Wheelock   CC, 6 pp., Princeton

July 23, 1929

Dear Wolfe:

I was greatly delighted and touched by your fine letter of July 19. I wish I could answer it as it deserves to be answered, but the rather unusual pressure in the office just now, which means that I have to work every evening as well, makes the writing of letters a luxury beyond my reach at the moment.

I think you know that both Mr. Perkins and myself have the greatest admiration for your genius and an almost fatherly solicitude for the fortunes of your work in the world. Now that we have come to know you through our meetings together in the office, we count you with pride among those friends for whom we have real affection. I'm afraid years do not bring always the feeling of greater wisdom and assurance, but if we can be of any help by virtue of our longer experience in the work-a-day world, you know that you may look to us for it.

I am so glad to see that you are happy at Ocean Point and that you feel the exhilaration which one has always, I think, in the presence of the sea. Some day I shall present you with a book of mine containing some poems about the sea. I was sea-born, just as Eugene was hill-born.

Now to business. With your permission I'm not going to show you the 256 pages that we have. There were hardly any corrections in the revised galleys and I have checked up all that there were most carefully. I think you have enough on your hands now, and that any further kind of proof will only be confusing and distracting. Page proof after this will be made direct from original galleys, and this page proof we will want you to see.

I received this morning corrected galleys 73 to 78, inclusive, also corrected revised galleys 71 and 72, also manuscript and foul galleys. All of these have been carefully attended to. I also received corrected galleys 79 to 90. I have a confession: the manuscript covering these galleys was lost by myself in a taxi-cab, together with original printer's set of proofs. I had read all the galleys of this set except one, and I can assure you that no part of the manuscript was omitted from the galleys except one or two places which you and Mr. Perkins had decided to omit. Of this I can be absolutely positive, as I went over the whole manuscript with the galleys before it was lost. I am terribly sorry.

You must follow your own judgement entirely in the matter of cutting the boys-going-from-school scene. You need not worry about the correctness of quoted lines or of words in foreign languages, as I will take care of all of that here; but you must watch very carefully the names of your characters, for I may slip up on these now and then.

I'm sorry, but since you leave the matter to us, it still seems best to cut the passage on galley 80, as we originally had done. This passage doesn't add anything more to what has already been said, and in our opinion it would be likely to cause trouble.*

I sent you yesterday galleys 109 to 115, inclusive, together with manuscript.

Now, my dear Wolfe, I can write no more but this letter brings you all sorts of good wishes. If my communications seem dry and matter-of-fact, please know

*In the absence of galleys it is impossible to identify this passage.

that I am not really so by nature, but that I'm working under terrible pressure here just now during the absence of Mr. Perkins.

> As ever,
> Yours sincerely,
> J. H. W.

To
Mr. Thomas Wolfe
c/o Mrs. Jessie Benge,
Snow Cottage, Ocean Point
Boothbay Harbor, Maine

P.S. Please excuse this hurriedly-written note, dear Wolfe.
J. H. W.

■ ■ ■ ■

TO: John Hall Wheelock   ALS, 22 pp., Princeton
24 June 1930   Guaranty Trust letterhead, Paris

Everything moves, everything moves, changes, goes on from place to place—and of the women of the everlasting earth

Dear Jack: Thanks very much for your fine letter—I can't tell you how touched and grateful I was. I'm not going to write you a long one now—I'll do that later when things have settled a little more. Briefly, this has happened: I have been in Paris almost all the time since I landed with the exception of a few days in Rouen—this not because I love Paris, but because after two weeks of casting around, moving from one hotel to the other, I suddenly decided that we spend too much of our lives looking for ideal conditions to work in, and that what we are after is an ideal condition of the soul which almost never comes. So I got tired and disgusted with myself went to a little hotel—not very French, I'm afraid, but very touristy—and set to work. I've been doing five or six hours a day for almost two weeks now—the weather is hot and sticky, but I sweat and work—its the only cure I've found for the bloody hurting inside me. Dear Jack, its been so bad I can't tell you about it: I feel all bloody inside me—but have faith in me, everything's going to be all right. What do you know about it? I am writing a book so filled with the most unspeakable desire, longing, and love for my own country and ten thousand things in it—that I have to laugh at times to think what the Mencken crowd and all the other crowds are going to say about it. But I can't help it—if I have ever written anything with utter conviction it is this—dear Jack, I <u>know</u> that I know what some of our great woe and sickness as a people is now, because that woe is in me—it is rooted in myself, but by God Jack, I have not written a word directly about myself yet God knows what Maxwell Perkins will say when he sees it, but I've just finished the first section of the first part—it is

called <u>Antaeus</u>,* and it is as if I had become a voice for the experience of a race:
It begins "Of wandering forever and the earth again"—and by God, Jack, I
believe I've got it—the two things that haunt and hurt us—the eternal wandering, moving, questing, loneliness, homesickness, and the desire of the soul for a
home, peace, fixity, repose. In Antaeus, in a dozen short scenes, told in their own
language, we see people of all sorts <u>constantly in movement</u>, going somewhere,
haunted by it—and by God, Jack, it's the <u>truth</u> about them—I saw it as a child,
I've seen it ever since, I see it here in their poor damned haunted eyes:—Well
there are these scenes—a woman telling of the river—the ever-moving river—
coming through the levee at night, and of the crippled girl clinging to the limb,
of the oak, and of then how she feels the house break loose and go with the tide,
then of being on the roof-top with Furman and the children, and of other houses
and people—tragedy, pity, humor, bravery, and the great wild savagery of American nature; then the pioneer telling of "the perty little gal" he liked, but moving
on because the wilderness was getting too crowded; then the hoboes waiting quietly at evening by the water tower for the coming of the fast express; then a rich
American girl moving on from husband to husband, from drink to dope to
opium, from white lovers to black ones, from New York to Paris to California;
then the engineer at the throttle of the fast train; then a modest poor little couple from 123d St—the woman earning living by painting lampshades, the man
an impractical good-for-nothing temporarily employed in a filling station—
cruising in their cheap little car through Virginia and Kentucky in autumn—all
filled with details of motor camps, where you can get a shack for $1.00 a night,
and of "lovely meals" out of cans—whole cost $0.36—etc; then a school teacher
from Ohio taking University Art Pilgrimage No. 36 writing back home "—didn't
get your letter till we got to Florence . . . stayed in Prague 3 days but rained
whole time we were there, so didnt get to see much, etc", then Lee coming
through Virginia in the night on his great white horse; then the skull of a pioneer
in the desert, a rusted gun stock and a horses skull; then a Harry's New York Bar
American saying "Jesus! What a country! I been back one time in seven years.
That was enough. . . . Me, I'm a Frenchman. See? But talking, telling, cursing,
until he drinks himself into a stupor—then a bum, a natural wanderer who has

---

*"Antaeus, or A Memory of Earth" was intended as a prologue for "The October
Fair." "Antaeus" was suspended on Maxwell Perkins's advice and later rewritten for *Of
Time and the River.* See Wolfe's *Antaeus or A Memory of Earth,* edited by Ted Mitchell (n.p.:
David Strange/Thomas Wolfe Society, 1996).

Antaeus, son of Earth (Gaea) and Sea (Poseidon), was the Libyan wrestler who
was unbeatable when he remained in contact with the earth; Heracles defeated Antaeus
by lifting him off the ground. For Wolfe, Antaeus represented the themes of wandering and the search for a father.

been everywhere; then a Boston woman and her husband who have come to France to live—" Francis always felt he wanted to do a little writing. . . . . we felt the atmosphere is so much better here for that kind of thing; then a Jew named Greenberg, who made his pile in New York and who now lives in France having changed his name to Montvert, and of course feels no homesickness at all, save what is natural to 4000 years of wandering—and more, and more, and more! Then amid all this you get the thing that does not change, the fixed principle, <u>the female principle</u>—the <u>earth again</u>—and, by God, Jack, I know <u>this is true</u> also. They want love, the earth, a home fixity—you get the mother and the lover—as the book goes on, and you see this incessant change, movement, unrest, and the great train with the wanderers rushing through the night outside you get the eternal silent waiting earth that does not change, and the two women, going to bed upon it, working in their gardens upon it, dreaming, longing, calling for men to return upon it. And down below in the mighty earth, you get the bones of the pioneers, all of the dust now trembling to the great trains wheel, the dust that lived, suffered, died, and is now buried, pointing 80 ways across 3000 miles of earth—and deeper than all, eternal and enduring, "the elm trees thread the bones of buried lovers" Through it all is poetry—the enormous rivers of the nation [drinking] the earth away at night, the vast rich [stamina] of night time in America, the lights, the smells, the thunder of the train—the savage summers, the [fierce] winters, the floods, the blizzards—all, all! and finally the great soft galloping of the horses of sleep! Mr Perkins may say that the first part is too much like a poem—but Jack, I've got it [loaded] with these stories of the wanderings of real people in their own talk, and by God, Jack, a <u>real unified</u> single story opens up almost at once and gathers and grows from then on. The chapter after Antaeus is called at present <u>Early October</u>, and begins "October is the richest of the seasons"—it tells about the great barns loaded with harvest, the mown fields, the burning leaves, a dog barking at sunset, the smell of supper cooking in the kitchen—Oct is full of richness, a thousand things, then a section begins 'October is the time for all returning'—(which is true, Jack)—it tells how exiles and wanderers think of home again, of how the last tourists come back on great ships, of how the old bums shiver in their ragged collars as the newspaper behind the Public Library is blown around their feet, and of how they think of going South; it tells of the summer girls who have gone back home from the resorts; of the deserted beaches; of people lying in their beds at night thinking "Summer has come and gone—has come and gone"—then in the frosty dark and silence, they hear the thunder of the great trains. Then the October of a persons life— the core, the richness, the harvest, and the sadness of the end of youth.

By God, Jack, I'm just a poor bloody homesick critter, but when I think of my book sometimes I have the pride of a poet and a master of man's fate. Don't sigh and shake your head and think this is a welter of drivel—I've slapped these things down wildly in my haste but I tell you, Jack, this book is not incoherent—

it has a beautiful plan and a poetic logic if I am only true to it. <u>I have not</u> told you the thousandth part of it; but I hope you can see and believe in the truth and worth of it—and then if you do, please pray for me, dear Jack, to do my best and utmost, and to write the kind of book I want to write. In case you should doubt my condition, I am perfectly sober as I write this, it is a hot day, and I am now going back to my little room to work like hell. I have really not told you <u>about</u> my book—all this has been [coming] in the sweat and heat of the last few days, and this letter, however crazy, has made things clearer for me. I shall not leave Paris until I finish that first section—then I'm going like a shot to Switzerland, I think. I wont waste time moving about—I have a horror of moving now at all. Reeves,* the English publisher was here, took me around to see Aldington, Michael Arlen,† and other lit. lights—I was so unhappy at the time I have not been back since—although they [were] very nice. Reeves wants me to come to England and stay with him, the book is coming out there next month, but I've a horror of reading more reviews—I don't want to do anything more about it. Hope and pray for me, dear Jack—write me soon and talk to me. I've said nothing about you, forgive me, I'll write you a regular letter later.

 With love and best wishes to everyone.

Tom Wolfe

Write me <u>here</u>—the mail will be sent on

Dear Jack—I'm sending this on a day or two later—I guess I've really started—six hours a day, kid

June 24, 1930

This is my schedule if you can call such a way of living a schedule—up at noon, to Bank for mail, write letters, have lunch, (and bottle of wine!), buy a book—go home and work from four or five until 10 at night. Then out to eat, walk—back at midnight or one o'clock read—work until three or four

■ ■ ■ ■

FROM: John Hall Wheelock   TLS, 4 pp., Harvard

July 23, 1930

Dear Tom:

 A day or so ago I got your postal card telling of the man in Brooklyn who sent you fourteen closely-typed pages listing two or three thousand alleged mistakes in

---

*A. S. Frere-Reeves (1892–1984), editor at Heinemann.

†Richard Aldington (1892–1962), British imagist poet and novelist; Michael Arlen (1895-1956), British society novelist.

"Look Homeward Angel". I hope you will send it on to me so that it can be checked up here* I don't doubt that one of the tribe who make a profession of this sort of thing could find a great many errors, typographical and other, if he went over the book with a fine-tooth comb; but then this much could be said of any book, however carefully edited. Unless author and publisher are willing and prepared to devote the rest of their natural lives to the ideal of absolute letter-perfection as regards every semicolon and spacing, there must always be errors.

I was awfully glad, dear Tom, to get your fine long letter of June 24, which I would have answered long ago had it not been for pressure of work and other events. Your daily schedule in Paris sounds good to me and I am tempted to cast off all responsibilities and follow you over.

Of course the tremendous and exciting thing in your letter is the news about the new book—the fact that it is going forward, that you are working on it, and that it is growing from day to day. What you tell me about it stirs me deeply and I can see from the tone of your letter and the mood out of which it is written, that you have got started. Nothing can stop you now I think. There is only one way for a man to work and that is his own natural way, without thinking much about it, and above all without the slightest regard for what others might or will think. You'll always have to pour out your work at white heat, great slags of it, and shape it up afterwards when the more critical part of your mind is clear. At the same time I don't doubt that your experience with "Look Homeward Angel" will stand you in good stead and that you'll find yourself able to rein in a little more as you go along.

One of the sad things about a daily job is that one hasn't the time even to write letters to one's friends–I mean real letters, like the one you have written me. Perhaps you can tell from this how much your letter meant to me. I know that a great book is in process and if there's anything more cheering to know about than that, I have yet to discover it. In many ways, too, it now seems that your going abroad has given you just the right setting for the sort of thing you're trying to say. It brings all these feelings to a focus, to a poignancy which I am sure is nearly unbearable but which will be reflected magnificently in your story.

Dear Tom, we all miss you. We speak of you very often and I have even imagined, on occasions, that I heard your voice in the outer office. I wish it might have been so.

*The list is in the Scribners Archives at Princeton. The errors and inconsistencies were not emended in the plates of the first edition.

Max is away for a few days and I'm kept pretty busy. We've had some very hot weather but, as you know, the hotter it gets the better I like it. I must have a dash of nigger blood.

All sorts of good wishes, dear Tom.

As ever,

Your friend,

Jack.

P.S. I hope the "Angel" goes well in England. I've read one splendid review so far, but based upon the American edition.

■ ■ ■ ■

TO: John Hall Wheelock   ALS, 6 pp., Princeton
Grand Hotel Bellevue letterhead

Geneva, Aug 18, 1930

Dear Jack: Thanks very much for your good letter. There is very little that I can say to you now, except that 1 I have stopped writing and do not want ever to write again. The place that I had found to stay—Montreux—did not remain private very long: 2 Fitzgerald told a woman in Paris where I was, and she cabled the news to America—I have had all kinds of letters and cables speaking of death and agony, from people who are perfectly well, and leading a comfortable and luxurious life among their friends at home. In addition, one of Mrs Boyd's "young men" descended upon me, or upon Montreux, and began to pry around. This, of course, may be accident, but too many accidents of this sort have happened.

3 The English edition has been a catastrophe: some of the reviews were good, but some have said things that I shall never be able to forget—dirty, unfair, distorted, and full of mockery. I asked the publisher not to send any reviews, but he did all the same—he even wrote a special letter to send a very bad one, from which he said he got no satisfaction. Nevertheless the book is selling fast and they continue to advertise. All I want now is money—enough to keep me until I get things straight again. It is amusing to see the flood of letters and telegrams I began to get from "old friends" who were "simply dying to see me" when the first good reviews came out in England—it is even more amusing to see how the silence of death has settled upon these same people recently—I want to vomit, I should like to vomit until the thought and memory of them is gone from me forever.

There is no life in this world worth living, there is no air worth breathing, there is nothing but agony and the drawing of the breath in nausea and labor until I get the best of this tumult and sickness inside me. I have behaved all right since I came here—I have lived by myself for almost 4 months now and I have made no enemies: people have charged me and my work with bombast, rant, and noisiness—but save for this letter to you I have lived alone, and held my tongue, and kept my peace: how many of them can say the same? What reward in the world can compensate the man who tries to create something: my book caused hate and rancour at home, venom and malice among literary tricksters in New York, and mockery and abuse over here. I hoped that that book, with all its imperfections, would mark a beginning; instead it has marked an ending. Life is not worth the pounding I have taken both from public and private sources these last two years. But if there is some other life, and I am sure there is, I am going to find it. I am not yet 30, and if these things have not devoured me, I shall find a way out yet. I have loved life and hated death, and I still do.

I have cut off all mail by wiring Paris, and I am going to stay alone for some time to come. I know that that is the only way. Write me if you can The address is The Guaranty Trust Co, Paris. I hope this finds you well and that you get a good vacation

Ever yours,
Tom Wolfe

■ ■ ■ ■

FROM: John Hall Wheelock   CCS, 6 pp., Princeton

August 28, 1930

Dear Tom:

I was distressed and saddened by your letter of August 18, but at the same time I could not help being pleased that you have sufficient confidence in me to unburden yourself thus frankly as to a real friend, which I hope I am. Although the bitterness and vehemence of your letter was something of a shock, I must confess that I was not entirely surprised. As we get older there are fewer and fewer things that surprise us. Then, too, I have some understanding of the excitements, sufferings, and nauseas to which the man who is trying to do the almost impossible is subject.

I'm awfully sorry, dear Tom, that you have been bothered by all these people and I can sympathize with your feeling—at having your privacy broken into this way. It sometimes does seem as if privacy and solitude were conditions which have been permanently lost for any of us. There is nothing quite so depressing— almost degrading—as the constant intrusion upon one's state of mind by well-meaning and otherwise-disposed "friends". Can't you make another move, in great secrecy, and escape all this sort of thing, for a while at least?

I find it more difficult to feel with you in your decision not to write any more, and if I really believed this decision to be final and not the reaction from a mood, I should be more than unhappy. You are one of the few men of genius writing in English to-day. I am not saying that there are no faults in your first book; doubtless there are many which might be pointed out by careful analysis; but they are all faults which are the reverse of great qualities, qualities very rare to-day, such as vigor, profusion and vitality. Your book has had a remarkable reception in this country and has moved thousands of people. At the age of thirty you have taken your place among the best writers of our day, and have all the future before you in which to discipline your art and progress to even finer things. Your book is doing excellently in England, from all reports, and had a review in the <u>London Times</u> which might be considered flattering from any source, but from this particular source (usually so captious towards American work) amounts to superlative praise. Why in God's name should you allow yourself to be cast down by a few unintelligent or prejudiced English reviews? The greatest writers of all periods have been subjected to just this sort of thing but have had the courage and the serenity to come through it and to weigh it for what it is worth, which isn't much. I hardly think you will go the way of Keats, you are built of more vigorous stuff, without forfeiting any of his sensitiveness. It would certainly be a tragedy if the forces of ignorance and second-rate criticism were going to prove stronger than the creative energy of our best men. Yet your confession would seem to imply that such was the situation. I know this frame of mind will be very temporary with you.

I think you will need only one thing, Tom, and that is isolation from the artificial world of letters—not from the actual world. Don't receive any reviews; don't read any reviews; don't see any literary or writing people; enjoy life as you go along and devote a part of your time to regular work on your new novel, proceeding with it serenely or stormily as the mood may take you, but in absolute nonchalance where the opinions of literary critics are concerned.

Dear Tom, isn't it a grand thing to be a poet or a writer and you are both! Surely you must realize the tremendous impression that your book has made, both here and in England, and is destined to make in other countries too (we received yesterday an interested letter from a German publisher). Yet even if your book had had the most unfriendly reception, or had fallen absolutely flat, you ought not be prevented from going forward with what you had in mind. There will be moods of depression and even despair, but then you can't expect to achieve anything as important and as fine as a really good book without suffering on the way. I wish we could have a good talk; it would be so much more satisfactory than a letter. I shall be thinking of you very often during my vacation at the seashore, and hoping that things are a little less oppressive.

Many good wishes to you, dear Tom. As ever,

Yours,

<u>J. H. W.</u>

To Mr. Thomas Wolfe,
c/o Guaranty Trust Company,
4 Place de la Concorde,
Paris, France.

■ ■ ■ ■ ■

FROM: John Hall Wheelock   TLS, 3 pp., Harvard

March 1, 1935

Dear Tom:

This is a short line, on stationery from an office by this time quite familiar to you, to wish you every good thing one friend can wish another. I hope that you're going to have a glorious time and that you may combine with it some of the rest that you surely deserve. I think you ought to give yourself such a rest before you tackle any new work—though I know it will be hard for you to keep away from writing that long.

We're all looking forward with confidence and excitement to Friday, March 8. As you know, I feel and have felt all along that this book is going to have a material success as well as every other kind. To my mind it is one of the few really great books to come out of America, and I think it has qualities which are so overwhelmingly good, so full of life and so genuine in their force and conviction that no reader of any feelings at all will be able to resist it. I think you ought to feel very proud and happy to have written such a book.

We are going to miss you, dear Tom, and the office will seem very lonely. I shall think of you and look forward to your return. It has been the greatest happiness to have any part, however small, in getting "Of Time and the River" ready for publication.

My mother joins with me in sending you affectionate greetings and best wishes.

As ever your friend,
Jack

To
Mr. Thomas Wolfe
Ile de France
French Line,
New York City.

■ ■ ■ ■ ■

FROM: John Hall Wheelock   TLS, 2 pp., Harvard

April 16, 1936

Dear Tom:

I know that you're at work and that I oughtn't to disturb you, at this time, even with a letter, but I have just been rereading, in its book form, your magnificent

"The Story of a Novel",* and I feel that I really must tell you how deeply it affected and impressed even a hard-boiled editor, upon rereading. The book is unique. I can think of no other instance where a great writer has shared so generously with others his own experience in becoming a writer, his own torment and exaltation in the process of creation. And you've done it so superbly. The book is really profound—what it has to say is of such tremendous significance to every writer. This "Story of a Novel" is one of the finest introductions to and interpretations of your work that the general reader could have. I'm sure that it's going to bring you new readers and that it will become a classic of its kind. There certainly has never been a book like it.

You see I have to let you know my very strong feelings after a critical rereading, but this letter is sent with the strict understanding that it is not to be answered. We'll probably be seeing each other before long.

With many good wishes, dear Tom,

As ever,

Jack

To
Mr. Thomas Wolfe,
865 First Avenue,
New York City.

■ ■ ■ ■

FROM: John Hall Wheelock   TLS, 4 pp., Harvard

October 8, 1936

Dear Tom:

I want to thank you with all my heart for the splendid letter you have written me about my book. It is a letter that a writer would be proud and happy to receive from any source, but coming from yourself it is precious beyond words.[†] The feeling that your overgenerous praise is undoubtedly, though unconsciously, influenced by our friendship —is "tainted by friendship", in the words of a certain critic —doesn't make it any less welcome. You couldn't have said anything that would please me more than the words you write about finding a man, rather than merely an author, in these poems. I feel that I could have made the book less vulnerable to detailed criticism, and more perfect from the point of view of a selection merely, by omitting a number of the poems which, nevertheless, I felt were needed to give the rounded impression of a human being and his life.

---

*Wolfe's book-length essay published by Scribners in 1936.
†Wolfe's letter has not been located.

As for your remark about your indebtedness to me for some image, phrase or rhythm, I can only smile and attribute that, too, Tom, to your desire to make me happy, and to your generous imagination, for, much as I should like to claim the honor, I cannot really feel that I am entitled to it.

The younger school of reviewers have already reduced me to mincemeat: notably in the <u>New Yorker</u>, wherein I am informed that it is "démodé" to write about love and that the religious emotions of awe and reverence are just a lot of tripe. The kind of love poetry which is written to-day, and is therefore of course the best, is along the lines of

"I had an aunt

Who loved a plant

   But you're my cup of tea."

Another reviewer states that the book is worse than nothing, that it is positively evil. Here is one of the Harvard boys writing about the sea and about dawn in the city, while his fellow human beings are starving to death—a poet who seems unfamiliar with the dialectic of materialism and of the whole proletarian ideology. I'm trying very hard to look at this criticism impartially and to find out just how much of it is true and applicable, but it's difficult even at so early an age as fifty to dislocate your mind sufficiently to make these readjustments. Another reviewer tells me that the book is "a good example of a certain kind of genuine poetic feeling". I wonder how different kinds of genuine poetic feeling there are? I am also told that I should write with more "violence, venom, and scorn", and yet it would be difficult, perhaps, to maintain these emotions on all subjects.

But all this is beside the point. I wanted to thank you, Tom, for your letter, which means a great deal to me and has left a glow in my heart.

As ever,

Your friend,

Jack

To

Mr. Thomas Wolfe,

865 First Avenue,

New York City.

■ ■ ■ ■

Unmailed Wolfe Letter

TO: John Hall Wheelock   AL draft, 3 pp., Harvard

Early September 1929

Dear Mr Wheelock: I like to write, rather than to speak, the things I feel and believe most deeply—I think I can say them more clearly that way, and keep them better.

In the last few months, when I have come to know you, I have observed again and again the seriousness with which you would deliberate even the smallest changes in my book. As time went on I saw that this slow and patient care came from the grand integrity of your soul. Consequently, when you presented me with a book of your poems on the day when we had finished our work together on my novel, this simple act was invested with an importance and emotion which I can not describe to you now—every one of the subtle and rich associations of your character went with that book of poems, I was profoundly moved, profoundly grateful, and I knew that I would treasure this book as long as I live.

When I got out on the street I opened it and read your inscription to me and the magnificent lines that follow it.* In this inscription you speak of me as your friend. I am filled with pride and joy that you should say so. I am honored in knowing you, I am honored in having you call me friend, I am exalted and lifted up by every word of trust and commendation you have ever spoken to me.

You are a true poet—you have looked upon the terrible face of Patience, and the quality of enduring and waiting shines in every line you have written. The poets who are dead have given me life; when I have faltered I have seized upon their strength. Now I have by me living poetry and a living poet, and in his patience and in his strong soul I shall often abide.

I have now read all the poems in your book—I think I have read them all several times. But true poetry is a rich and difficult thing—we invade it slowly, and slowly it becomes a part of us. I have read few books as often as three or four times, but there are poems I have read three or four hundred times. I do not presume therefore to offer you a glib criticism of poems I shall read many times more—and I do not presume to think you would be seriously interested in my feeling. But there are some of your poems that are already communicated to

---

*JHW inscribed *The Bright Doom* (1927) to Wolfe with lines from his poem "Noon: Amagansett Beach":

    for

      Thomas Wolfe

    in friendship and admiration—

    "Loneliness—loneliness forever. Dune beyond dune,

        Stretches the infinite loneliness—pale sand and pale

            sea-grass,

    Pale beaches, mile upon mile. In the immensity of noon

        A hawk moves upon the wind. Clouds darken and pass."

                              John Hall Wheelock

    August 26,
    1929
  (Harvard).

me—I dare to say <u>entirely</u>—and that have become a part of the rich deposit of my life.

I wish to say that <u>Meditation</u> seems to me one of the finest modern poems I have ever read—<u>modern</u> only in being written by a man now living. When I read this poem I had that moment of discovery which tells us plainly that we have gained something precious—it has now become a part of me, it is mixed with me, and some day, in some unconscious but not wholly unworthy plagiary, it will come from me again woven into my own fabric.

Notes

1. Eugen Sandow (1867–1925), strongman who performed in theaters.

2. Henry Wadsworth Longfellow, "The Builders."

3. Charles E. Carryl, *Davy and the Goblin; or, What Followed Reading "Alice's Adventures in Wonderland"* (Boston: Ticknor, 1885).

4. At 3 West Forty-sixth Street, Manhattan; antiquarian dealer John S. Van E. Kohn specialized in first books by American authors.

5. Neither Mrs. Wheelock's bound copies nor separate issues of *The Morristonian* have been located.

6. "Silence," *Harvard Monthly*, 40 (March 1905), 30.

7. Hagedorn became a poet, novelist, and biographer. The Theodore Roosevelt Association was chartered by Congress in 1920.

8. Biggers (1884–1933) became a very successful writer of mystery and detective fiction. He was the creator of Charlie Chan.

9. New York: Boni & Liveright, 1926.

10. *Makers and Finders* (New York: Dutton, 1936–1952).

11. Knopf published the book in 1943.

12. *Reminiscences of Adventure and Service: A Record of Sixty-five Years* (New York: Scribners, 1927).

13. *The Art of Thinking* (New York: Simon & Schuster, 1928); *Under the Volcano* (New York: Reynal & Hitchcock, 1947); Musil, *The Man Without Qualities* (New York: Coward-McCann, 1953); *Journey to the End of Night* (Boston: Little, Brown, 1934).

14. Zaturenska, "The Strange Victory of Sara Teasdale," in *The Collected Poems of Sara Teasdale* (New York: Collier Books / London: Collier-Macmillan, 1966), xvii–xxxii.

15. Edward James, ed., *Notable American Women 1607–1950: A Biographical Dictionary,* (Cambridge: Harvard University Press, 1971), 3: 435–436.

16. Edward Burlingame retired as editor of *Scribner's Magazine* in 1914. His son, Roger Burlingame, was a Scribners editor from 1914 to 1926.

17. Charles Francis Dunn (1875–1962) was the Scribners reader of unsolicited manuscripts. Although JHW does not credit him with the discovery, Dunn reportedly found Alan Paton's *Cry, the Beloved Country*. JHW says that Dunn first recognized the genius of Wolfe's *O Lost* (published as *Look Homeward, Angel*), but Perkins credited that discovery to editor Wallace Meyer.

18. Brownell joined the firm in 1888 and remained as editor and literary advisor until his death in 1928.

19. Perkins died on 17 June 1947.

20. See Donald Hutter, "The Repository: A Remembrance of Scribner's," *Yale Review,* 78 (Summer 1989): 629–653. For biographical sketches of the Scribners who were heads of the house, see John A. Garraty and Mark C. Carnes, eds., *American National Biography* (Oxford: Oxford University Press, 1999), 19: 523–530.

21. See Matthew J. Bruccoli, *The Fortunes of Mitchell Kennerley, Bookman* (San Diego, New York and London: Harcourt Brace Jovanovich, 1986), and Daniel Boice, *The Mitchell Kennerley Imprint: A Descriptive Bibliography* (Pittsburgh: University of Pittsburgh Press, 1996).

22. New York: Scribners, 1935.

23. *Mrs. Eddy: The Biography of a Virginal Mind* (New York: Scribners, 1929).

24. Millay's poem "God's World" was collected in *Renascence* in 1917. Wheelock's poem appeared in the October 1921 issue of in *Scribner's Magazine.*

25. Anne Knish and Emanuel Morgan, *Spectra: A Book of Poetic Experiments* (New York: Kennerley, 1916).

26. Probably the American painter and miniaturist William J. Whittemore (1860–1955).

27. *The Bohemian: A Tragedy of Modern Life* (1878) and *Hesperus and Other Poems* (1880).

28. Joseph Bucklin Bishop, *Theodore Roosevelt and His Time Shown in His Own Letters* (New York: Scribners, 1920).

29. *The Life of Emerson* (New York: Dutton, 1932).

30. *The Pilgrimage of Henry James* (New York: Dutton, 1925).

31. By Eric Wollencott Barnes (New York: Scribners, 1956).

32. *Who Tells Me True* (New York: Scribners, 1940).

33. *Interpretations: A Book of First Poems* (New York: Kennerley, 1912).

34. "Whispers of Immortality" (1920).

35. *Vachel Lindsay: A Poet in America* (1935); *Whitman* (1937); *Mark Twain: A Portrait* (1938).

36. New York: Scribners, 1951.

37. *Poems, 1955–1958* in *Poets of Today VI* (New York: Scribners, 1959).

38. *In an Iridescent Time* (New York: Harcourt, Brace, 1959).

39. New York: Scribners, 1948.

40. *Systematic Theology* (1951–1963) was published as three volumes in one by the University of Chicago Press in 1967.

41. New York: Scribners, 1937.

42. Garden City, N.Y.: Doubleday, 1947.

43. "Non Sum Qualis Eram Bonae sub Regno Cynarae."

44. New York: Harcourt, Brace & World, 1967.

45. *The Mystery of Hamlet* (tetralogy) was performed in April 1949. It was published as *The Mystery of Hamlet, King of Denmark* (New York: Wheelright, 1950).

46. *The Collected Poems of John Peale Bishop,* edited by Tate, and *The Collected Essays of John Peale Bishop,* edited by Wilson, were published by Scribners in 1948.

47. *John Keats* (Boston: Houghton Mifflin, 1925).

48. Published by Scribners in 1953.

49. *New and Selected Poems: 1932–1967* (Indianapolis: Bobbs-Merrill, 1967).

50. Carl R. Dolmetsch, *The Smart Set: A History and Anthology* (New York: Dial, 1966).

51. Probably *Modern Painting: Its Tendency and Meaning* (New York: John Lane, 1915).

52. *The Creative Will: Studies in the Philosophy and the Syntax of Aesthetics* (New York and London: John Lane, 1916).

53. Zabel was author of only one published book, *Craft and Character: Texts, Methods and Vocation in Modern Fiction* (New York: Viking, 1957).

Index

"Builders, The" (Longfellow), 17, 247
Burlingame, Edward L., xxii, 75, 247
Burlingame, Roger, xxii, 52, 75, 76, 113, 247
Bury, Basil, 106
Bury, John, 106
Bury, Patrick, 108
Butler, Arthur Pierce, 18
Bynner, Witter, 99–100
Byron, George Gordon, Lord, 38

Cable, George Washington, 58, 77, 78
Caldwell, Erskine, xvii, 90–91
Caldwell, Taylor (Janet Miriam Taylor Holland Caldwell Reback), 187n, 187–90, *188*
California, 23, 109, 122, 137, 140, 141–42, 164, 191, 205
Call (newspaper), 37
Cambridge, Mass., 21, 30, 33, 178
Cambridge University, 3, 72, 93
Campbell, Mrs. Patrick (Stella), 140–43
Campbell, Patrick, 142–43
Canada, 231
Canary Murder Case (Van Dine), 205
Captain Craig (Robinson), 143n, 143–44
Carlyle Walk, London, 184
Carmel, California, 191
Carnivore, The (Slavitt), xviii
Carryl, Charles E., 17, 247
Carson City, Nev., 109
Céline, Louis-Ferdinand, xvii, 68
Central National Bank, New York, 4, 21
Central Park, New York, 40
Century (magazine), 44, 89, 105, 178, 199
Century Company, 36, 105, 123, 199
Chagall, Marc, 202
Charles Scribner's Sons. *See* Scribners
Chatto and Windus (publishers), 185
Chaucer, Geoffrey, 61, 209
Chelsea Hotel, New York, 151, 153
Cheyne Walk, London, 184
Chicago, Ill., 110, 111, 112, 113, 171, 172, 207, 208
Childers, Erskine, 180
"Chinese Nightingale, The" (Lindsay), 95

Christ. *See* Jesus Christ
Christian Science, 98–99, 128
Chrysler Building, New York, 163, 164
"Church's One Foundation, The," 7
Clothing's New Emperor and Other Poems, The (Finkel), *86*
Clurman, Harold, 158
Collected Essays of John Peale Bishop, The (ed. Wilson), 186, 248
Collected Poems (Gilder), 105
Collected Poems (Humphries), 206
Collected Poems of John Peale Bishop, The (ed. Tate), 186, 248
Collected Poems of Sara Teasdale, The, 70, 247
College of Physicians and Surgeons, 4
Cologne, Germany, 44
Colum, Molly, 172–73, 179, 200
Colum, Padraic, 115, 172–73, 179, 200
Columbia University, xix, 192
Columbus, Christopher, 19
Comedy Club, New York, 138
Coney Island, New York, 166
Conklin, Margaret, 70, 72, 74
Conrad, Joseph, 208, 209
Convent of the Blue Nuns, Rome, Italy, 115
Copeland, Charles Townsend, 23, 35–36
Corfu, 103
Cornell University, 41
Cory, Daniel, 116–17
Cosmopolitan (magazine), 89
Cosmopolitan Club, New York, 111
Craft and Character: Texts, Methods and Vocation in Modern Fiction (Zabel), 208, 249
Crane, Hart, 175
Crane, Mrs. Murray, 173
Crane, Murray, 173
Creative Will: Studies in the Philosophy and Syntax of Aesthetics, The (Wright), 203, 249
"A Critical Introduction" to *Poets of Today I* (JHW), *86*
Cromwell sanitarium, 71
Crosby, Ernest, 21, 22
Crosby, Howard, 21
Crosby, Maunsel, 21, 22, 30
Crosby, Mrs. Ernest (née Schieffelin), 22
Cross, Wilbur, 217

Index

Index